JOSHUA LEVINE has written seven bestselling history books, including several titles in the Forgotten Voices series. *Beauty and Atrocity*, his account of the Irish Troubles, was nominated for the Writers' Guild Book of the Year Award. *On a Wing and a Prayer*, his history of the pilots of the First World War, has been turned into a major television documentary. He has written and presented a number of programmes for BBC Radio 4. Most recently he acted as historical adviser on Christopher Nolan's movie *Dunkirk*. Born in the Bahamas, he was a criminal barrister in a previous life. He lives in London.

PRAISE FOR JOSHUA LEVINE:

'Joshua Levine has a natural gift for narrative description'
Daily Express

'Fascinating and thoroughly entertaining'
Observer

'A first-class portrait of a traumatic and tragic time'
Sunday Telegraph

DUNKIRK

The History Behind the Major Motion Picture

JOSHUA LEVINE

WILLIAM
COLLINS

William Collins
An imprint of HarperCollins*Publishers*
1 London Bridge Street
London SE1 9GF

WilliamCollinsBooks.com

First published in Great Britain in 2017 by William Collins

5

A catalogue record for this book is available from the British Library

ISBN 978-0-00-822787-6

Printed and bound by CPI Group (UK) Ltd, Croydon, CR0 4YY

MIX
Paper from
responsible sources
FSC™ C007454

FSC™ is a non-profit international organisation established to promote
the responsible management of the world's forests. Products carrying the
FSC label are independently certified to assure consumers that they come
from forests that are managed to meet the social, economic and
ecological needs of present and future generations,
and other controlled sources.

Find out more about HarperCollins and the environment at
www.harpercollins.co.uk/green

To Lionel who inspired me.

To Peggy whom I hope to inspire.

To Philip Brown, Eric Roderick, Harold 'Vic' Viner
and Charlie Searle with thanks.

Contents

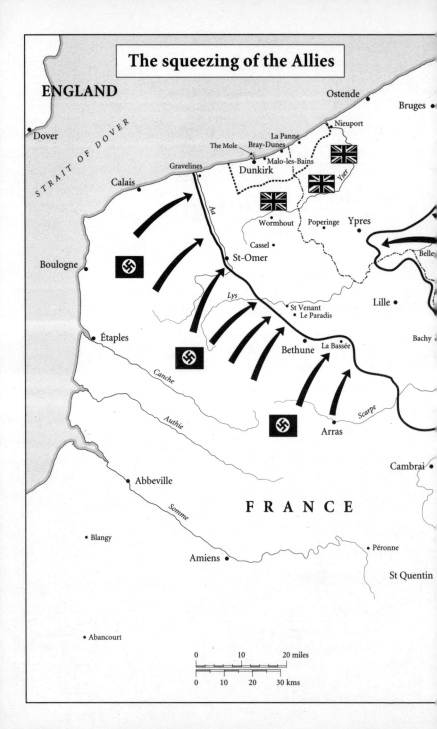

The squeezing of the Allies

ENGLAND

Dover

STRAIT OF DOVER

Ostende

Bruges

Nieuport

La Panne

The Mole   Bray-Dunes

Gravelines   Malo-les-Bains

Dunkirk

Yser

Calais

Aa

Wormhout   Poperinge   Ypres

Cassel

St-Omer

Belle

Boulogne

Lys

St Venant

Le Paradis

Lille

Étaples

Bethune   La Bassée

Bachy

Canche

Arras

Scarpe

Authie

Cambrai

Abbeville

FRANCE

Somme

Blangy

Péronne

Amiens

St Quentin

Abancourt

0	10	20 miles
0	10	20	30 kms

Preface

One afternoon, sitting in the National Archives in Kew, I opened a file containing a report by Commander Michael Ellwood. Commander Ellwood was in charge of communications during the Dunkirk evacuation, and he wrote, in passing, of a Marconi transmitter/receiver that was used for a very short time before it broke down – due to 'sand in the generator'.

This seemed surprising. How had sand got inside this precious piece of equipment? The Marconi TV5 was a sizeable box, and the memory of Laurel and Hardy delivering a piano in *The Music Box* flashed through my mind. Had two particularly clumsy ratings dropped it on the beach? Had Captain William Tennant, the Senior Naval Officer Dunkirk, yelled at them in frustration when they told him what they had just done to his only piece of transmitting equipment? Or did they stay quiet and hope that somebody else got the blame?

A short while later, in May 2016, I was standing at the shore end of the Dunkirk mole, very close to where Captain Tennant had placed his headquarters. Looking around, I could see parts of the Dunkirk beach cluttered with soldiers

– or men who looked like soldiers. There were warships out to sea, and a white hospital ship, clearly marked with red crosses, was berthed at the end of the mole. Black smoke billowed in the distance, and the sea frontage had been camouflaged to remove any traces of the late twentieth century. Dunkirk was looking remarkably as it had in late May 1940.

Something else was striking, though. The wind had picked up and sand was whipping everywhere. It was clogging hair and stinging eyes. Most people were wearing goggles and shielding their faces – and I suddenly realised that *nobody had dropped the transmitter*. There had been no clumsy ratings. Sand had been blown into the generator in May 1940 just as it was now blowing into everybody's eyes and ears. By spending time at Dunkirk, I was learning things about the original event that I could simply never have learned otherwise.

This is why I would urge anybody interested in the story of the evacuation to visit Dunkirk. Walking along the beaches and up the mole, exploring the perimeter where French and British troops kept the Germans at bay, visiting the excellent War Museum, the deeply moving cemetery and Église Saint-Éloi with its bullet- and shrapnel-pitted walls – these are all activities that will bring the events of May and June 1940 to life. The landscape retains the story, and fills in the gaps between words.

With this book, I have tried to tell a different story, or at least a wider story. Just as a visit to Dunkirk will make you think differently about the evacuation, so this book tries to explain events by placing them within a richer context – not merely military, but also political and social. It will try to give a sense of what it was to be a young soldier in 1940, and of the importance of youth culture, in its different forms, in the build-up to war. It will focus on the fighting (and sometimes lack of fighting) that led to the evacuation. And it will explore the effect of the evacuation, up to its very latest manifestation – the 2017 Chris Nolan film.

I have been lucky enough to work as historical adviser on this film. It was a pleasure to do so – partly because I enjoyed meeting so many interesting and enthusiastic people. But mainly because it has brought an under-appreciated piece of history to life in a remarkable way. In the last chapter, you will read of the efforts taken by director, producer and heads of department to be as true as possible to the historical event. By making those efforts, they have allowed the spirit of the evacuation to be recreated as vividly and as truly as I think it ever could be. The result allows us to experience the story for what it actually was – a hard and desperate fight for survival that kept the world free.

Nothing could be more important than that. I urge you to remember, as you watch, that without the real Tommys, Georges and Alexes, we would be living in a far darker world today. And many of us would not be living at all.

Joshua Levine
April 2017

'I Don't See It as a War Film.
I See It as a Survival Story'

An Interview between Joshua Levine
and Director Christopher Nolan

Joshua Levine: You're a British person who works in America. When you said you wanted to make this very British subject into a movie, what did people say?

Christopher Nolan: I had the script finished before I told anyone. Emma [Thomas – producer of *Dunkirk*] knew. She had originally given me your book [*Forgotten Voices of Dunkirk*] to read. We had made a Channel crossing many years ago with a friend of ours (who's actually in the film in one of the boats) in the spirit of re-enacting that historic journey. It was one of the most difficult and frankly dangerous-feeling experiences I have ever had. I was very grateful to get back in one piece, and that was without people dropping bombs on us. It was literally just the Channel, the elements and the three of us on a small boat.

JL: And you made that crossing as an homage?

CN: Yes. We did it a little bit too early in the year. It was Easter, I think it was April rather than May. It was a little too cold and we went over to Dunkirk specifically, but not as massive history buffs. We knew the story – we had grown up with it and our friend had a sail boat, and he said let's just do it. It turned out to be very, very difficult (at least for me and Emma) venturing out into the Channel in a small boat. It's a considerable thing to do. The idea of doing it and knowing that you're heading into a war zone is unthinkable really. And that's where the analysis of what Dunkirk means as mythology, or as modern mythology, or whatever you want to call it, can't be overstated. By actually getting on a boat and making that trip you can glimpse the bravery of the people who did it. It's just such a courageous thing for them to have done.

Emma and I talked about it years later and started reading first-hand accounts. We were curious about why no one had made a film about it – in modern times. It's one of the greatest human stories. It's universal, I think. So I did a lot of reading, danced around how to go about it and why people hadn't in the past. Ultimately we came to the conclusion that the reason people hadn't was because it was a defeat. And it's an expensive film. It's big. It's an epic any way you slice it up. We tried to approach it in a very intimate way, but it's an epic and so you need the resources of the industrial Hollywood machine behind it, and getting those resources channelled into a tale, however great, of defeat was a little tricky. But actually what drew us to the story is that it's not a victory, it's not a battle. It's an evacuation. It's a survival story.

So I don't see it as a war film. I see it as a survival story. That's why we don't see the Germans in the film and why it's approached from the point of view of the pure mechanics of survival rather than the politics of the event.

JL: It doesn't feel like a war film. I remember reading about George Orwell's Room 101, which contains the worst things in the world from your own personal perspective, this face-less enemy which is the nightmare of your imagination, it's whatever terrifies you. And the film is almost a horror film, or a psychological horror film, or something like that?

CN: It's a suspense film, but we try and push the visceral suspense as far as we can. So you get into the language of horror films, definitely.

JL: There's almost an implied contract that if you're going to make a film about the Nazis in any way you have to show them for what they were. And you haven't done that.

CN: No. Well, when I was first writing it – it was a crawl at the beginning, but it tells you what's going on – I used the word Nazi constantly and had people referring in the dialogue to Nazis. I wanted to continually remind the modern audience how evil and awful the enemy was and get them alongside. And then at some point – I think it was in my discussions with Mark Rylance, who first came aboard the project – I realised that because I had made the decision to never actually show Germans, even referring to them was pointless. You don't want to be in a middle ground. That is to say that you either have to try and address the entire concept of Nazi evil and ideology, or you have to completely circumvent it by not showing them, by having them be subliminal creatures in a way, having them as an off-screen menace. It's like the shark in *Jaws*, maybe you see the fin but you don't see the shark. And that way your mind, and even your ethical sense of who you are identifying with in the film, automatically makes them the worst thing possible out there.

JL: The audience can run with their imagination and take it wherever it goes. But because this film will be seen by a lot of young people who know nothing about the Second World War at all, is there an obligation to underline who the Nazis were?

CN: I think the responsibility is to not present a misleading portrait of the Nazis, but Nazism is notable by its absence and being notable I think is the proper thing. You want the feeling of crisis and jeopardy in Europe. You want the feeling of these British and French soldiers on the ground at a crucial moment in history. You want to feel like this is the absolute crisis point. I did that, from a cinematic point of view, by not personalising, not humanising the enemy, which most war films, one way or another, tend to want to do at some point. Even as far back as *All Quiet on the Western Front* there's a thread in war films of wanting to be sophisticated, wanting to humanise the enemy. But of course when you put yourself in the position of a soldier on that beach, for the vast majority their contact with the enemy is extremely limited and intermittent. Most of what you are seeing is bombs dropping. Most of what you are hearing is gunfire from a couple of miles away, which must have been more terrifying than we can really imagine as it gets closer and closer and closer. What we are trying to do with the sound mix right now is to figure out how to create that audio space, so that the battle appears to be ten miles away, then seven miles away, then four miles away, and how absolutely terrifying it would have been for the guys there on the beach.

It's what you don't know that is important in the film. So, in the expositional scene we give hopefully just enough historical information. The idea is that [the characters] Tommy and Gibson wouldn't know anything about what was going on and then they'd be given disquieting scraps of information like 'we're trying to get forty-five thousand people off the beach', 'there are four hundred thousand people on the beach' and then you get that 'OK, every man for himself' feeling. I was interested in the idea of what people wouldn't know rather than explaining everything we know now. If you're inside an event, particularly back then, when you didn't have smartphones and everything, it's pretty difficult to get any perspective on what's going on. One of the most moving things about the Dunkirk story to me – in fact, definitely the single most moving thing – is that when these guys finally were rescued, when they finally made their way home, they went home with a sense of shame. That they went home, the vast majority of them, thinking they were going to be a huge disappointment to the British people back home and then found that they were welcomed as heroes was to me one of the most extraordinary turnarounds, emotionally, in history, and it was because they didn't know what was going on. So we have them reading Churchill's speech in the newspaper. They wouldn't have been in Parliament, they wouldn't have been able to do what films do traditionally, which is to cut to Winston Churchill speaking to the Cabinet or preparing his speech. They were just going to get it from the newspapers, so they find out after the fact what it is that they've been through.

JL: Are there any modern parallels? Are people going to see it as something that happened *x* years ago or are they going to see it as something that could happen again?

CN: One of the great misfortunes of our time, one of the horrible, unfortunate things with the migrant crisis in Europe, is that we are dealing once more with the mechanics and the physics of extraordinary numbers of people trying to leave one country on boats and get to another country. It's a horrible resonance but it's very easy in our technologically advanced times to forget how much basic physics come into play. Reality is insurmountable. If you have a vast number of people in one place and they need to get someplace else and they can't fly and they have to get on boats – to overcrowd the boats, with that human desire for survival … it's unthinkably horrible to see it on our front pages in this modern day and age. But it's there. With that going on in the world today, I don't think you can in any way dismiss the events of Dunkirk as being from another world or another era.

JL: So what war films do you like?

CN: One of my favourite films – one of the films I most admire – is Terence Malick's *Thin Red Line*. It has almost no relevance to this film whatsoever, but it has had relevance to a lot of my other films. I think *Memento* is heavily indebted to *Thin Red Line*. We did actually screen it before this film, but it wasn't relevant except in one key textural, stylistic sense, which is that it is timeless. It feels very accessible and contemporary even though it's about World War II, and that was certainly something that we wanted to try and achieve in the texture of this film, but as far as the artistic underpinnings and the way in which it tells the story it felt very unrelated. I didn't look at too many war films. We looked at Spielberg's *Saving Private Ryan*, which was also instructive because it has a horror movie aesthetic. It has an approach to intensity and gore that's so absolute and successful that you realise that you have to go elsewhere. You can't try and compete with that film. It would be like trying to compete with *Citizen Kane*. I mean it's an absolute. That's the horror of war right there. So we went more in a suspense direction. I didn't watch too many war films because I read – I think it's reprinted in the liner notes of the Blu-Ray on the Criterion Edition of *Thin Red Line* – a piece of writing about war films by James Jones, who wrote the novel of the *Thin Red Line*, and it's humbling. This is somebody who had been at war and had written about war and he exposes the devices, the bullshit of war movies in a merciless way that to a filmmaker sitting down to write a film set during a real moment in history was extremely daunting. One of the things he says is 'What more can be said about war after *All Quiet on the Western Front*?' So I went back to look at *All Quiet on the Western Front*, which I had not seen in many, many years. It's incredible how all-encompassing it is as a statement about war, how horrible war is. Even though the craft of filmmaking was more in its infancy than now – it's black and white, it barely has sound – it's extraordinarily well made. And by virtue of the fact that it's about Germans but made in the Hollywood system, the anti-nationalist point of view is so powerful, so strong. And that's what elevates it above any other anti-war film made since. It's so relentless in its depiction of how awful war is, it's so unsparing in its depiction of how nationalist myths, jingoistic myths, propagate the idea of war as glorification. I don't think they'd ever have been allowed to do that if it was made about the Americans and the British.

JL: So is your film a sort of successor to that?

CN: No, not at all. Because I did that reading, that research, it pushed me further in the direction that I had already been heading, not making a war film but making a survival story because that was what I felt confident of doing. I have not fought in a war. It's my worst nightmare. I can't imagine doing that. So to me *Dunkirk* becomes a survival story. The terms of the success or failure for me are survival, and that's why when one of the soldiers at the end says 'all we did was survive', the blind man replies 'That's enough.' Because in the terms of Dunkirk, that <u>was</u> the definition of success. Which is where Churchill's 'Inside this defeat there's victory' comes from. That's the particular situation I felt confident trying to tell.

JL: Do you have anyone in your family who fought?

CN: My grandfather died in World War II. He was a navigator on a Lancaster.

JL: Good Lord. Do you know how many missions he survived?

CN: He survived forty-five. He was meant to retire, but I think he died on the forty-sixth. After forty-five, they would then go and instruct new pilots and he was right there. He's buried in France, and we went to visit his grave while we were making the film, which was very moving. He was in his thirties when he died and he was the old man of the crew, they looked up to him as a father figure. I mean they were kids. They were eighteen, nineteen.

JL: Do you watch your films again?

CN: I do, yes.

JL: And when you watch them do you judge them? How do you watch a film you made several years ago?

CN: You wind up watching them for various reasons fairly soon after you finish, for the video release, for this and that, all kinds of technical reasons. And these days my kids are interested to see *The Dark Knight* or whatever and I'll sit and watch it with them. But the reasons go away over time and you stop seeing the films. It's a very long time since I have seen *Memento*. There are filmmakers who never watch their films. But I'm interested to because they change over time as you get further away from them. You start appreciating them in a more objective way – what's good, what's bad – and they become a little bit more of their time, I suppose.

JL: Yes.

CN: Which isn't a cheerful thought, because you don't want to think of yourself as ageing and being very much of your time, but you are ...

JL: But how could you be anything else?

CN: Yes, it's what we all are. But your highest aspiration is to make a film that feels timeless.

JL: Are you worried that the story of Dunkirk is going to be – certainly for a while, for a generation – *your* story of Dunkirk?

CN: That brings with it a responsibility, yes, and I am certainly mindful of it. But it's probably one of the reasons why the film doesn't attempt to be comprehensive. We don't deal with the politics of the situation. We don't deal with the larger worldview around it because I think it would be too daunting a responsibility to try and own a complex piece of history that you can't actually distil into a two-hour dramatic narrative.

I'm comfortable presenting the visceral experience of Dunkirk and having that define for a period of time, for the next few years, people's ideas of what the experience might have been. I feel qualified to do that, because we researched and we were able to film it comprehensively. But regarding the wider implications of the story, of the history itself, I don't want to take that on. And I don't think the film pretends to. The film has a quality of simplicity that allows you to imagine more stories. And that's very, very deliberate. That's part of the reason for the structure. We want to allow people the space to understand that there are many, many more experiences of these events.

JL: This is something that I have written in the book:

> For every individual who stood on the beach or on the mole, or retreated clinging to a cow, there was a different reality. Set side by side, these realities often contradict each other. To take one element of the story; the beaches covered a large area, they were populated by many

thousands of people in varying mental and physical states over nearly ten intense days of rapidly changing conditions. How could these stories *not* contradict each other? The whole world was present on those beaches.

To me that feels like the essence. Do you agree with that?

CN: Yes. I think the film is very much based on that same assessment of the illusive nature of individual subjective experience defining objective reality. Which is a connecting thread with all the films I've ever made. They are all about individual experiences, potential contradictions with objective reality, and the film tries very strongly to leave space for the seemingly infinite number of experiences and stories that would contradict each other or comment on each other in different ways. We tell three stories that intersect at a point. We show the point when they come together and they are very, very different experiences. Watching a Spitfire pilot ditch from the other Spitfire, it looks calm and controlled, but to actually go through that as you do later in the film is completely different. A massive contrast. That is something that's always fascinated me about human experience.

JL: We went on a trip round parts of Britain meeting Dunkirk veterans. What did you learn from that?

CN: Absolutely vital things. But what was interesting was that although when we were talking to those people I was honoured and humbled, I wasn't necessarily inspired or aware in the moment exactly what I was going to get out of these conversations. I knew it was a smart thing to do. We needed to talk to people who had actually been there if we were going to presume to portray their experience. It's really only when I look back at the film now … when I look at the scene where they watch the guy walk into the water, I don't know what that guy's doing, whether he's killing himself or whether he thinks he can actually swim out. But the reason I don't know is because I think I even asked him [the veteran] 'Was he killing himself?' and he didn't have an answer. This was a direct thing he had seen.

JL: Did the man himself even know what he was doing?

CN: I don't know. Exactly.

JL: We like to pin a certainty on everything – 'This is what he's doing' – and actually we don't even know why we do what we do half the time. And in a situation like that, where the pressures are unimaginable …

CN: A lot of what I got from the conversations with those amazing people was confidence that things that we were intending to do were supported by people's experience. Different people talking about being on the mole, people getting off the boat, the chap bringing water to Dunkirk, which meant getting off the boat and then not being able to get back on the same boat. It's just this nightmarish feeling of chaos. Ordered chaos, I suppose you'd call it, or the almost bureaucratic chaos that was apparent on the mole. It's very interesting listening to people talk about that. And also with that chap who, although he wasn't a civilian, he'd come over from England to supply water – one of the things that fascinates me is the mechanics. This is why Tommy is trying to go to the loo at the beginning, because those things are interesting; the logistical things. Where are you going to get food from? Water? It's something that was never planned and is being done ad hoc and so hearing the accounts of somebody who came over with water and saw all the fires from a distance and knew he was going there. That's an omnipresent image in the film: heading towards these burning fires. It's on the horizon. It's the last place you want to go. There were all kinds of things I got from those conversations. They seeped in over time. I think it was very informative asking as you did what their interpretation of the Dunkirk spirit was, because there were such different interpretations. Three very distinct interpretations, as I remember. One was the little ships representing the idea of the Dunkirk spirit. Another was, I can't remember the words he used, but he basically said it was complete bullshit. And then the last chap we were talking to, he related it to the people holding the perimeter who were left behind. And they were all three absolutely definitive in their own interpretation: that's what it is, that's what it means.

JL: Absolutely. I remember one said, 'You were only worried about yourself.'

CN: Yes. I think he was one of the most interesting people to talk to. What he implied to us was that he'd gone through a set of experiences of which he was not proud, but which he firmly felt were in the norm of that situation for the people that were there. I felt that he wasn't in any way saying he had done anything wrong or different, but that there were things which shouldn't be talked about, which were best left there. And for me the whole relationship between Alex and Tommy and Gibson was that moment. It's not meant to be judgemental of people. I felt that there was a window which opened up on to the privacy of that subjective experience.

JL: I find it interesting that when you get to a certain age the order of things often disappears. Stories no longer move from beginning to end. Time becomes increasingly irrelevant. For me, as a barrister and now a writer, I instinctively want to reorder people's stories, make logical sense of them. But you're coming from a totally different perspective, which I find very interesting. You've dealt so much in your films with the nature of time that – to you – there was something very honest about this.

CN: Very much. My job is to tell a story in a very disciplined and ordered manner, whether it's chronological or not, and I wouldn't have a job if it were natural to people conversationally. The reality is that people's nature is not to be able to relate their experiences in an absolutely coherent manner, for whatever reason. So storytelling, in whatever form, always has value in society because it's a particular skill. It's putting something into a different form, and that's why the guy not telling us about that specific experience creates an interesting hole in our knowledge which I think is much more expressive than the words would be. Whatever happened, I think he was aware on some level that it would either sound trivial to us, because perhaps he had just sworn at an officer, for example, or it would seem truly shameful, and we wouldn't be able to understand. Whatever it is, his subjective experience, by becoming a story, would be greatly reduced. I find it very powerful and thought-provoking to think of it as a little gap in our knowledge. It confirms everything that the research suggested, which is that there was an enormous range of experience.

One

Survival

In the early summer of 1940, Anthony Irwin was a young officer in the Essex Regiment. As his battalion carried out a fighting retreat towards the French coast, held up by civilian refugees, targeted by guns and aircraft, pressured by approaching German infantry, Irwin, like most of his fellow officers and men, was experiencing war for the first time.

One afternoon, under attack from German bombers, he saw his first dead bodies. The first pair upset Irwin – but the second pair made him vomit, and appeared in his dreams for years afterwards. The difference was not in the manner of their deaths or even the severity of their wounds. It was in the second pair's 'indecent attitude'. Naked, demeaned, bloated and distorted, they embodied something worse than death.

That evening, his battalion was under attack again. Overwhelmed, a young private began crying. Irwin took the boy aside, intending to lead him away. But the private, rigid with misery, refused to move. The only thing to do, decided Irwin, was to knock him out. He ordered a sergeant to take a swing at the private's chin – but the sergeant missed, cracking his knuckles on a wall. The private suddenly came to life and ran, but was chased down by Irwin who tackled him, and punched him in the face. The boy was now unconscious.

Irwin slung the private over his shoulder and carried him down to a nearby cellar. It was dark inside, and Irwin shouted for somebody to bring him a light. In the relative quiet, Irwin heard surprised voices, a man's and a woman's, and his eyes slowly focused on a soldier in the corner of the cellar having sex with a Belgian barmaid. Who could blame them, wondered Irwin. With death so close, they were grabbing hold of life.

Irwin was among hundreds of thousands of officers and men of the British Expeditionary Force retreating through Belgium towards the coast. They had sailed to France following the declaration of war on Germany on 3 September 1939. After months of 'phoney war', the German Blitzkrieg in the west had been launched on the morning of 10 May, and the bulk of the British forces was hurried into Belgium to assume prearranged positions along the River Dyle. There they formed the Allies' left flank, alongside the French and Belgian armies, facing Hitler's Army Group B. Further to the south, the Allies' right flank was protected by the mighty Maginot line, a series of heavily defended fortresses, blockhouses and bunkers along the French border with Germany.

For a few short days in May 1940, the Allies and the Germans, broadly equal in military terms, seemed destined to act out another war of trenches and attrition. If experience could be trusted, the Germans would soon be hurling themselves at heavily defended Allied lines.

But the Allied commanders were instead offered a sharp lesson in modern warfare. Between the strongly held Allied flanks was the Ardennes forest, theoretically impregnable, and weakly defended by the French; only four light cavalry divisions and ten reserve divisions protected a hundred-mile front. And the Germans had a plan to exploit this front.

First formulated by Lieutenant General Erich Manstein, the plan had been through seven drafts by May 1940. It involved an initial attack on Holland and northern Belgium, drawing the Allies into a trap. For at the same time, the main German attack would come further south at the very weakest point of the Ardennes front. Led by Panzer tank divisions, it would begin by crossing the River Meuse, pushing through the area around Sedan and surging north-west for the coast, splitting the French armies in two and joining up with the northern attack to encircle the British Expeditionary Force.

The Manstein Plan was extremely risky; breaking through a wooded area was a huge logistical challenge, and the Panzer tank was a largely untested weapon. The plan's success depended on unprecedented speed and intensive air support, but, above all, it depended on surprise. If the French learned of it in advance, it would surely fail. In January 1940, however, the Belgians had captured a copy of the previous German plan – to launch the main assault in Holland and Belgium. This was a straightforward repeat of Germany's First World War strategy – and the Allies had no reason to believe that the Germans were now considering an alternative.

The level of risk involved in the Manstein Plan was so great, the break from traditional practice so complete, that most German generals refused to countenance it. It gained, however, an influential supporter in General Franz Halder, Chief of Staff of Army High Command. And, crucially, it had the support of the man whose opinion ultimately mattered in Nazi Germany – Adolf Hitler. The attack was ordered to go ahead.

In the event, the French were taken by complete surprise. Armoured forces, spearheaded by Lieutenant General Heinz

Guderian's Panzer Corps and devastatingly supported by the Luftwaffe, plunged through enemy lines, tearing a massive hole in French defences. German tanks began to race through France unchallenged. This is why, just days after taking up their positions in Belgium, British soldiers – clearly able to hold their own against the Germans – were being ordered backwards. There must, they thought, be a localised reason. Had the Germans broken through in a nearby sector? Or was their particular battalion being sent to the rear for some misdemeanour?

At first, British units retreated in stages, from one defendable line to another. Sometimes an entire division was pulled out, free to plug a distant gap. As the retreat gathered pace, confusion increased, and rumours began to circulate. One of these rumours proved true – an almighty breakthrough to the south was threatening to outflank the British army. But for most of the retreat there was no suggestion of evacuation, nor mention of the now legendary name *Dunkirk*.

All sorts of soldiers found themselves on the move, from elite guardsmen to untrained labour troops. Some went on foot, marching in battalion strength or stumbling alone. Others travelled in trucks, on horses, tractors and bicycles. One intrepid group was observed riding dairy cattle. Under fire and lacking supplies, the men of the British army were in every kind of physical and mental state.

One man, Walter Osborn of the Royal Sussex Regiment, was in a particularly difficult situation. Having sent the Prime Minister, Winston Churchill, an anonymous letter asking for 'some leave for the lads', he had been sentenced to forty-two days' detention for using 'language prejudicial to good order and conduct'. He was now engaged in a fighting retreat with his comrades – but he was at a disadvantage. Whenever the fighting stopped, he was locked up in a nearby barn or cellar to continue serving his sentence. This did not seem fair. As he complained to a regimental policeman: 'A man's got a right to know where he stands!'

Even more unusual was the small soldier sitting in a truck on the road to Tourcoing. In steel helmet and khaki great-coat, carrying a rifle, the soldier looked like any other. The uniform may have hung a little, but that was hardly unusual. Private soldiers weren't expected to dress like Errol Flynn in *The Charge of the Light Brigade*. The odd thing about this soldier was her marriage to a private in the East Surrey Regiment.

The soldier was Augusta Hersey, a twenty-one-year-old French girl. She had recently married Bill Hersey, a storeman in the 1st East Surreys. They had met in Augusta's parents' café when Hersey was stationed nearby, and despite neither speaking a word of the other's language, they had fallen in love. Hersey had asked Augusta's father for her hand by pointing at the word *mariage* in a French–English dictionary and repeating the phrase 'Your daughter …'

Hersey was fortunate to have a sentimental company commander who agreed – against any number of regulations – that Augusta could dress in army uniform and retreat with his battalion. This was how the couple found themselves, almost together, fleeing the German advance. But their retreat had no definite objective until Lord Gort, the British commander, reached the brave conclusion that the only way to save a percentage of his army was to send Anthony Irwin, Walter Osborn, and the rest of the British Expeditionary Force, towards Dunkirk, the one port still in Allied hands, from where some of them could be hurriedly transported home by ship.

As they arrived at Dunkirk, soldiers were confronted by an unforgettable scene. Captain William Tennant, appointed Senior Naval Officer Dunkirk by the Admiralty, sailed from Dover to Dunkirk on the morning of 27 May to coordinate Operation Dynamo. He entered a town on fire, its streets littered with wreckage, every window smashed. Smoke from a burning oil refinery filled the town and its docks. There were dead and wounded men lying in the streets. As he walked on, he was confronted by an angry, snarling mob of British soldiers, rifles at the ready. He managed to defuse a difficult situation by offering the mob's ringleader a swig from his flask.

Another naval officer arrived in Dunkirk two days later. Approaching from the sea, he was struck by one of the most pathetic sights he had ever seen. To the east of the port were ten miles of beach, the entire length blackened by tens of thousands of men. As he drew closer, he could see that many had waded into the water, queuing for a turn to tumble into pitiable little boats. The scene seemed hopeless. How, he wondered, could more than a fraction of these men hope to get away?

Yet the closer one came to the beaches, and the more time one spent on them, the clearer it became that there was no single picture and no single story. An officer of the Royal Sussex Regiment recalls arriving on the beach, and being smartly saluted by a military policeman who asked for his unit before politely directing him into a perfectly ordered queue. A young signalman, on the other hand, was greeted with the words, 'Get out of here before we shoot you!' in another queue. And a Royal Engineers sergeant watched a swarm of desperate soldiers fighting to get onto a boat as soon as it reached the shallows. In a desperate attempt to restore order before the boat capsized, the sailor in charge drew his revolver and shot one of the soldiers in the head. There was barely a reaction from the others. 'There was such chaos on the beach,' remembers the sergeant, 'that this didn't seem to be out of keeping.'

For every individual who stood on the beach or on the mole (the long breakwater from which most troops were evacuated), or retreated clinging to a cow, there was a different reality. Set side by side, these realities often contradict each other. To take one element of the story – the beaches covered a large area, they were populated by many thousands of people in varying mental and physical states over nearly ten intense days of rapidly changing conditions. How could these stories *not* contradict each other? The whole world was present on those beaches.

And the reality was no tidier once the soldiers were on boats and ships sailing for Britain. Bombed and shot at by the Luftwaffe, shelled by coastal batteries, fearful of mines and torpedoes, the men might be on their way to safety – but it had not yet arrived. An officer in the Cheshire Regiment was one of thirty aboard a whaler being rowed from the beach to a destroyer moored offshore which would then ferry them home. As the whaler drew close, the destroyer suddenly upped anchor and headed towards England. Overcome by emotion, an army chaplain leapt up in the whaler and yelled, 'Lord! Lord! Why hast thou forsaken us?' As he jumped, water began to pour into the boat, and everyone simultaneously screamed at him. Seconds later, in answer to his prayer – or possibly in answer to the exceptionally loud noise just made by thirty men – the destroyer turned round and came to pick them all up.

In the event, the vast majority of the British Expeditionary Force was brought safely home from Dunkirk. Most of those were carried by naval ships or large merchant vessels; the famous little ships (some crewed by ordinary people, most by sailors) were mainly used to ferry the soldiers from the shallow beaches to the larger ships moored offshore. But had these soldiers been killed or captured, Britain would surely have been forced to seek a peace settlement with Hitler, history would have taken a far darker course, and we would all be living in a very different world today.

This helps to explain why Dunkirk – a disastrous defeat followed by a desperate evacuation – has come to be seen as a glorious event, the snatching of victory from the jaws of a worldwide calamity. Whereas Armistice Day and most other war commemorations are sombre occasions focusing on loss, Dunkirk anniversaries feel more like celebrations, as small ships recreate their journeys across the Channel. Dunkirk represents hope and survival – and this is what it represented from the very start.

When the evacuation began, so dire was Britain's military situation that, as in Pandora's Box, only hope remained. On Sunday 26 May, a national day of prayer was observed. Services in Westminster Abbey and St Paul's Cathedral were mirrored in churches and synagogues across Britain, and in the London Mosque in Southfields.

In his sermon, the Archbishop of Canterbury asserted that Britain both needed and deserved God's help. 'We are called to take our place in a mighty conflict between right and wrong,' he said, suggesting that Britain's moral principles were invested with sanctity because 'they stand for the will of God.' God was with Britain, and He alone knew how the evil enemy would be beaten. It is little wonder that the evacuation, quickly dubbed miraculous by Winston Churchill, assumed a quasi-religious quality. The Archbishop had been right, it seemed, Britain *was* favoured by the Lord. This confirmed the views of such writers as Rupert Brooke and Rudyard Kipling, and it helped give rise to a concept that has survived the last seven and a half decades: Dunkirk Spirit.

Defined as the refusal to surrender or despair in a time of crisis, Dunkirk Spirit seems to have asserted itself spontaneously. As they arrived back in Britain, most soldiers saw themselves as the wretched remnants of a trampled army. Many felt ashamed. But they were confounded by the unexpected public mood. 'We were put on a train and wherever we stopped,' says a lieutenant of the Durham Light Infantry, 'people came up with coffee and cigarettes. We had evidence from this tremendous euphoria that we were heroes and had won some sort of victory. Even though it was obvious that we had been thoroughly beaten.'

Nella Last was a housewife from Lancashire. In early June she wrote in her diary:

> This morning I lingered over my breakfast, reading and rereading the accounts of the Dunkirk evacuation. I felt as if deep inside me was a harp that vibrated and sang ... I forgot I was a middle-aged woman who often got tired and who had backache. The story made me feel part of something that was undying.

The emotional outpouring did not please everybody, however. Major General Bernard Montgomery, commander of 3rd Division during the retreat, was disgusted to see soldiers walking around London with an embroidered 'Dunkirk' flash on their uniforms. 'They thought they were heroes,' he later wrote, 'and the civilian public thought so too. It was not understood that the British Army had suffered a crashing defeat.' A German invasion was expected, and exhibitions of pride and self-congratulation did not sit well with Montgomery. But for the majority, while Britain still had a fighting chance of survival, the returning soldiers were glorious heroes.

Some civilians baulked at the euphoria too. An old woman watched the shattered troops disembarking at Dover on 3 June. 'When I was a girl,' she said, 'soldiers used to look so smart and would never have gone out without gloves.' The Mass Observation reporter to whom she spoke noted a flat, unemotional atmosphere in the town. 'I can only describe it,' he wrote, 'as no flags, no flowers and unlike the press reports.'

However widely felt, the authorities were keen to encourage the sense of emotion and relief – and this was something that Winston Churchill understood instinctively. Oliver Lyttelton, later to be a member of Churchill's War Cabinet, describes great leadership as the ability to dull the rational faculty and substitute enthusiasm for it. In 1940, on a careful evaluation of the odds few would have acted decisively. But despite not being the cleverest of men, Churchill had the ability to inspire the country. He made you feel, says Lyttelton, as though you were a great actor in great events.

On the evening of 4 June, radio listeners heard a report of the Prime Minister's speech, given earlier in the day to the House of Commons. The speech did not attempt to ignore reality; Churchill spoke of the German armoured divisions sweeping like a scythe around the British, French and Belgian armies in the north, closely followed by 'the dull brute mass' of the German army. He spoke of the losses of men and the overwhelming losses of guns and equipment. He acknowledged that thankfulness at the escape of the army should not blind the country 'to the fact that what happened in France and Belgium is a colossal military disaster'.

But Churchill also described 'a miracle of deliverance, achieved by valour, by perseverance, by perfect discipline, by faultless service, by resource, by skill, by unconquerable fidelity'. If this is what we can manage in defeat, he was suggesting, imagine what we can achieve in victory! He then spoke of his confidence that Britain would be able to defend itself against a German invasion:

> We shall fight on the seas and oceans, we shall fight with growing confidence and growing strength in the air, we shall defend our Island, whatever the cost may be, we shall fight on the beaches, we shall fight on the landing grounds, we shall fight in the fields and in the streets, we shall fight in the hills; we shall never surrender …

Inspiring though these words must have sounded (the front page of the next morning's *Daily Mirror* barked 'WE NEVER SURRENDER'), they hint at a difficult future. Fighting in streets and hills implies guerrilla warfare: the sort of fighting to be engaged in once the Germans had already gained a foothold in Britain. Beyond this, though, Churchill was implying that Britain had strength in reserve. And while this might serve as a reassurance to her own people it was also meant as a message to the United States. We will hold the fort, Churchill was saying, until you come and join us. But please don't wait too long …

Joan Seaman, a teenager in London, remembers being scared in the aftermath of Dunkirk. But when she heard these words, the effect was transforming. 'When people have decried Churchill, I've always said, "Yes, but he stopped me being afraid!"' George Purton, a private in the Royal Army Service Corps, had just struggled back from Dunkirk. He could not share Churchill's opinion of the evacuation, but he knew 'a splendid bit of propaganda' when he heard it.

The next evening, 5 June, another BBC broadcast boosted the nation. Novelist and playwright J. B. Priestley gave a talk after the news. It was much chummier than Churchill's, delivered as though knocking back a drink in the saloon bar with friends. In his Yorkshire accent, Priestley mocked the typical Englishness of the Dunkirk evacuation, the miserable blunder having to be retrieved before it was too late. He sneered at the Germans: they might not make many mistakes, but they didn't achieve epics either. 'There is nothing about them,' he said, 'that ever catches the world's imagination.' Warming to his theme that the British are lovable, absurd and quixotic, he spoke of the most 'English' aspect of the whole affair: the little pleasure steamers called away from their seaside world of sandcastles and peppermint rock to a horrid world of magnetic mines and machine guns. Some of the steamers had been sunk. But now they were immortal: 'And our great grandchildren, when they learn how we began this War by snatching glory out of defeat, and then swept on to victory, may also learn how the little holiday steamers made an excursion to hell and came back victorious.'

In Priestley's talk – and in other reactions to the evacuation – pride can be sensed in perceived British traits: modesty, comradeship, eccentricity, a belief in fairness, a willingness to stand up to bullies, and an effortless superiority. One does not, after all, want to be seen trying too hard. As Kipling once wrote:

Greater the deed, greater the need
Lightly to laugh it away,
Shall be the mark of the English breed
Until the Judgment Day!

The emerging story of Dunkirk was being shaped to fit the sense of national self. When, after all, had a plucky little army last hurried towards the French coast, desperate to escape an arrogant and vastly more powerful enemy, only to succeed against the odds and fight its way to freedom? During the Hundred Years War, of course, when the English won the glorious Battle of Agincourt, fought, according to Shakespeare, by the 'happy few', the 'band of brothers'. If a sense of English self had been born at Agincourt, the Dunkirk story needed very little shaping.

Prevailing public attitudes can be gauged by the reaction to a play that premiered two weeks after the evacuation. *Thunder Rock*, starring Michael Redgrave, opened at the Neighbourhood Theatre in Kensington. Its author, Robert Ardrey, described it as a play for desperate people – and it was an instant hit. Theatre critic Harold Hobson recalls that it had the same effect on its audience that Churchill's speech had on his. It proved so popular that it was secretly bank-rolled by the Treasury and transferred to the West End – emphasising the blurred line between spontaneous spirit and its imposition by the authorities.

The plot revolves around a journalist, disillusioned by the modern world, who has retreated to a solitary life on a light-house on the American lakes. There he is visited by the ghosts of men and women who drowned on the lake a century earlier as they headed west to escape the problems of their own times. As the journalist and the ghosts speak, the parallels become clear; just as they should have engaged with the problems of their age, so should he now do the same. He resolves to leave the lighthouse and rejoin the wartime struggle. In a closing monologue, he rehearses the issues so relevant to the modern audience:

> We've reason to believe that wars will cease one day, but only if we stop them ourselves. Get into it to get out ... We've got to create a new order out of the chaos of the old ... A new order that will eradicate oppression, unemployment, starvation and wars as the old order eradicated plague and pestilences. And that is what we've to fight and work for ... not fighting for fighting's sake, but to make a new world of the old.

Such lofty social ambitions reveal how Dunkirk Spirit was mutating. The initial sense of relief (that defeat was not inevitable) and pride (in an epic last-ditch effort) was combining with political realities to become something more complex and interesting. If Adolf Hitler was a symptom rather than a cause of the problem, then with victory must come a better and fairer world.

But for all the words spoken and written, perhaps Dunkirk Spirit's most impressive manifestation was in the realm of British industry. In the immediate aftermath of the evacuation, the need for greater industrial effort was fully acknowledged by workers. This rare convergence of management and workforce, reflecting a shared interest in survival, was perhaps the apex of Dunkirk Spirit. At the SU factory in Birmingham, responsible for building carburettors for Spitfire and Hurricane fighters, output was doubled in the fortnight after Dunkirk. Official working hours stretched from eight in the morning to seven in the evening, seven days a week – but many workers stayed at their benches until midnight and slept on the factory premises. Such a state of affairs would have been unimaginable at almost any other time in the last century.

When the Blitz – the Luftwaffe's bombing campaign against Britain – seized the country for eight and a half months between September 1940 and May 1941, 'Dunkirk Spirit' and 'Blitz Spirit' merged into a single idealised mood, the indiscriminate bombs emphasising the need to pull together. But the essence of both was the instinctive realisation that life truly mattered.

In the immediate post-war years, the concept of Dunkirk Spirit was sometimes called upon to decry the supposed British trait of trying hard only when something becomes necessary, but more recently, it has been used in its earliest, simplest sense. In December 2015, for example, retired picture framer Peter Clarkson pulled on a pair of swimming trunks and went for a swim in his kitchen after heavy rains flooded his Cumbria home. 'This is how we treat these floods!' he shouted as he breast-stroked past the cooker, explaining that he was trying to 'gee up the neighbours with a bit of Dunkirk Spirit'. And when Hull City made a winning start to the 2016–17 Premier League season despite injuries to leading players and the lack of a permanent manager, midfielder Shaun Maloney ascribed results to 'Dunkirk Spirit' at the club.

But Dunkirk Spirit reached its high water mark during the 2016 Brexit referendum campaign, when the country was almost overwhelmed by references to the period. As Peter Hargreaves, a leading donor to the 'Leave' campaign, urged the public to vote for Brexit, he harked back to the last time

Britain left Europe. 'It will be like Dunkirk again,' he said. 'We will get out there and we will become incredibly successful because we will be insecure again. And insecurity is fantastic.' Nigel Farage, meanwhile, not satisfied with invoking Dunkirk, tried to restage it by sailing a flotilla of small ships up the Thames, bearing slogans like 'Vote Out and be Great Britain again'.

But these are the words and actions of people in current situations, with modern agendas. How do veterans of the evacuation describe Dunkirk Spirit? What did – and does – it mean to them?

For the most part, they relate it to their individual experiences. Robert Halliday of the Royal Engineers arrived in France at the start of the war and was evacuated from Bray Dunes on 1 June. As far as he is concerned, the essence of Dunkirk Spirit was the units of British and French soldiers fighting fiercely on the Dunkirk perimeter. 'The guys who were keeping them [the Germans] at bay and letting us through were as good as gold!' he says. He recalls soldiers calling out as he passed – 'Good luck, off you go!' His eyes sparkle as he remembers these events. Dunkirk Spirit remains very real to him. It was, he says, 'wonderful'. George Wagner, who was evacuated from La Panne on 1 June, relates Dunkirk Spirit to survival. 'We wanted to survive as a country. It was about comradeship and everyone together helping.'

Not everybody agrees. Ted Oates of the Royal Army Service Corps was rescued from the Dunkirk mole. Asked if Dunkirk Spirit means anything to him, he simply shakes his head. And far from experiencing Dunkirk Spirit, George Purton feels that the British army was effectively betrayed. 'We were sent into something,' he says, 'that we couldn't cope with.' He remembers Dunkirk as a time of isolation. 'There was so much happening and you were concerned about yourself only. How the hell am I going to get out of this?'

Dunkirk holds a semi-sacred place in Britain's collective conscience. It has spawned conflicting experiences and attitudes. It inspires strong emotions, not only among veterans but in those born years afterwards, with only a folk memory of the event and a politically convenient interpretation. How then does a modern filmmaker approach it?

Chris Nolan, one of the most respected directors currently working, has written and directed a feature film set during the evacuation. It was a story with which he was already familiar. 'I think every English schoolboy knows it,' he says. 'It's in your bones, but I thought it was time to go back to the original source.'

Reappraising the Dunkirk story, Chris built up questions about what had really happened. 'I was assuming, as modern, cynical people do, that when I looked into it, what I would find would be disappointing. That the mythology of Dunkirk Spirit would fall away and there would be a more banal centre.' But as he unpeeled the layers, he found something unexpected: 'I realised that the simplifications actually expose a truth, because the bigger truth, the wood for the trees, is that an absolutely extraordinary thing happened at Dunkirk. I realised how utterly heroic the event was.'

Heroic – but not straightforward. 'When you dive into the real life of the story, what it would really have been like to be there, you find that it's an incredibly complicated event. The sheer numbers of people involved – it was like a city on the beach. And in any city, there is cowardice, there is selfishness, there is greed, and there are instances of heroism.' And the fact that heroism occurred alongside negative behaviours, that it flourished in spite of base human nature, makes it all the more affecting and powerful. 'That,' says Chris, 'is what true heroism is.' Yet for all the individual acts, he sees the Dunkirk evacuation as a communal effort by ordinary people acting for the greater good. This, he says, makes the heroism greater than the sum of its parts. And it is ultimately his reason for making the film.

Another attraction is the sheer universality of the story. 'Everybody can understand the greatness of it – it's primal, it's biblical. It's the Israelites driven down to the sea by the Egyptians.' This offers an ideal background for what he calls 'present-tense characters', anonymous individuals without unwieldy back stories. 'The idea is,' he says, 'that they can be anonymous and neutral, and the audience can encounter them, and become wrapped up in their present-tense difficulties and challenges.'

Chris sees himself as proxy for the audience while making the film. 'What I'm feeling and how I choose to record what I'm feeling – the way in which I'm acquiring the shots – fires my imagination about how to put the film together.' If he has a visceral reaction, he feels he's on the right track. 'I'm sitting in the cinema watching it as I shoot it,' he says. And for him, to tell the story well it has to be shot from the point of view of the participants – on land, in the air, and at sea. Which means that on the little ships, almost all of the shots he eventually used are from the deck, while on the aircraft, cameras are carefully mounted in places where the audience can see what the pilot sees. 'You want things to feel real, and you want them to be experienced. Pure cinema, to me, is always a subjective experience.'

The enemy barely makes an appearance in the film. German soldiers appear only very briefly, and even then the audience barely sees their faces. But this, as Nolan points out, reflects the reality of the situation, the subjective experience of the men on the beach. 'When you look at first-hand accounts, close contact with the enemy was extremely sporadic for most British soldiers. I wanted to put the audience in the boots of a young inexperienced soldier thrown into this situation, and from the accounts, they did not stare into the eyes of Germans. I wanted to be true to that and embrace the timeless nature of the story. The reason the story has sustained generations of interpretation and will continue to do so, is because it's not about the Germans and the British, it's not about the specifics of the conflict. It's about survival. I wanted to make it as a survival story.'

In fact, the actual enemies of most of the British soldiers (at least those not defending the Dunkirk perimeter) were aeroplanes, artillery guns, submarines, mines and gunboats. And a battle against an unseen enemy that can't be fought, touched, or often even seen, creates an unusual war film. In fact, in Chris's eyes, it is not a war film at all. 'It's more of a horror than a war film. It's about psychological horror, about unseen threats. The guys on the beaches had very little understanding of what was happening and what would happen – and I want the audience to be in the same position.'

Another enemy was time. 'It is the ultimate race against time,' he says. 'But set against that, you have the length of time of the event, comprising boredom, stasis, things not happening. They're stuck and this is where the tension comes from, where the adrenalin comes from. Making a film about people standing in line on a bridge to nowhere, time becomes everything.'

Chris Nolan may want his audience to feel as baffled and uninformed as the young men queuing under fire for a place on a boat home, but as the author of a history book on the same subject, I do not. I want to paint a vivid picture of the event, offering readers rather more clarity than two soldiers offered Pilot Officer Al Deere of 54 Squadron after he had crash-landed on the beaches on 28 May:

'Where are you going?' asked Deere.
'You tell us,' said one of the soldiers.
'You're evacuating, aren't you?'
'We don't know.'

Before examining what happened, though, I want to place the event in its historical context, and so it is important to find out more about the lives of young people in the years leading up to the war. What, we will ask next, did it mean to be young in an age of uncertainty? Where did Dunkirk *come from*?

Two

Quite Like Us

The story of Dunkirk amounts to more than a frenzied month of soldiers and sailors, tanks and beaches, ambitious politicians and quivering generals. It is more, even, than an intense drama of personal and national survival. It is the story of the men and women involved, their backgrounds, and the experiences that formed them. It is a story of the approaches used by different nations to overcome the misery of the 1930s, and how these led to the evacuation of an army as another strained to destroy it. And it is a story of the rising importance of youth, politically, economically and militarily.

We begin the story in Britain. We will move to Germany, and finish in the United States. We will observe similarities and the contrasts. And we will wonder who we might have been, and how we would have coped.

The United Kingdom

Nineteen-year-old Thomas Myers was evacuated from the Dunkirk beaches on 31 May 1940. Recalling the event, years later, the Durham Light Infantryman remembers behaving like an ostrich, trying to bury his head (and other parts) in the sand, as bombs, bullets and shells flew down. He managed to stay calm, unlike the unlucky few whom he saw panicking and running about aimlessly.

But despite his coolness under fire, Thomas was not an experienced soldier. Five years earlier, aged fourteen, he had left school in County Durham on a Friday afternoon and walked up the pit road to meet the manager of the Dean and Chapter Colliery. At three o'clock on the following Monday morning he started work as a coal miner.

Thomas's father and his two older brothers were miners. 'In this area you were bred for the mines,' he says. Asked whether he was happy doing it, he says, 'You were born to it. You were a miner. You go in the mine. There's nothing else.'

Thomas started work just as his father had before him. He was given no training; he was simply told to collect a pit pony and go and find an older boy. Thomas's job, it turned out, was to collect tubs of coal, recently filled at the coalface, attach them to the pony by harness, and pull them several hundred yards to a spot where they were mechanically hauled to the surface. He would then collect empty tubs and drive them back to be filled. This cycle would repeat itself over his seven-and-a-half-hour shift.

Thomas remembers his first night in the mine: 'Timber supports were holding the roof which was trying to come down, cracks would show, and I was frightened to death. The noises! When I was on my own! It was very frightening for a boy of fourteen to go in the mine under those conditions.'

A short while later, Thomas's fears about safety were confirmed when a boy was killed doing the very same job. The boy had been asked by a hewer to carry a drill in his empty tub. As his pony galloped along, the tub slid off the road and the drill shot up in the air, driving itself through the boy's body. Thomas was horrified when he heard the news. 'I'm going there no more,' he told his brother that evening. 'You're going back again tomorrow!' he was told. 'You've got to get over this!' Shortly afterwards, when yet another boy was killed, Thomas was the first person there. 'What a scene!' he says. 'There wasn't a body. He had been pulled to bits.'

In the year that Thomas started work, an average of four miners were killed every day in Britain. Coal mining was the nation's most dangerous peacetime occupation. And even when a miner had worked his way up to hewer, the work was no safer. Hewers had to work in tiny seams, sometimes as narrow as twelve inches wide, lying on their sides, hacking at coal with an elbow tucked inside a knee. 'You get the coals out the bloody best you can,' a Durham miner told BBC interviewer Joan Littlewood in 1938. 'If you hear the ceiling coming down, you have to get out of the way. But the only way to be really safe is to let the flaming coal stay there ...'

Life was difficult as well as dangerous. Miners returned, caked in coal and sweat, to small homes without bathrooms. Most washed in little tubs in the kitchen. The author W. F. Lestrange spent some time in a house, like Thomas's, lived in by a family that included three miners. The woman of the house, he wrote, 'spent most of her time fighting vainly against coal-dust-smeared walls and furniture and floors in the intervals of boiling water for the three successive bath-times'.

Life was no easier across the Irish Sea. Politically, Northern Ireland was (and still is) a part of the United Kingdom; geographically, it is a part of Ireland. Harry Murray started work at Harland and Wolff shipyard in Belfast in 1937. 'People used to earn their pay or they didn't get it,' he says, 'and if they didn't earn it, they were sacked and that was it.' Harry worked out in the open, in all weathers, drinking tea from a can, with a half-hour break to eat, play dice or pray. And his future was dependent on the goodwill of the foreman. 'He used to get brought in butter, eggs, money, just so people could keep their job,' Harry says. 'If the foreman didn't like your face, that was good enough to put you out ... and if you were unemployed, it was ten times worse to survive.'

Yet as odd as it may sound, Harry Murray was a fortunate man. The Northern Ireland government was intended, in the words of its first Prime Minister, to be 'a Protestant government for a Protestant people'. And as a Protestant, Harry was guaranteed access to basic housing and a lowly paid job in industry. An Ulster Catholic had no such security. Harland and Wolff had not employed Catholics since the early twentieth century, and they no longer bothered applying for shipyard jobs. These had become the natural preserve of Protestants, passed from father to son, from uncle to nephew.

So although Ulster Protestants received lower wages than their English counterparts, and often lived in houses without mains water and gas lighting, they could be considered – in relative terms – privileged. It was, after all, better to be second than third class.

Even in London, the beating heart of the British Empire, ordinary life was hard. In 1939, the average Londoner lived to the age of sixty-two, compared with eighty-two today. Two per cent of Londoners attended university in 1939; today, the figure is 43 per cent. In 1934 Sister Patricia O'Sullivan arrived in east London, where she lived among the families of sailors. One of her chief memories is of the importance of pawn shops to local people. When a man went to sea, he would not be needing his suit for a while, so he would take it to the pawn shop. On his return, he would redeem it, and pawn items brought back from distant parts of the world. Sister Patricia would often furnish poor homes with the things sailors had brought home and pawned.

One of those homes belonged to Doris Salt. Doris's husband had been killed by a drunk driver in a stolen car. The circumstances meant that she received no insurance money. 'It was just make-do with me for years,' she says. 'I had to learn to make a good meal out of more or less nothing. People pooh-pooh sheep's head, oh no, they wouldn't eat that, but we used to thoroughly enjoy it.' Florence Muggridge, from Poplar, knew a woman whose husband was killed working in the docks. 'Miserable bugger, we were going out tonight,' said the woman on hearing that she was now a widow. But, says Florence: 'You didn't expect anything, you see? That's the whole point. People had to fend for themselves in ways that are unheard of now.'

It is possible to view modern life – from a western perspective, at least – as a succession of choices. But for most young Britons living in the first decades of the twentieth century, fewer choices existed. They followed their father's trade, lived near their birthplace, and married for convenience as often as for love. Yet in Britain in the 1930s – as in Germany and the United States – economic tremors would begin to shake social foundations. Young people's attitudes and expectations started to change, and a generational gulf would emerge.

But for change to occur, a catalyst had to appear – and that catalyst was, as elsewhere, the depression. As author Ronald Blythe points out, Britain's inter-war years took place against a huge, dingy, boring and inescapable backcloth – unemployment. All sorts of people suffered as a result.

Trevor, a seventeen-year-old from south Wales, had wanted to become an engineer, but when his father lost his job, he was forced to leave school to become an errand boy. This was intended to be a temporary arrangement, but Trevor's father had failed to find another job, and now Trevor too was out of work. He spent his days playing table tennis in an unemployment centre.

In 1933, the number of unemployed in Britain reached three million, and it remained high until the outbreak of war. Alfred Smith, from south London, lost his job in 1935. Three years later, despite being in his mid-thirties, he was described in *Picture Post* magazine as having a lined face, sunken cheeks, and looking down as he walked – 'the typical walk of the unemployed man'.

Alfred lived with his wife and three young children in a two-room flat, of which one of the rooms was partitioned. On a typical day, the family ate bread and margarine for breakfast, stew or boiled fish with potatoes and bread for dinner (the midday meal), and more bread and margarine in the evening. The Smiths rarely ate fresh fruit or vegetables – not because they were too expensive, but because they were less filling than bread and potatoes. Unemployed people in Britain were more likely to be malnourished than underfed.

In 1935, 45 per cent of British army recruits were considered unfit to serve. Five years later, when American journalist William Shirer was working as a special correspondent with the German armed forces, he was introduced to a group of British soldiers taken prisoner shortly before the Dunkirk evacuation. Describing them as a cheery lot (one said, 'You know, you're the first American I've ever seen in the flesh. Funny place to meet one, ain't it?'), Shirer writes that what struck him most was 'their poor physique'. The depression affected Germany and the United States with equal (if not greater) severity, but the young British male seems to have showed the effects most visibly. Military training had not, believed Shirer, made up for bad diet, and lack of fresh air and exercise.

George Orwell, that unsurpassed chronicler of British working-class life, noted that almost the worst evil of unemployment, beyond even financial hardship, was 'the frightful feeling of impotence and despair'. Trevor, the seventeen-year-old from Wales who now spent his days playing table tennis, was a case in point. 'I'm here every day at ten and play till dinner-time,' he told W. F. Lestrange, 'and there's nothing to do in the afternoon, either, so I come up here and play whenever the table's free. Ping-pong. Knocking little celluloid balls about. That's my life! All I'll ever do is play ping-pong. When I was a kid I thought I'd be … wanted to be …' At that point, tears welling up, Trevor ran from the room.

Life was made harder still for the unemployed with the introduction of the Means Test, ensuring that the jobless would have regularly to justify themselves to a stranger, a government employee, who would stand in a family's front room asking questions about a suspiciously new-looking overcoat. The unemployed man could afford neither secrets nor pride.

People sometimes tried to evade the Means Test; a young person living with parents might give a false address in an attempt to claim a separate allowance. On the other hand, assistance was sometimes mistakenly withdrawn. Orwell tells of a man seen feeding his neighbour's chickens while the neighbour was away. It was reported that the man now had a job, and his money was withheld. And there was little official sympathy for those who slipped through the net. When a man travelling the country looking for work was caught stealing two loaves of bread, he told the bench that temptation was difficult to avoid. 'That is what you say,' said the magistrate. 'I will teach you something different. You will go to prison for two months with hard labour.'

Arguably, though, it was the women who suffered most. The wife of an unemployed man still had to try to maintain a home. She often ate too little so that the children had enough, she dealt with the debt and rent collectors, and she had to manage her husband's diminished sense of self-worth. And as Orwell noted, the average working-class man never did a stroke of housework – even when at home all day. Yet such women were not above being patronised; Sir F. G. Hopkins, president of the Royal Society, delivered a speech to fellow members in 1935, declaring that 'what the English housewife in the poorer classes needs most is to be taught the art of simple but good cooking'.

With the dearth of any workable system of welfare, and the lack of understanding between society's classes, it was to be expected that extreme political parties began to attract support. The British Union of Fascists, led by the opportunistic Oswald Mosley, consisted overwhelmingly of young working-class men under thirty. Its members marched through areas where they were sure to provoke local people. In October 1936, a huge mob, headed by Mosley, marched through the East End of London, where they were predictably confronted on Cable Street by a young mob of anti-fascists, enraged at the invasion. The ensuing fight led to the arrest of more anti-fascists than fascists, allowing Mosley to present his men as victims of aggression. The result was an increase in new members.

At the end of the march, Mosley spoke to his followers. 'The government surrenders to Red violence and Jewish corruption,' he said. But the fascists would *never* surrender. 'Within us is the flame that shall light this country and later the world!'

Interviewed on BBC radio in 1989, Mosley's widow, Diana (one of the eccentric, entitled Mitford sisters), claimed that her husband had not really been anti-semitic at all. Rather, by preventing him and his followers from marching, the Jews had provoked him. (In the same interview Diana remembered Hitler – 'He was extremely interesting to talk to ... he had so much to say ...')

Shortly before Cable Street, Diana's father, Lord Redesdale, had given a speech to the House of Lords, protesting at ignorant British attitudes towards the Nazis. The most common mistake, he claimed, related to the Nazi treatment of Jews. The reality was that no Germans interfered with the Jews so long as they behaved themselves. And if the Germans felt that the Jews were a problem, Redesdale said, they should be allowed to deal with that problem as they thought best. Had the Nazis arrived in Britain, they would clearly have had ready-made support among the upper ranks, as well as the lower orders.

Another extreme – communism – was gaining support among young Britons. One of these, Winston Churchill's nephew, Giles Romilly, wrote, 'Youth has a clear choice. Either they must side with the parasites and exploiters ... or with the working class to smash the capitalist system and lay the foundations of the classless society.'

In 1936 and 1937, thousands travelled to Spain to fight against Franco with the International Brigades. Once again, the vast majority were young working-class men – though not all. Penny Fiewel was a nurse working in Hertfordshire. A colleague asked her if she would volunteer for Spain: 'I said I knew nothing about Spain – I didn't know anything. She said I wanted educating, so she told me all about Spain, how the nuns were taking Franco's side, and of course, it grabbed my heart – I was young and very emotional.'

Penny soon found herself in a field hospital on the front line, treating terrible injuries and teaching Spanish nurses to do the same. When bombs first fell near her operating theatre, it was invaded by civilians desperate for shelter. One man collided with her in the dark, and as she pushed him away, her fingers became sticky. When the lights were back on, she saw that half of the flesh on the man's face had been blown away. Long before Hermann Goering launched the Luftwaffe's raids against London in September 1940, Penny Fiewel was experiencing the brutality of area bombing. The Spanish Civil War – as illustrated by Pablo Picasso – was teaching the world to dread the bomber.

Months later, Penny was badly wounded during a raid. Waking up in a barn, naked except for bandages wound tightly around her chest and abdomen, she was in terrible pain. And as she lay recovering in hospital, the raids continued. 'These were nightmare days,' she says.

The war was ultimately won by Franco's nationalists, with help from the Germans. This was a clear violation of a non-intervention agreement signed by Germany – and a warning of the dangers of trusting Hitler. But just as Britain's leaders were tentative in their handling of the economy, so they were tentative in their handling of the Führer.

This was understandable. Britain had won the First World War – but her economy had been badly damaged. (As of 2017, astonishingly, the country still owed a large amount of First World War bond debt.) The greatest loss, however, was human. Much of Britain's young male generation had been killed, wounded or traumatised, and the nation's leaders were desperate to consign the war to history. They wanted to believe in a new peaceful world order based on the League of Nations – and were reluctant to focus too closely on events in Germany. Equally, they did not want to impose the high taxes that would be needed to rearm. Overall, therefore, it was easier for collective heads to remain in the sand where they could ignore the war cries of men such as Winston Churchill.

And although Britain's politicians disapproved of Hitler's methods, they did not initially identify him as an existential threat. As future United States President John F. Kennedy explained in his 1940 book, *Why England Slept*, 'It is only fear, violent fear, for one's own security … that results in a nation-wide demand for armaments.' Such fear did not exist in Britain until it was almost too late.

Germany, by contrast, could hardly rearm quickly enough. And the two nations' respective pre-war attitudes, one conservative and placatory, the other radical and ruthless, would come to a head in the events of May and June 1940.

But for all the difficulties Britain and her people faced in the years leading up to war, there was another – more positive – story emerging. Just as in America, and, in its own dark way, Germany, a distinct youth culture was forming. 'Youth has broken out like a rash,' stated a *Picture Post* leader in early 1939. Everybody, it claimed, was talking about 'youth', from journalists to politicians to church leaders: 'What causes all this present chatter about "youth"? It is partly that we are in an age of transition, and older people are stamped by the institutions in which we have lost faith. We hope that youth will do better!'

Here is a striking similarity between our three nations. The depression and the apparent failure of the previous generation were allowing the young to forge a new identity. But in Britain, this new identity was being exercised by single wage-earners, aged fourteen to twenty-four, who had more expendable income than any other sector of society. The nation's burgeoning youth culture would not have grown so quickly had it not offered such a boost to the economy.

A survey conducted in 1937 in a deprived area of Manchester concluded that working children from even the poorest families 'would have holidays and outings and new clothes, while probably the parents, the mother certainly, stayed at home and wore old clothes'. We are witnessing the birth of the teenager – before the word was even coined. For, by keeping a considerable amount of their earnings to themselves, these young people had a far superior standard of living to the older members of their family.

Much of their money was spent watching (mainly American) films. Most young people watched at least one film a week, some watched many more. And not only did they watch films, they learned from them. They copied fashions and hairstyles, accents and attitudes. Boys wore slouched fedoras, girls delivered Scarlett O'Hara-style putdowns. According to the diary of a girl from a working-class Manchester suburb, an average 1938 Monday evening was spent watching a George Formby film with a friend, discussing the film (as well as boys and clothes), and then returning home to listen to dance music and talk to her family – about films.

Plenty of teen money was spent in dance halls. George Wagner (a sapper who would be evacuated from La Panne in May 1940) was sixteen in 1936, when he became a regular dance hall attendee. Despite being a shy boy, dancing was his chief hobby. 'It was a place where you met all the girls,' George says, 'that was the main thing.'

Wearing suit, tie and waistcoat, bought by his mother (he had only graduated to long trousers at fourteen), George would walk a few miles to the Palace Ballroom in Erdington with three of his closest friends. The dances were run by Harry Phillips, who would walk around the floor, partnering boys and girls. No alcohol was served, so any of George's friends who wanted a drink would have to go to a local pub and lie about their age. A five-piece dance band played popular American music – George's favourite song was 'Deep Purple' – as young men plucked up their courage to approach young women. George says:

> You used to chat them up, see if you could take them home. I didn't have a particular girlfriend, not in them days, I was too young. I would walk them home and probably have a little snog when you got up to the gate. But they were very looked after in them days. Sometimes parents would be watching out of the window in the lamplight. 'Come on! You're late!'

So what were the differences between young wage-earners of this period and those of previous generations? Their instincts had not changed, but their behaviour had. They were now keeping far more of their wages to spend on themselves, and they had their own interests and pursuits. Before the First World War, there were very few – if any – pursuits that appealed only to the young. The music halls and cheap theatres were equally popular with all ages. It is hard to overestimate the growing independence and importance of youth at this period – and without the depression, it is hard to imagine how such developments could have taken place.

But at the same time, we should be careful not to ascribe our own modern attitudes to 1930s teens. We may want to imagine that they were 'just like us', but the truth is more nuanced. At the same time as he was learning about girls, George was very much a boy of his own time. He and his friends loved nothing more than pitching a tent in a field, pinching a bit of coal from the railway to start a fire, and cooking whatever they found in the fields. George would find an acorn, poke a straw into it, fill it with cigarette ends, and use it as a pipe. 'If my mother had known,' he says, 'I would have got a thick ear.' Youth attitudes may have been changing, but most young people remained innocent by today's standards.

And we should also remember that young people were not alone in experiencing new pleasures and entertainments. Entirely British in flavour, accessible to all ages, a popular culture was also developing. It took the form of cheap luxuries and diversions available to people who could not afford the essentials. This, according to Orwell, was the logical result of the depression, as the manufacturer's need for a market coincided with the half-starved populace's need for cheap distractions:

A luxury nowadays is almost always cheaper than a necessity. One pair of plain solid shoes costs as much as two ultra-smart pairs. For the price of one square meal you can get two pounds of cheap sweets. You can't get much meat for threepence but you can get a lot of fish and chips … And above all, there is gambling, the cheapest of all luxuries. Even people on the verge of starvation can buy a few days' hope by having a penny on a sweepstake.

These trends are still with us today – although many of the specific diversions have now disappeared. Two British dances, enjoyed by all ages, in the late 1930s, were the Lambeth Walk and the Chestnut Tree. One was a pastiche of cockney culture, the other was based on a nursery rhyme. Compared with the primal danger of Swing, that edgy American import, these dances were cosily British in their eccentricity.

In Blackpool, the country's favourite seaside resort, the diversions were equally British. One involved a woman named Valerie Arkell-Smith. Masculine in appearance, Arkell-Smith had spent years passing herself off as a retired army colonel – and had married an unsuspecting woman in the process. Following Arkell-Smith's release from prison for making a false statement on her marriage certificate, an impresario signed her up to feature in a Blackpool sideshow. Billed as a woman who had recently had a sex-change operation, Arkell-Smith lay in a single bed, while a young woman lay alongside her in another bed, the two beds separated by flashing Belisha beacons. The conceit was that the pair had recently married but Arkell-Smith had placed a £250 bet that, for twenty-one weeks, they would not touch one another. Spectators paid twopence to view the odd, sexless bedshow, shouting obscenities at the 'couple'.

Another sideshow was stranger still. Harold Davidson had been the rector of the parish of Stiffkey in Norfolk. He had been defrocked after an ecclesiastical court found him guilty of immoral conduct with a variety of women. Outraged at the verdict, Davidson had first embarked on a hunger strike (in an attempt to prove that God would not allow him to starve) before sitting for months in a barrel on Blackpool Promenade, trying to raise enough money to launch an appeal. The following year, he abandoned the barrel, and chose to appear inside a lion's den at Skegness Amusement Park. This would be the end of the ecclesiastical road for the ex-Vicar of Stiffkey; the lion turned on him, and ate him in front of a paying audience.

It is often repeated that the 1950s gave rise to American-inspired youth culture, as well as a popular culture of cheap luxuries – but the pre-war period was clearly there first. And just as the American and German economies recovered as the 1930s wore on, so the general standard of living in Britain improved considerably.

One measure of this was the growing vibrancy of particular areas – such as Soho in London's West End. The traditional French and Italian cafés and restaurants were joined by Chinese, Spanish and Hungarian restaurants. Considering that in 1939, less than 3 per cent of Londoners had been born abroad (compared with 37 per cent today), Soho was a genuine hub of cosmopolitan activity. A *Picture Post* feature noted expanses of cheese, garlands of sausages, rows of straw-covered Chianti bottles, tins of anchovies, olives and fruits, dishes of sweets and coloured beans, and glittering espresso machines. 'The shop windows of Soho,' it observes, 'are crammed, gay, glowing and vivid.' Even more surprisingly, Denmark Street, on the other side of Charing Cross Road, housed a Japanese community, where the truly intrepid could eat Japanese food. This is not a picture one readily associates with the 1930s.

Similarly, at this time, recognisably modern jobs emerged. Bill Taylor could neither read nor write – yet he worked as a long-distance lorry driver. When his firm gave him a delivery note, he would study a map for the place name that most resembled the one on the note. Then he would draw a straight line between his start point and end point, and circle every large town on the way. When he arrived in each town, he would stop and ask the way to the next. 'None of the guv'nors I worked for ever knew I couldn't read,' he says, although he admits that 'it had been easier when I'd started on the horses because some of the horses knew where they were going.'

One perk of Bill's job was the existence of 'lorry girls' who hung around the cafés. 'You'd take them from one town to another,' he says. 'Sometimes they'd stop with you a whole week, sleep with you and keep you company.' In return the driver bought the girls food and cigarettes. 'When the wives found out,' says Bill, 'a lot of marriages broke up.'

Sam Tobin, meanwhile, was a door-to-door vacuum cleaner salesman in north London. On Monday mornings, before setting off on the road, he would join fellow salesmen in a motivational singsong:

> *All the dirt, all the grit,*
> *Hoover gets it every bit,*
> *For it beats as it sweeps as it cleans ...*

Sam's day then became a struggle to be allowed into suburban homes, where he would demonstrate his vacuum cleaner on samples of sand that he carried with him. 'It was pretty soul destroying,' he says, 'and if it was bad weather, or if Electrolux salesmen had done your territory, it was very difficult to get a demonstration anywhere.'

But perhaps the most modern job under way in Britain was being carried out by a recent Jewish immigrant from Poland. Joseph Rotblat was a physicist working in the field of radioactivity who arrived in Britain in April 1939. Earlier in the year, he had read about Frisch and Leitner's discovery of nuclear fission, and it had occurred to him that a staggering release of energy might be possible if a chain reaction could be triggered in a very short time. Initially, he pushed this idea – for an atomic bomb – out of his mind, so concerned was he by the horrifying prospect of creating what would now be called a weapon of mass destruction. But by the time he arrived in Britain, Rotblat had figured that the Nazis might be working on a bomb, making it his duty to share his thoughts with British scientists. 'Perhaps, in my own mind,' he says, 'I was the first person to develop the concept of the nuclear deterrent.' As a result, Rotblat approached Sir James Chadwick, the discoverer of the neutron. Chadwick approved of the idea, and granted Rotblat two assistants. The dark march of atomic progress had begun.

But for all the period's changes, the most anticipated and dreaded was the outbreak of war. Many young men began volunteering to join the British army, while limited conscription was introduced for twenty- and twenty-one-year-olds in April 1939. In the last war, volunteers had joined up enthusiastically, keen to fight for King and Country, eager to put the Kaiser in his place. A quarter of a century on, emotions were more muted. Nevertheless, the 1939 generation showed itself, on balance, to be quietly dutiful and aware of the need to confront Germany.

But there were many who joined up oblivious to the political situation, unconcerned with any sense of duty. Thomas Myers, the young Durham coal miner with whom we began this chapter, joined the Territorial Army in early 1939, because, he says, it was the fashionable thing to do. 'Everybody wanted to be in the Territorials, it was chaotic there were that many joining.' Yet he had no interest in politics. 'I didn't know war was coming,' Thomas says, 'I didn't know anything about Hitler.'

When pressed, he adds that he joined in order to get the occasional weekend away, and evening out. To young men trapped by work and community, the army offered a break from monotony and social restrictions. It offered adventure. George Wagner, the keen dancer from Erdington, says, 'We joined and it was something to do. On top of that, you got paid a bounty, and on top of that, once a year, you used to go away for a fortnight training. It was great.'

Anthony Rhodes, a young Royal Engineers officer, was given a long-serving army batman (a servant). Rhodes describes this man as seeking a niche, a quiet place where he could rest in indefinite seclusion. There were peacetime soldiers, in other words, who were attracted to the army by its *lack* of adventure.

And to some, the army provided a solution. Thomas Lister, a young man from Durham, had not been able to settle down to anything. At the age of fourteen, he had been sent by his father for an interview with an electrical engineer. He had taken one look at the workshop floor – 'it looked like the jaws of hell' – before walking away. He became an errand boy for Burton's Tailors before becoming 'a bit fed up with it'. After that, he had a spell as a wholesale fish salesman. But without a calling, or any particular direction, he would find the enforced discipline and comradeship of the army attractive. And it solved the problem of what he would do with his life – temporarily, at least.

Germany

To be young – and racially pure – in Adolf Hitler's Germany was to be important. In Hitler's eyes, the country's future greatness depended on its young people – but it wasn't their intelligence or initiative that he looked to encourage. Clever weaklings were not going to improve the country's situation. Tough, healthy and strong-willed boys and girls were needed. 'The weak must be chiselled away,' he said in 1938, 'I want young men and women who can suffer pain. A young German must be swift as a greyhound, as tough as leather, and as hard as Krupp's steel.' And though it would never be publicly admitted, they must also be brainwashed to adopt his ideology. Pure by blood, stripped of free will, they were going to make Germany great again.

In 1938, over 80 per cent of young Germans were members of the Hitler Youth organisation. Childhood ended for this generation at the age of ten with admission to the organisation's junior branch. From that moment on, children became the political soldiers of the Fatherland. Boys and girls had separate sections, preparing them for lives as soldiers, housewives and bearers of the Nazi worldview.

The Hitler Youth even had an internal secret police – an infant Gestapo – responsible for rooting out disloyalty and denouncing members. In one case, Walter Hess reported his own father for calling Hitler a crazed maniac. The father ended up in a concentration camp while Walter was promoted for showing admirable vigilance. Hitler, meanwhile, was being worshipped as a secular god by boys and girls who would recite an incantation based on the Lord's Prayer:

> Adolf Hitler, you are our great Führer. Thy name makes the enemy tremble. Thy Third Reich comes, thy will alone is law upon the earth. Let us hear daily thy voice and order us by thy leadership, for we will obey to the end and even with our lives. We praise thee! Heil Hitler!

Melita Maschmann was a member of the League of German Girls, the female branch of the Hitler Youth. Aged eighteen in 1938, she began working as a press officer for the organisation. In November, after attending a rally in Frankfurt, the head of the local SS asked her if she wanted to come with him. Something exciting, he said, was going to happen that evening. Tired, she decided against it. The next morning, she could see broken glass and smashed furniture strewn everywhere. Finding a policeman, Melita asked what had happened. He told her that this was a Jewish area, and that 'the National Soul had boiled over'.

Melita was witnessing the aftermath of Kristallnacht – Crystal Night – named for the glittering glass shards strewn across the streets. Instigated by the Nazi leadership, mobs of stormtroopers and Hitler Youth set out to vandalise synagogues and Jewish-owned properties throughout Germany and German-controlled areas. Michael Bruce was an English newspaper correspondent in Berlin. He followed a mob as it moved towards a synagogue. Before long, the building was on fire, and people cheered as they ripped wood from the façade to feed the flames inside. The crowd continued to a nearby Jewish shop. Men and women, howling with exhilaration, started hurling concrete blocks through the doors and windows, fighting to get inside to loot the stock. Bruce noticed an old Jewish woman being dragged from her house, and ran to help another reporter pull her free. The mob then moved off towards a hospital for sick Jewish children, where the leaders – many of them women – attacked hospital staff as the young patients were forced to run barefoot over broken glass. Bruce described the spectacle as 'one of the foulest exhibitions of bestiality I have ever witnessed'.

Riots and attacks erupted on an astonishing scale. Bernt Engelmann was a seventeen-year-old living in Düsseldorf, about to join the Luftwaffe. As young thugs smashed up an apartment owned by a Jewish family in his building, he stood outside wondering whether to confront them. The police were nearby but were refusing to interfere. Eventually, Bernt ran inside the apartment and tried to sound authoritative.

'You're in charge here?' he barked at the ringleader. 'You're through here, right?'

'That's correct, we're finished here.'

To Bernt's relief, the youths left. But throughout the attack a little girl – the daughter of the family – had been hiding inside the apartment. Relieved that the youths hadn't seen her, Bernt went looking for her parents while his mother put her to bed with a sleeping pill. Finding the parents on the street, he reassured them that their daughter was safe, and persuaded them to spend the night with non-Jewish friends – who embraced them wordlessly as they hurried into their apartment.

As Bernt returned to his building, he watched the body of a Jewish doctor being brought out of a house. 'He put up a good fight,' said a bystander. As he crunched his way over broken glass and discarded belongings, Bernt saw people with full bags, hiding in alleyways. He couldn't tell whether they were fleeing Jews or cringing looters.

On Steinstrasse, he met a cowering couple – a woman and a child. Telling them not to be afraid, he led them to the house of a notable Nazi who was secretly harbouring Jews before smuggling them abroad. Bernt left them there and went home, where along with sympathetic neighbours he began to clear up the mess in the Jewish family's apartment.

Walking through Düsseldorf in the midst of this state-led anarchy, he noted people's reactions: 'It's a disgrace! The police just stand by and do nothing!' 'We Germans will pay dearly for what was done to the Jews last night!' And one reaction that lands awkwardly on modern ears, but was common at the time: 'They shouldn't have done that! I'm sure the Führer doesn't approve!' But there were many more bystanders who said nothing, concealing their fear or apathy or support for the system.

Throughout Germany, Austria and the Sudetenland, hundreds of synagogues were destroyed, thousands of shops were smashed and looted, houses were torn apart, Jews were attacked, and tens of thousands of Jewish men were arrested and sent to concentration camps. It is probable that several hundred Jews were murdered, although we will never know for certain.

The government quickly announced that these had been spontaneous riots – the 'boiling over of the National Soul' observed by the Frankfurt policeman – and that the Jewish community was entirely to blame. It would therefore be fined the equivalent of $400 million, while all insurance payments would be confiscated.

Kristallnacht marked the start of concerted violence aimed at ridding Germany of Jews. It paved the way for mass exterminations. And the overwhelmingly passive reaction of citizens reassured the government that they could take further – and more extreme – action in the future. To take the example of Melita Maschmann, as she stepped gingerly over broken glass in Frankfurt, she was perfectly aware that something terrible had happened. But she quickly rationalised it. The Jews, she knew, were enemies of the German people. Perhaps this event – whatever it had been – would teach them a much-needed lesson. And then she put it completely out of her mind.

Almost six years earlier, on the January day in 1933 when Adolf Hitler came to power, Melita had been an ordinary fifteen-year-old girl without political opinions or racial prejudices. Germany itself was quite unlike the fanatical country it would become. On that day, Melita sat with a dressmaker – whom she liked very much – as the woman altered one of Melita's mother's dresses to fit her. The dressmaker was working class and interesting and *different*. She had a hunched back and walked with a limp. She wore a metal swastika on her coat. She talked about this man Hitler, how he was going to make Germany fairer, how class differences wouldn't matter any more, how servants would be able to eat at the same table as their rich employers. The dressmaker's eyes came alive as she spoke of the 'National Community'.

Melita was struck emotionally by what she was hearing, moved by the idea of a future in which 'people of all classes would live together like brothers and sisters'. However odd it may seem that Nazism – the most wicked and hateful political ideology of the twentieth century – could once have been thought to represent social justice and protection for the weak, this was how it was portrayed in 1933.

Later that evening, Melita and her brother went into the centre of Berlin where they watched the Nazi Party's victory celebrations. For the second time in a day she was enthralled, but this time it was the torchlit procession that gripped her. The flickering flames, the red and black flags, the feet marching as one, the prominence of boys and girls like herself, the aggressively sentimental music, all of these played their part. Almost overcome by a wave of hope and solidarity, she felt euphoric. And when a young man suddenly leapt from his marching column to punch somebody standing next to her, her instinctive horror was laced with rapture. As she explains:

'For the flag we are ready to die' the torch-bearers had sung. It was not a matter of clothing or food or school essays, but of life and death ... I was overcome with a burning desire to belong to these people for whom it was a matter of life and death.

In the end, though, it was neither the politics nor the spectacle that converted Melita to Nazism – though they were the chief contributing factors. The deciding feature was teenage rebellion.

Melita's parents were conservative. They supported the old social order, and they had little interest in young people or the rights of workers. They had raised their daughter strictly, expecting her obedience just as they expected it from their servants. Even before her political conversion, Melita had come to resent their attitudes. Nazism was a timely antidote. With its emphasis on youth and working people, and the radical certainty of its message, it stood for everything that her parents did not. For Melita's generation in Germany, rebellion was not Elvis Presley, the Beatles, David Bowie or Public Enemy. It was Adolf Hitler.

But there were other, more prosaic reasons why young people became enthusiastic Nazis. They had, for example, little faith in existing institutions and forms of government. Democracy – which had no great tradition in Germany – had presided over successive crises. In 1922, a loaf of bread cost three Reichsmarks; the following November it cost eighty billion Reichsmarks. Workers began to receive their salary twice a day so they could afford to eat both lunch and dinner. And the depression of the early 1930s left six million people unemployed and a government so toothless that its people lacked the most basic services.

The National Socialists, with their charismatic leader, their understanding of propaganda and their racial mysticism, cleverly communicated their offer of work, bread and political stability. It was a straightforward offer, and in the circumstances an attractive one. But by accepting it, the people allowed the Nazis to trample over previously established boundaries. And the further the Nazis trampled, the more implicated the people became, to the point where any behaviour at all could be justified, or had to be ignored.

At school, Melita Maschmann's closest friend, who entered her class in the spring of 1933, was Jewish. She became close to the girl – despite knowing her religion. They came to share an interest in literature and philosophy. And while they didn't discuss religion, they shared stories of their respective youth groups. But Melita's brainwashing soon began.

Rather than analysing Germany's experience of the First World War for its military and economic failings, German children were taught to blame defeat on being 'stabbed in the back' by Jews. 'International Jewry' was blamed for both capitalism and communism, and thus for all the world's problems. Melita sat through a series of lectures on Jewish religious teachings, in which a supposed expert taught that Jews were responsible for the ritual murder of Christians. And though she claims that she saw through the lecturer's nonsense, she could not – or would not – step back sufficiently to acknowledge her own brainwashing. She laughed at the man and his words, but failed to question their purpose.

The relentless indoctrination ultimately worked. Melita came to believe in the bogeyman Jew, the Jew as a concept. He was indeed to blame for capitalism, communism and everything besides. His blood was corrupting, his spirit was seditious. And Adolf Hitler was sure that the indoctrination would work. In 1933, he said, 'When an opponent says, "I will not come over to your side," I calmly say, "Your child belongs to us already ..."'

But because she felt comfortable with her Jewish friend, Melita could not accept that she would come to any harm. When she learned that Jews were being dismissed from their professions and confined to ghettos, she rationalised that it was only 'the Jew', the bogeyman, who was being persecuted. And despite being an intelligent young woman, the rationalisation worked for her.

Denial of reality was a common defence mechanism among Germans. Bernt Engelmann knew a Jewish doctor who was visited by a young German stormtrooper. 'There was nothing wrong with him really,' the doctor explained. 'His throat was a little inflamed, probably from shouting "Heil" so much.' In fact, the stormtrooper just wanted to talk. Perhaps he wanted to ease his guilt. He told the doctor what he had been doing recently, which included helping to rig an election by filling in over five hundred ballot papers. As he left, the stormtrooper spoke seriously. 'I have nothing against you. I want you to know that.' And then he gave a Nazi salute, said 'Heil Hitler!' and walked out. As Heinrich Himmler once said in a speech to concentration camp guards, 'Every German has his favourite Jew.'

Once the Nazis were in power, it was a matter of days before freedoms began to disappear from every sector of life. The Enabling Act allowed Hitler to make laws without recourse to the Reichstag, freedom of speech was abolished, concentration camps were introduced, political parties were banned, trade unions were destroyed, beatings were administered, and books reflecting an 'un-German spirit' were burned. In a speech to Berlin students at a book-burning, Joseph Goebbels said:

The future German man will not just be a man of books, but a man of character. It is to this end that we want to educate you. As a young person, to already have the courage to face the pitiless glare, to overcome the fear of death, and to regain respect for death – this is the task of the young generation.

Here is the key to Nazi intentions. Young people faced a future of action, sacrifice, certainty and obedience – with no room for individuality. As head of the German Labour Front, Robert Ley, declared, 'such a thing as a private individual does not exist.' Hitler went further, privately describing how, from the age of ten until adulthood, a German youth would be sent from one militaristic organisation to another, until he or she was a 'complete National Socialist'. Once this had been achieved, he said, 'they will never be free again as long as they live.'

Hitler's ambition could be seen taking shape. Christabel Bielenberg, a British woman living in Hamburg, was a committed anti-Nazi. After two years of National Socialist rule, she observed how the youngsters she saw hiking the country roads were now dressed in dreary Hitler Youth uniforms, with identical haircuts: short hair for the boys and plaits for the girls. Individualism, she noted, seemed to have evaporated. But she was also forced to admit that people seemed more cheerful, and were behaving more politely. Fear of a financial crisis seemed to have passed, and a sense of national self-respect was returning.

Optimism was not visible everywhere, of course. In April 1936, Bernt Engelmann was sitting in a train carriage as it passed through Duisberg. At the time, the long-distance 'Adolf Hitler roads' were being built, and two construction workers were sitting opposite him, moaning to each other about the project. Into this mix came a young female member of the National Socialist Women's League. 'Heil Hitler!' she said cheerfully to everybody, and sat down. For a while, she read her newspaper while the men continued moaning. 'Is this whining really necessary?' the woman said suddenly. 'You should be grateful that you have work and thank the Führer for getting rid of unemployment!'

The men stared at her, before one of them spoke. He explained that they were on compulsory service with just ten days' holiday a year, their accommodation was a straw mattress in a wooden barracks, their food was abysmal and their pay was low and regularly falling lower. In fact, the man said, he was earning less than he had before the Nazis came to power, and was no longer even allowed to carry out his own trade.

The young woman was silent for a while. Finally she spoke, protesting that Germany had regained its strength, that Hitler had achieved miracles, and that the people now had hope. 'You must have faith in the Führer!' she said.

We have already noted the quasi-religious quality of the Dunkirk evacuation, but this pales beside the secular sanctity of the Third Reich, where Hitler and the Fatherland stood for God and Heaven. The young woman was invoking Hitler just as a Christian invokes Jesus or a Muslim invokes Allah. And two years later, shortly before Kristallnacht, Melita Maschmann was having another of her euphoric, quasi-religious experiences, this time at a meeting of leaders of the League of German Girls. The sense of being young, of belonging, of loving each other, of sharing a common task

– making Germany great again – filled her with overwhelming joy.

But Melita's greatest joy and intoxication were to come once the war had begun on 1 September 1939 with the invasion of Poland. Depicted in Germany as a legitimate action to liberate Germans living in occupied territories, the invasion saw Melita being sent in an official capacity to a town on the Polish border. Arriving by train, she was seized by a feeling of invulnerability. All sense of fear dropped away as she felt an identification with something greater than herself. Fulfilling Robert Ley's ideal, she was no longer an individual. She had become Germany.

But it was not just fear that Melita lost when the war began. She was sent, in 1940, to Wartheland, an annexed area containing a large number of Jews and Poles and only a small minority of Germans. Together with a Hitler Youth leader, she was driving across the Warta river when they became stuck. Stranded, with the waters rising, their car was eventually towed to safety by a team of gaunt, bearded men who lived locally. These, it turned out, were Jews forced to live together in ghetto fashion. Once ashore, the Jews worked busily to clean the car of mud and slime. And just as Melita was about to climb in again, one of the men stopped her; he had found one more tiny piece of dirt that he wanted to remove.

When the man had finished, Melita and the Hitler Youth leader drove away without saying a word to the Jews who had gone out of their way to help them. She had not even looked them in the face. She despised them for being Jews and for wanting to help those who despised them. But she was also ashamed of her attitude. She knew she should have thanked these people.

But how could she acknowledge their humanity? They were not individuals. And nor was she. She had become Germany.

The United States

The Germans, of course, were not the only western people to suffer economic difficulties between the wars. The United States had undergone a great stock market crash in 1929, and suffered a grinding depression for years afterwards. Nearly all levels of society were affected. But as wages dropped and work became harder to come by, it was the poorest who experienced the greatest suffering.

With Franklin D. Roosevelt's 'new deal for the American people', and specifically the introduction of the National Youth Administration, members of the struggling generation were finally offered hope. They were provided with grants in return for part-time work, allowing them to remain in high school and college. And they were placed in job training programmes or full-time work by local Youth Administration offices.

This was a large-scale federal programme which, to some, seemed un-American in its focus on collective welfare. Indeed, with his youth organisations and work camps for young people, his conservation projects stressing the importance of physical fitness and the outdoor life, and his myriad new agencies and regulations, Roosevelt's initiatives could seem remarkably similar to Adolf Hitler's.

Certainly, both leaders inherited ravaged economies. They were both trying to restore their nations' self-respect as well as their finances. And they were both placing huge impor-tance on their young people. The young were the bearers of national resurgence, and they were set aside for special treatment.

But that is where the similarities end. In Hitler's Germany, the state set about stripping away the individuality of its young people. A young German faced a future of service and obedience to the Fatherland, its needs eclipsing his or her own. Roosevelt's initiatives may have been collective, but he had no desire to brainwash America's youth. His New Deal offered individual growth alongside the nation's. And how could it have offered anything else in America – a country built on self-reliance and self-expression?

We are very used, nowadays, to youth culture coming out of America before spreading around the world. And it was in the late 1930s, as Roosevelt's measures had their impact and the depression started to ease, that genuine youth culture was first seen. While jazz music had been popular for some time, this was the period when it exploded into Swing and spread among all levels of society. And while the word 'teen-ager' would not be used for a few more years, and rock and roll was still a decade and a half away, the right music, the right clothes and the right attitudes took on a new importance among American 'teens' (a word that *was* in use).

In large part this was thanks to the New Deal. Three-quarters of those aged between fourteen and eighteen were now staying in high school, a far higher proportion than ever before. No longer so influenced by their parents, or at all by their senior workmates, they began to create a distinct identity inside their teen bubble. When sociologist August Hollingshead conducted a study of the young people in a midwestern town (called Elmtown to disguise its identity) he was able to look inside the bubble. One girl, a misunderstood teenager years before the breed was identified, said about her parents, 'Sometimes they just don't understand what kids want to do, and they think we ought to act like they acted twenty years ago.'

Other subjects referred to clothes and style. 'Janet's a big girl,' said one, 'and she doesn't dress right; so she just isn't accepted.' Peer pressure was intense, and dressing right was possible because high school students had a disposable income. They lived at home, usually received money from their parents, and often had part-time jobs. Without rent or bills to pay, there was no excuse for not dressing 'slick', as one Elmtown girl put it. And even young people without money, living on the small amounts paid by the National Youth Administration, were keen to spend what they had to look good. American materialism, after all, has a proud history.

The Elmtown study is interesting in relation to sex and marriage, revealing that it was a badge of honour among many boys to be sexually active. 'A boy who is known or believed to be a virgin is not respected,' writes Hollingshead, and he describes a clique of lower-class boys calling themselves 'The Five Fs'. This near-acronym stood for 'Find 'em, feed 'em, feel 'em, fuck 'em, forget 'em'.

A girl, on the other hand, had to tread a dangerously thin line between 'having some fun' and becoming 'free and easy'. 'Mary' told Hollingshead about going to a dance with a young man. At the dance, she decided that the boy 'could have it' but she would have to get drunk to go through with it. So the couple drove to a bar where Mary drank a double bourbon and three double whiskies, before driving to an isolated spot. 'Oh, it was wonderful!' said Mary. Over the next few months, she had affairs with five other men, going on at least four dates with each before 'becoming intimate'.

She was adamant that none of the boys had known in advance that 'she knew what it was all about'. And then, at the age of eighteen, she married a twenty-year-old mill worker. Mary's brief but intense adventures were over.

Yet for any social changes, it was the music that really marked out the new youth culture. Swing music had a terrifically fast tempo, and sounded terrifying to older white listeners. It encouraged wild, out of control dancing, even solo dancing without a partner. Numbers like Benny Goodman's 'Sing Sing Sing' had a brutal, thumping drumbeat. Hep cats (aficionados) used jive (slang) when beating up the chops (talking). They wore wild drapes (clothes) and spent hard (enjoyable) blacks (nights) in the Apple (Harlem). But despite – and because of – its edgy street culture background, Swing became hugely popular with young white audiences.

On the evening of 16 January 1938, Swing crossed over into the mainstream, when Benny Goodman's orchestra played Carnegie Hall, New York City's most prestigious concert venue. Asked how long an intermission he wanted, Goodman said, 'I don't know. How long does Toscanini have?' And when, several months later, a hundred thousand people of all races attended a Swing Jamboree in Chicago, music seemed to be lifting the nation. 'Swing,' reported the *New York Times*, 'is the voice of youth striving to be heard in this fast-moving world of ours.' It was the voice of hope as America finally emerged from the depression.

But it would be a mistake to think that the young had moved beyond their elders. A poll conducted by the American Institute of Public Opinion in 1940 asked young people across the country, 'Would you favor changing to a different form of government if it would promise you more in the way of a job?' Eighty-eight per cent of the sample answered 'No'. 'Ours is the only sound form of government,' said one respondent, speaking for most.

Young Americans may have grown more optimistic over the 1930s, they may have developed their own culture, but they were happy to remain American. And to a real degree, they were the benchmark by which the new Europe measured itself. Their culture was worshipped and copied in Britain, reviled and banned in Germany. But as detached as they were making themselves, they would not ultimately be able to escape the tensions brewing in Europe. The new world had not yet outgrown the old.

Three

The Long and the Short and the Tall

On 3 September 1939, British Prime Minister Neville Chamberlain announced that Britain was at war with Germany. The Royal Air Force had already flown a small advance party to France. The next day, further advance parties set sail from Portsmouth. Within a week, the men of four divisions were arriving at French ports – just as their fathers and uncles had done a little over a quarter of a century earlier.

But promptness does not indicate readiness. Major General Bernard Montgomery, commander of 3rd Division, writes that the British Army 'was totally unfit to fight a first-class war on the continent of Europe'. Britain was justifiably renowned for her Royal Navy; she had contributed fully to the development of aerial warfare. But the army that crossed to France in September 1939 was both undermanned and underequipped.

As recently as April 1938, the government had determined that Britain's response to a European war would be chiefly naval and aerial. Her land forces would not be sent to Europe; they would defend Britain and her still widely spread Empire. But by the start of war, a desperate reappraisal and a frantic burst of rearmament and troop training had taken place.

Conscription had been introduced. There was a massive amount of catching up to be done.

In fact, the nation's soldiers were to be engaging in modern warfare against armoured divisions, yet most of their anti-tank rifles would prove useless, knocking out more British shoulders than German tanks. And though the British army had been the first to use tanks, on the Somme in 1916, 1st Armoured Division would not be ready to cross the Channel for many months. Through the period to the Dunkirk evacuation, the British had very few effective tanks. Only the Matilda Mark II – with its 2-pounder cannon, impressive speed and thick armour – was a match for the best French and German tanks. Montgomery, a divisional commander, wrote that he did not see a single British tank throughout the winter. Put simply, when the British Expeditionary Force sailed to France, it was not ready to go to war.

Despite this, in November 1939, Lord Gort, commander-in-chief of the BEF, told journalist James Lansdale Hodson, 'I have never had the smallest qualm about the outcome of this war.' Gort was a buoyant man and he was doing his best to buoy the country. But beyond the state of his army, he had another major problem. As head of the Expeditionary Force, he was answerable to the local French commander, General Georges, who was in turn under the command of French supreme commander General Gamelin. On the face of it, this was acceptable given the relative size of the forces, but in practice it meant that the BEF could be treated in a subordinate fashion. The latest plans and reports could be withheld, advice and opinions could be ignored. Gort had a responsibility to keep a close watch on his ally.

The British Expeditionary Force, as we have seen, was chiefly made up of young men whose attitudes were formed during the depression, who were influenced by the growing youth culture, and who joined up for reasons ranging from a search for excitement to an escape from unemployment. But the BEF was a broad church. Cyril Roberts, a lance sergeant in the Queen's Royal Regiment, was the son of a black Trinidadian father and a white mother from Lancashire, disowned by her family for marrying a black man. At a time when roughly 0.0003 per cent of the British population was black or mixed race, Cyril was unusual not only in the BEF, but in British society as a whole.

Growing up in south London, Cyril and his brother, Victor, learned to stand up for themselves. 'If you were the only black kid in the class,' says Cyril's daughter, Lorraine, 'you just had to get on with it.' But the boys had a role model. Their father, George, had served with the Middlesex Regiment in the First World War, becoming known as 'The Coconut Bomber' for his grenade-tossing ability, a skill he inadvertently picked up (so the story went) while knocking coconuts out of trees in Trinidad.

An apprentice telephone engineer before the war, Cyril followed his father into the army, joining up under age, and finding himself promoted above older, more experienced men. 'He was very calm and organised,' says Lorraine. 'He had an air about him. He could take command and people did as they were told.'

Cyril's battalion sailed from Southampton, reaching Le Havre early the next morning. These young men, like so many others, were travelling abroad for the first time. What should they expect? What would France look like? Would it be *different*?

Second Lieutenant Peter Hadley, of the Royal Sussex Regiment, noted an atmosphere of undisguised excitement among his men as they crossed the Channel. They were like children on a Sunday school outing. But after only a short time in France, Hadley began reading letters from his charges to their parents and girlfriends, expressing disappointment that the people and the houses seemed very much the same as those in England.

Cyril Roberts' battalion had a similar experience. At first, the soldiers crowded the train windows as they sped through northern France. But they were very soon bored, and drifting away to play cards. Arriving at their destination at Abancourt in the Pas de Calais, the men were set to work building railway lines. It was hard, physical labour, carried out with pick and shovel, without any mechanical assistance. And this, as far as they were concerned, would be the extent of their role. They were not trained for fighting.

Shortly before its outbreak, most people in Britain were strongly in favour of war. And once it had begun, the majority believed that Hitler's bluff had now been called. We have heard what Lord Gort told a journalist in November 1939. Victory was certain, and everybody from the commander-in-chief to the man on the Clapham omnibus thought so. Of course, many of these people had also believed that the last war would be over by Christmas.

But war was also welcomed for personal reasons. Fred Carter had been an unemployed concreter before joining the Royal Engineers. He viewed the war as an opportunity to return to his old trade – or something very similar. John Williams of the Durham Light Infantry felt actively sorry for the 'poor sods' not in the army, condemned to their ordinary little jobs while he and his mates got the glory and the girls.

Listening to Chamberlain's announcement in his Surrey mess, Jimmy Langley, a Coldstream Guards subaltern, admits that he half-expected a couple of armed Germans to burst through the door. And for a very few Britons, the action *did* begin straight away. Winifred Pax-Walker was an eighteen-year-old Londoner who hoped to become a movie actress. She was travelling to Montreal with her mother on the Anchor-Donaldson ocean liner *Athenia*.

That evening, as the ship was sailing two hundred miles west of Ireland, a note was posted announcing that war had been declared. At dinner, an authoritative-sounding man, who had been gassed in the last war, told Winifred and her mother that *Athenia* would be safe from attack. The Germans, he said, would not attack until the ship was returning from North America packed full of armaments. Travelling away from Britain, they had nothing to worry about. Just as the man finished speaking, the first of two German torpedoes struck *Athenia*.

Hitler had given orders that no passenger ships were to be attacked; but it seems that the commander of U-30, a German submarine, mistook *Athenia* for an armed merchant cruiser, zigzagging as she was with all lights blacked out. Fearful of the consequences for a peace settlement, German propaganda minister Joseph Goebbels quickly denied any German responsibility.

Winifred and her mother had been hoping to escape the war. And yet it had found them within hours. As *Athenia* began sinking, stern first, their lifeboat failed to lower properly, and nobody could find the plug for its bung-hole. These problems resolved, passengers started to descend two at a time, causing the lifeboat's ladder to break. Seamen had to fish people out of the water with boat-hooks. Winifred's mother was picked up off the ship's deck by a sailor and thrown into the boat. Winifred made her own way down.

In the dark, the lifeboat encountered a Norwegian freighter, *Knut Nelson*, and the passengers were brought on board. As they sailed towards Galway in Ireland, the freighter's captain told Winifred, 'You British! You're always at war! Be like Norway! Keep out of all these things!' A little later, as the freight's tender approached Galway harbour, Winifred overheard two middle-aged English ladies chatting away as though at a Women's Institute meeting. 'Of course, my dear,' said one, 'you have to pour the pink icing over the cake …'

One hundred and twelve of *Athenia*'s passengers were killed in the attack. In its aftermath, a few ocean liners continued to cross the Atlantic. On board the Cunard liner *Aquitania*, it was said that American passengers nervously prayed for the crossing to end peacefully – while British passengers sat in the Palladium Lounge determinedly discussing the weather.

By 27 September, 152,031 British soldiers (and 60,000 tons of frozen meat) had safely reached France. John Williams was surprised to see so many bright lights in French towns, utterly different from blackout conditions in England. 'All these bars and brothels with lights on!' he remembers. William Harding was touched by the warm welcome the Royal Artillery received. Marching through the streets of Cherbourg, the soldiers were showered with flowers by people leaning so far out of windows they seemed about to fall.

And once they had reached their destination, east of Lille on the French side of the border with Belgium, the men started to dig in, and to consolidate houses and pillboxes. They behaved as though they were settling down – even though they were not intending to remain. Once the anticipated German attack began, they were to move seventy-five miles east to take up new positions on the River Dyle in

Belgium. There were a number of reasons for this; the French wanted to keep the fighting away from their industrial areas, the British did not want the Germans to establish airfields within striking distance of southern England, and both nations wanted Belgium as a partner. But because Belgium professed neutrality, the French and British were not permitted to enter Belgian territory until the start of the attack, and so, for the time being, they built entirely pointless defences.

For Winston Churchill, Belgium's position was a source of frustration. In January 1940, he compared neutrality in the face of a sabre-rattling Germany with feeding a crocodile. Each neutral country was hoping that feeding the crocodile enough would ensure its being eaten last. Still, it is hard not to sympathise with Belgium; had she gone to war, the Germans would have used that as a pretext to invade. As Oliver Harvey, British minister in Paris, observed in January 1940, 'Germany will invade Belgium if it suits, whatever Belgium does.'

And so British troops built their meaningless Gort line. The winter trenches were so wet, and the water table so high, that infantrymen ended up digging breastworks practically naked from the waist down, with canvas wrapped around their feet. Richard Annand, a Durham Light Infantry officer, found that if he joined in with the digging, his men responded and worked harder. His brigadier quickly ordered him out of the trench. His job, he was told, was to supervise his men – not to become one of them. By blurring the lines, he was queering the pitch for members of his class. Nevertheless, Annand returned to the trench and continued to muck in. Eventually the brigadier reappeared, murmuring angrily to the colonel, 'I notice you have some well-spoken private soldiers in your battalion.'

The winter of 1939 was particularly cold, and soldiers' living conditions were poor. Finding their barn overrun by rats, men of the Royal Corps of Signals built raised beds out of materials they had to hand – wood and telephone cables. Colin Ashford remembers washing and shaving in a freezing algae-filled pond as cattle drank from it. Percy Beaton of the Royal Engineers had to clean up a billet that French soldiers had been using. 'There was excreta all over the place,' he says. 'The French had obviously wiped their backsides with their hands and wiped it down the wall.'

And once British soldiers started to wear battledress, replacing the more formal service dress worn previously, their overall discipline declined. Battledress had no buttons to shine, and although boots still needed polishing, and cotton webbing still required blanco, soldiers were no longer, says John Williams, 'the smart, button shining people we'd been the month before'.

For some it was difficult even to look presentable. 'My battledress was very dodgy,' says Royal Engineer Fred Carter. In the quartermaster's stores he had been issued with a uniform several sizes too big, and he tried to make all the necessary alterations himself. He was, unfortunately, not much of a tailor.

Battledress consisted of a greenish-brown jacket and trousers in wool serge, worn by officers and men alike (although officers wore it open-necked with a tie). At this early stage of the war, it bore very few distinguishing marks or insignia. Officially, the only insignia allowed were slip-on titles on the shoulder (with a regiment's name in black letters on khaki cloth), a plain fabric rank badge, and a plain fabric trade badge. Reflecting their elite status, Guards regiments were allowed to wear coloured shoulder titles. Helmets, meanwhile, could be worn with or without hessian camouflage covers.

Such standardisation of uniform was intended to offer as few clues as possible to a curious enemy. (The only evidence of personal identity were the green and red identity tags worn round the neck, bearing the soldier's name, number and religion.) This being the army, however, the rules were quickly tested. Some regiments continued to wear old-style metal shoulder titles, others wore coloured shoulder titles, and others still wore sleeve 'flashes' in different patterns and colours. So while the majority of British soldiers at Dunkirk would have looked uniformly spartan (particularly when wearing the plain, heavy greatcoat), there would have been plenty of exceptions.

One exception was the Queen's Own Cameron Highlanders, the only British Expeditionary Force regiment to wear the kilt in France – despite being officially forbidden to do so. The tartan was known as Cameron of Erracht, although it would often have been obscured by 'kilt aprons'. These were plain kilt covers, tied round the waist. With their prominent frontal pouches, they gave the wearer the air of a khaki kangaroo.

Army food was rarely savoured. There was no Army Catering Corps until 1941, and according to George Wagner, the thickest bloke was usually picked to do the cooking. Wagner's company cook, known as 'Mad Jack', was known for his indigestible curry. 'Anybody who volunteered could become a cook,' says Norman Prior of the Lancashire Fusiliers, who has memories of the unenthusiastic volunteers dolloping out lumps of Maconochies stew – that unloved, tinned staple of the last war.

An alternative existed. British soldiers, raised on plain diets, were now in a country where food was savoured and celebrated, and where unusual animals were eaten with rich sauces. But, according to James Lansdale Hodson, the British were mostly unwilling to try anything new: 'Some … who have the opportunity of having a lunch such as soup, sardines, veal and coffee, much prefer egg and chips. They don't like omelettes much … It's fried eggs the soldiers want, not scrambled eggs.'

Scottish NCO Alexander Frederick paid five francs each evening for the same meal – a plate of egg and chips, a bowl of café au lait and a chunk of bread. Spending most of his spare time in a Normandy café run by a widow, John Williams had only one complaint: she could not fry an egg. 'So I went into the kitchen one day and asked whether I could show her.'

Not everybody conformed to the stereotype. Colin Ashford enjoyed trying new foods in Lille; the local cakes, he says, were far better than anything he ate at home. And he tried horsemeat and chips. 'It was all right …'

There were unfamiliar drinks on offer too. Estaminets were cafés serving alcohol where some men learned to drink wine and lager, while others settled for their usual dark beer. It was almost effeminate to drink light ale or lager, remembers John Williams. 'Nowadays, I see Marks and Spencer full of wines and it makes me laugh when I think of the days when wine was something rather strange that the French liked.'

And while Williams claims that British soldiers never caused any trouble, sometimes, of course, they did. In December 1939, a twenty-three-year-old military policeman, Lance Corporal Rowson Goulding, was charged with murder following a fight in an estaminet. A study of the court-martial transcript reveals some undisputed facts.

Goulding and four colleagues were drinking together in the Café de la Mairie in Drocourt when they became involved in a brawl with locals. Chairs and bottles were thrown, and minutes later shots were fired in the street, and a local man, Fernand Bince, was killed.

French witnesses to the brawl claimed that the soldiers were very drunk. They had started pouring their own drinks, breaking glasses, and taking cigars from behind the counter. When asked to pay, said the French, the soldiers resisted and started a fight. They were all eventually thrown out of the estaminet, but not before some of the locals – including Fernand Bince – had been injured.

The soldiers, on the other hand, denied being drunk. They claimed that one of their colleagues had been injured in an unprovoked attack by a local man – which had led to the brawl. They said that they had helped to carry their injured colleague outside, and that Goulding had been particularly angry about the incident.

Whichever version – if either – is accurate, it seems that Goulding then hurried back to his billet and seized a revolver from a colleague before returning to the café. Bince may too have fetched a gun before also returning to the café. There were no witnesses to subsequent events – but several shots were heard, and Goulding was seen dragging Bince down the street by the ankles. Bince died shortly afterwards in a British casualty clearing station. He had been shot once in the chest.

The court martial found Goulding guilty of murder and sentenced him to death. But two letters in mitigation sit on the court file. The first was dictated by Bince's mother and translated into English. She expresses the greatest sympathy for Goulding, and begs the authorities to show him mercy. 'I would not have his mother weeping for her son as I do for mine.'

The second letter, from the local mayor, also urges a reprieve. In touchingly flawed English, he writes: 'It certainly is not because a man has committed a grave fault that we shall cease to love the British Army. In taking into consideration my request, you will foster further the love and, this is why, with my respect, I would ask you to be as clement as possible for this poor Corporal.'

In the event, Goulding *was* reprieved. His sentence was commuted to life in prison. And these letters reveal a period when the French could forgive the British a great deal. As George Wagner says, 'They used to look on us as though we were saviours.'

But this attitude was not universal. When subaltern Anthony Irwin offered to mend a farmer's roof after a piece of ack-ack shell had fallen through, he was rewarded for his thoughtfulness with a hysterical tirade from the farmer's wife. Blaming the war on the British, she threw a pewter mug at Irwin's head.

The same officer was left in little doubt about French attitudes towards Germans. Billeted with a wine merchant and his family near Lille, one of the man's daughters, a woman of about thirty, angrily described her experiences in the last war when two German officers had been billeted with them. Whenever the Germans were dissatisfied with their food or wine, they would grab her, force her to sit inside the washing boiler, and threaten to burn her until they received something better. She endured this treatment for two years. John Williams, meanwhile, found himself billeted with two elderly sisters who ran a post office. They too had housed a German officer during the last war, a man who would regularly get drunk and vomit on the stairs. When one of the sisters had called him a drunken pig, she had been hauled in front of the commandant and imprisoned for several weeks. Her sister, she said, had come to the jail every day and dropped bread through the bars.

Yet for all the stories of German brutality, some of the current British troops could behave atrociously – not least of all those in the Auxiliary Military Pioneer Corps. In December 1939, the British adjutant general noted that the pioneers' behaviour was causing a deterioration in British relations with the French. The unit's men were old (with an average age of almost fifty), they lacked discipline (they had more courts martial than any other unit in France), they were often led by second-rate officers, and they worked as untrained labourers.

Percy Beaton, a Royal Engineer who worked alongside a company of pioneers, was both protected and intimidated by them. 'They looked on us as young and inexperienced soldiers,' he says, 'and they used to father us.' But he was extremely careful not to cross them after witnessing their treatment of an unpopular sergeant who was bundled out of an estaminet and dragged face down along a cobbled street. Afterwards, says Beaton, you couldn't recognise him. 'Only two slits and a little bit of mouth.'

Months later, during the latter stages of the retreat, John Williams halted a pioneer company as it hurried towards the coast; it was fleeing when it should have been fighting, and he said as much to the sergeant major running at its head. Unsurprisingly, the sergeant major disagreed. 'We're bloody well getting out of here!' he said.

'You should be bloody ashamed of yourself!' said Williams. 'You're a sergeant major in the British army and you're talking about getting out in the presence of all these men?'

Several pioneers aimed their rifles at Williams; they threatened to shoot him. Shaking with fear, he raised his own rifle. 'The first one who shoots, you won't stop me firing this! Now which one of you wants to die?'

Slowly, the pioneers backed down, and they took part in the defence.

A while later, Williams saw the sergeant major lying on a stretcher, with half a buttock missing. 'You said you were bloody well getting out of it, Sergeant Major?' he said. 'Well, I'm glad to see you *are* getting out of it!'

Yet for all the problems they would face in the future, a theme can be deduced from soldiers' accounts of the phoney war: it was a kind of holiday. 'We didn't think there was a war on,' says Williams.

British Expeditionary Force disciplinary records reveal very low rates of desertion throughout the period. In fact, after a warning was issued that troublemakers would be sent home to England, the behaviour of the Middlesex Regiment improved suddenly and noticeably.

For Anthony Rhodes, an officer with 253 Field Company of the Royal Engineers, an understated individual, the phoney war was 'amusing and interesting'. But he remembers a medical officer, an older man used to working hard in civilian life, for whom the period came as a great relief. It simplified the man's life, which now consisted mainly of 'eating, drinking, and what he called the carnal verities'.

Jimmy Langley remembers his platoon's delight, one Friday afternoon, on receiving their pay before the other platoons. Minutes later he was approached by his colonel, who expressed surprise at having seen No. 3 Company on a cross-country run. Langley stayed quiet, because what the colonel had actually seen was the company – with

Langley's platoon in the lead – running to the nearest brothel. It was a race that nobody wanted to lose.

David Elliott, of the Royal Army Medical Corps, remembers Rue ABC in Lille as a narrow cobbled street with brothels lining both sides. The doorways were cut in half like barn doors, with the lower half closed. Venturing inside one such establishment, Elliott found a dance hall and bar, where girls in G-strings drank with soldiers before taking them upstairs. 'It was a revelation to me,' says David, 'and to see two women together! Because even though I was nearly twenty-one, I don't think I'd ever heard the word lesbianism ...'

'Human nature being what it is, you just couldn't help yourself really,' says Royal Artillery gunner William Harding. He gave ten francs to a woman at the bottom of the stairs (twice the cost of a plate of egg and chips) and found the experience disappointing. 'The human touch wasn't there.

'I don't want to sound vulgar or anything,' Harding adds, 'but what the girls used to do before you went in, they'd come out of a room, and with a bit of a rag, she'd open her legs and wipe herself out. And she'd throw the rag down amongst the blokes waiting to go up. And there'd be a scramble for that piece of rag.'

There were clearly good reasons for staying away from brothels. Above all, there was the danger of venereal disease. Alexander Frederick had been warned by his father and other veterans of the last war to be careful about 'using the facilities'. But when a medical officer showed him a series of pictures of infected male genitals, his enthusiasm for the facilities seemed to vanish completely.

An unlikely hero in the fight against venereal disease was Major General Montgomery, who issued a controversial memorandum. 'If a man wants to have a woman, let him do so by all means,' wrote Monty, 'but he must use his common sense, and take the necessary precautions against infection – otherwise he becomes a casualty by his own neglect, and this is helping the enemy.' It was the army's job, Monty felt, to help soldiers remain disease free – by making condoms available for purchase, by providing 'prophylactic rooms' where men could clean themselves after an encounter, and by teaching soldiers enough French to buy condoms from a chemist and to ask directions to a licensed brothel. His memorandum was described as obscene by II Corps commander, Lieutenant General Alan Brooke, but significantly it was not withdrawn. 'I received from [Brooke] a proper backhander,' Monty later wrote, but 'it achieved what I wanted, since the venereal disease ended.'

For all the sexual activity tolerated – and tacitly encouraged – in France, there were plenty of young men shocked by such things. Before the war, Colin Ashford had studied Fine Art and graphic design at the prestigious Glasgow School of Art; he was now a private in the Highland Light Infantry, surrounded by people who swore incessantly, and whose only interests were drinking and sex. 'I never realised,' he says, 'that there were so many men with such low intelligence. I remember one sergeant major, and when you spoke to him, you could almost see him thinking.' Ashford and a few like-minded friends started using long words to befuddle the sergeant major. 'He ought to go around with a wreath of flowers on his head,' said a friend, 'to let people know his brains are dead.'

And beyond the fleeting sexual encounters, steady relationships and innocent flirtations took place. Percy Beaton 'walked out' for a while with a French girl who was chaperoned wherever she went. William Harding fell for a girl from

Nantes 'hook, line and sinker', but the relationship seemed over after his battalion was moved without warning. Days later, Harding was told that he had a visitor. Excited, he expected it to be the girl, and hurried along to meet her. But he received a surprise. 'It was her mum!' he says. 'She slung her arms round me and made such a fuss of me with tears running down her face.' She berated Harding for going away suddenly, and told him how much her daughter was missing him. As the scene played out, Harding's colleagues watched with glee. 'I had a terrible time from the chaps,' he says. 'They were saying that I was getting in bed between the mother and daughter. Oh, the terrible things they were coming out with!'

While the phoney war offered unexpected opportunities to British soldiers, it also had a symbolic resonance. These young men were living in, and later advancing and retreating through, areas where the last generation had fought and died. 'My father was severely wounded with shrapnel,' says Colin Ashford, 'and I was back in the same part of France.' He remembers seeing the old trench lines, and visiting British, French and German cemeteries. And just as visitors today are affected by the architecture and size of the cemeteries, so Ashford and his friends were surprised and moved. The difference of course, is that today's visitors do not fear a similar fate.

As Ted Oates moved through Belgium, he passed the Menin Gate, engraved with names of the Great War dead, and nearby he spotted an ice cream cart. He was on a recce with his quartermaster sergeant, Sergeant Richardson, a veteran of that war, and they decided that they would pick up an ice cream on their way back. But when they returned, the cart was gone; a German raid had frightened it away. Sergeant

Richardson would never return to England; his name is engraved on the Dunkirk memorial, a soldier with no known grave.

Soldiers were not the only servicemen in France, of course. The Royal Air Force, that happy amalgam of army and navy spared the discipline or rigidity of either, was also there. Four squadrons of Hurricane fighters, superb aerial gun platforms, were sent out in support. Roland Beamont was posted, with 87 Squadron, to Lille. The squadron's activity, he says, consisted of 'endless patrols looking for enemy reconnaissance, but we very, very seldom saw them'.

An Advanced Air Striking Force was also created and placed under French command. It consisted of two further Hurricane squadrons and eleven squadrons of medium and light bombers, and it saw rather more action. Billy Drake, flying a Hurricane with 1 Squadron, suddenly found a Messerschmitt Bf 109 coming at him. Despite it being his first encounter with the enemy, he managed to turn the tables; he was soon chasing the 109 as it raced away:

> He knew what he was doing: he was leading me into a trap, trying to make me fly under some high tension cables over the river. He pulled up to see whether I'd crashed – I hadn't. That was his mistake. I was able to catch up with him, give him a burst and, to the best of my knowledge, I forced him to crash land.

With its generous pay and dashing uniform, the air force had clear social advantages over the army – and it attracted a wide range of personalities. Vivian Snell moved to France with 98 Squadron in April 1940. He spent evenings in Reims, where he ordered a great deal of champagne at a fraction of the London price. A particular friend was Freddie Snell, an unrelated namesake who loved to 'whoop it up'.

Vivian Snell recalls Freddie passing an eventful weekend in a Reims hotel where the front door was locked every night at 11 p.m. Freddie did not appreciate this rule. 'If you lock the door,' he warned the staff, 'I'll open it.' Sure enough, that night, he shot the door open with his revolver. And when, the next day, the lounge pianist played on too long, Freddie lodged two bullets in his piano. But his grand gesture was still to come.

Freddie was supposed to return to the squadron on the Monday morning. Hours later, the squadron adjutant appeared in an attempt to lure him home. 'Come on Freddie!' he said. 'You know you should have been back this morning!'

'I can't come back! I'm dancing! Can't you see?' said Freddie, who was engaged with several girls at once. 'Why don't you dance too?' And, drawing his revolver, he fired at the ground all around the adjutant. Who did indeed begin to dance.

Freddie Snell was court-martialled. The Royal Air Force was known as a tolerant service – but it had its limits. And the fact was that an enormous number of crimes were taking place elsewhere. Almost as soon as the British Expeditionary Force landed in France, they began. From a smash and grab raid on a jeweller's to the theft of Rennes' only police car, the shadier members of the BEF went to work. The most common crime, however, was theft of army supplies. An organised chain developed; goods were stolen from the British depots, from the ports at either end, from the supply ships, from the French depots, from the trains, from the lorries, and from the eventual recipients. There was barely a secure moment in the life of any supply item, and the black market on both sides of the Channel was well supplied.

In September 1939, as I Corps Headquarters disembarked at Cherbourg, so many supplies were disappearing that every staff car had to be removed from the docks and kept under guard. Nothing was too big or too small to be stolen. Chief Inspector George Hatherill of Scotland Yard was sent to France, and his report was damning. 'At almost every port, railway siding and depot I visited it was the same story,' he wrote, 'vast quantities of all kinds of disposable commodities were disappearing, often within hours of being landed.' With immediate effect, five hundred army volunteers with police experience were withdrawn from their units to become supply escorts. Hatherill also recommended the creation of a Special Investigations Branch (SIB) within the Military Police (and within the navy and air force). As a result, fifty-eight officers and NCOs were recruited from Scotland Yard to work as military detectives. The SIB would become a large and effective organisation.

Theft, it should be noted, had been a way of life in the army since time immemorial. 'They'd pinch the milk out of a blind man's tea,' says a signaller, recalling how his knife and cap were taken – leaving him no option but to pinch someone else's. But beyond the widespread pilfering (and despite the best efforts of the Auxiliary Military Pioneer Corps) there seems to have been relatively little serious crime committed by the BEF in France. Examining court-martial figures for a random period in early March 1940, the most common offence was drunkenness – followed by violence against a superior, and theft. The prevalence of drunkenness seems unsurprising given that beer, wine and spirits were cheap, especially with the strength of the pound against the franc (£1 was worth 176.5 francs).

While not usually serious in itself, drunkenness could sometimes lead to graver offences. It probably played a major part in the murder committed by Lance Corporal Goulding, and it could certainly sour relations between soldiers and local people. But it could also compromise the army's ability to do its job. A company commander of the East Yorkshire Regiment was so drunk on the night of 9 May 1940 that he was rendered unfit for duty on the day the BEF finally advanced into Belgium. One assumes that this captain was not the only actor missing his entrance on 10 May. But such behaviour was one thing in a soldier, it was another thing altogether in an officer.

British army officers were expected to know how to behave. They had clear standards to uphold and responsibilities to fulfil, in return for which they were granted power over others and a more comfortable life. This, at least, was the theory. The novelist Anthony Powell, a second lieutenant in the Welch Regiment, writes of commanding a platoon that 'Thirty men are merely a responsibility without the least compensatory feeling of power. They only need everlasting looking after.' Perhaps – but it was also true that not every officer fulfilled his responsibility.

Some were vindictive. When a promising young Gordon Highlander turned down the chance to become a major's batman, explaining that he would rather remain with his friends, he was immediately sentenced to seven days confined to barracks. The slighted major had accused him of being improperly dressed; a bootlace could be seen poking from under his gaiter.

Others were negligent. In February 1940, four officers of the Royal Warwickshire Regiment were convicted of mutiny and unauthorised absence. The court martial concerned the drowning of a private during an assault boat exercise. All four officers were sentenced leniently: two majors were issued severe reprimands, and two second lieutenants reprimands. The battalion commander, meanwhile, was relieved of his position. These four officers – and the commanding officer – failed in their responsibilities. They had not looked after their men.

Given the manner in which the story of the Dunkirk evacuation is usually told, it can often appear that the entire British army was in France. This, of course, was not the case. There were conscripts and volunteers in Britain – and Mass Observation was keen to monitor their thoughts and attitudes. One recent conscript to the Royal Air Force reported regularly to the organisation. He revealed that while his colleagues were not 'deeply in love' with the RAF, they much preferred it to the army. Soldiers, he said, were generally acknowledged to have the worst lives.

He also noted that his colleagues were much less likely to underestimate the Germans than most civilians, who still thought the war would be quickly won. 'It is realised,' he said, 'that we have a tough nut to crack.' While Hitler was regularly described as a bastard, he did not hear a great deal of hatred expressed against the Germans, and he seldom heard political discussions, even though – or perhaps because – there were communists, socialists, and an ex-fascist among the conscripts. He noted that 'they like democracy but they know damn well that all we are fighting for is British capital.' Such cynicism is interesting, given that the conscripts' favourite member of the government was Winston Churchill – a politician who considered the war a fight for liberty and democracy.

The group's attitudes towards conscientious objectors were divided. Some dismissed them as 'unnatural and meet to be shot' while a surprisingly large number agreed that 'it requires a good deal of guts to be a conscientious objector and that we have taken the easy way out by following the crowd.'

Some conscientious objectors could never be accused of taking the easy way out. R. J. Porcas, from Norbury in south London, was a convinced pacifist who viewed conscription as training for the murder of his fellow human beings. Yet he refused to register as an objector – on the grounds that no tribunal had a moral right to judge him on a matter of conscience. The situation was similar, he believed, to medieval inquisitions judging a man for his religious beliefs.

Porcas was aware of the possible consequences of his action. In a letter to the Minister of Labour, he wrote that he was prepared 'to be handed over to the Military Authorities for them to see if they can break me'. Ultimately, however, Porcas did not have to play the part of martyr. He was acknowledged as a conscientious objector without having to appear before the tribunal, or even having to register. Such an enlightened decision (and the effort spent reaching it) reflects the gulf between First and Second World War attitudes to moral objection.

As a number of high-profile pacifists (such as A. A. Milne, author of *Winnie the Pooh*) modified their views and began supporting the war, others remained stubbornly committed to unilateral peace. Asked by an audience member at a public meeting whether he agreed with Hitler, Labour MP Rhys John Davies answered that he hated Hitler – as did the German people. He went on to argue that this would be the last war Britain would ever fight as a great power. In future, he claimed, 'we should be a sort of vassal state of America.'

An appalling judge of the present, Davies demonstrated notable prescience.

You did not have to be a pacifist to avoid conscription during the phoney war. You could be medically unfit for service. Or you could pretend to be. Jack Brack, a young Londoner suffering from heart disease, was rejected by a medical board in October 1939. Shortly afterwards, he became the central figure in an organised fraud, beginning when Maurice Kravis, the governor of a Brick Lane snooker hall, offered Brack money to impersonate him at his medical board. Brack duly appeared claiming to be Kravis – and gained him an exemption. There were plenty of other people keen to avoid service, and Brack was soon submitting to regular examinations under different names. Care was taken not to appear before the same board twice, but once Brack's face became known, the venture was doomed. Sure enough, he was arrested, along with everyone he had impersonated. Found guilty of conspiring to defeat the provisions of the National Service Act, he was sentenced to three years in prison.

In Burton-on-Trent, meanwhile, twenty-six-year-old Raymond Gould was sent to prison for failing to register for national service. The reason, according to his mother, was that he was too lazy to join up. Giving evidence in the case, a Ministry of Labour inspector alleged he had been forced to wait twenty minutes before speaking to Gould while his mother and sister persuaded him to get out of bed. Throughout the trial, Gould refused to speak; but the court was informed that he *could* speak, as he had recently been convicted of using indecent language at Derby Police Court.

Yet while people were avoiding service for many reasons, there was at least one man breaking the law in a desperate attempt to get *into* the army. Twenty-one-year-old north Londoner Samuel Martin was accused, at the Old Bailey, of sabotage at the factory where he made parts for submarines.

Martin was desperate to leave the factory to join the army – but his bosses refused. The following day, he assembled a pistol (an electrical device controlling the detonation of a torpedo) incorrectly, telling the foreman that he had lost interest in his work. The next day, he assembled a pistol with a crucial part missing. And then he made a mistake that, according to an expert witness, could not possibly have been made accidentally. Found guilty, and facing a severe sentence (sabotage was not far short of treason), Martin was bound over by the judge so that he could join up.

But as the months passed, the people of Britain, who had been expecting an Allied attack since the autumn, were beginning to wonder why nothing had happened. According to a Mass Observation report compiled shortly before the German offensive of 10 May, eight and a half months of inactivity had begun to demoralise the British people. Their previous confidence had declined, to be replaced by a range of attitudes to Hitler – varying from grudging respect to hatred of 'a sort of ultra-human devil, born to curse our days'.

And once the Germans attacked, their success both reinforced these attitudes and led to new ones: Hitler was clearly a military genius, a large section of the population now believed, and his war machine was invincible. Yet in reality, the Allies fielded a million more men than the Germans, and the French alone had more tanks and front-line aircraft. The legendary armoured divisions, those caravans of Nazi invincibility, actually constituted a small percentage of the army's overall strength, and contained mostly captured Czech and inferior training tanks. As for belief in Hitler's genius, nobody held this conviction with greater sincerity than Hitler himself, with disastrous future consequences for his armed forces.

But just as Germany's strength was becoming accepted wisdom in Britain, so was the weakness of the French Maginot line, and the foolishness of France's strategy. 'They sat pretty in their positions and waited for anything to happen,' says Peter Barclay, an officer of the Norfolk Regiment. Barclay visited the line, and came away critical of its effect on the troops' willingness to fight; it made them, he felt, far too defensive-minded. Other British soldiers who visited the line described it – in hindsight – as a mistake and a white elephant.

In fact, the Maginot line fully served its purpose; it was never breached. More significant, given subsequent events, are the myriad British officers and men who have related, in interviews and memoirs, withering appraisals of the French army itself.

Many of these memories may, of course, represent wisdom after the event, but some ring true. Captain Henry Faure Walker observed a lack of discipline and training among French soldiers while taking part in manoeuvres in 1939. He remembers a group of newly arrived reservists who, called to attention by an officer, began shouting, swearing and shaking their fists at him. The officer (a battalion commander) simply turned to Walker and shrugged his shoulders. Walker remained friendly with French officers throughout the phoney war; one of them told him, in the spring of 1940, that the morale of his men had sunk so low they would probably no longer fight. They had been keen enough in 1939, he said, but underpaid, bored and disillusioned for too long, they were now 'militarily useless'.

Given both that his officers were nervous about the possible performance of the French army, and that he was unlikely to be fully informed of developments by the French leadership, Lord Gort faced a difficult task; he must organise his own forces as efficiently as possible, and keep in regular and meaningful contact with the French. Otherwise danger lay ahead.

In the event, the Germans attacked on 10 May. Bemused citizens of the tiny state of Luxembourg watched columns of artillery, armoured vehicles, cars and tanks hurrying past on their way towards the Belgian frontier. A young German tank officer, Hauptmann Carganico, was making good progress until he reached a mined area at Bodange, just inside Belgium, where he and the rest of the column had to wait until a path could be cleared. The following day, he carried on, struck by the contrast between the Luxembourgers, well-fed and affluent, and the Belgians, poor and miserable.

After a while, a message came through on the radio warning of mines and enemy motorcycle troops ahead. Again the column stopped, until the commander of the lead platoon decided to fire at a number of mines lying visible on the road surface. Carganico heard a series of explosions, and the column was soon on the move again.

Tanks preferred to avoid towns, and so, a few miles further on, the column skirted around the edges of Neufchâteau. Reaching the top of a ridge, Carganico could see the village of Petitvoir in the valley below, its whitewashed little houses gleaming in the sun. Some firing came, first from the village and then from a wood to the left. Both died away. Belgian gunners could be seen on the slope beyond Petitvoir, trying to bring their artillery into action – but they were hit by machine-gun fire; some of them fell, the others ran away. All the while, a dense column of soldiers could be seen in the distance moving west, trying to escape the Germans' advance.

Carganico radioed to the brigade asking for fuel, and for troops to secure the flanks of the territory already captured, and then moved on. Suddenly, he heard the commanding officer shout, 'Halt!' His driver engaged the brakes, and Carganico realised that the tank was inches from tumbling into a pit nearly thirty feet deep, its edges overgrown with foliage. Having avoided a literal pitfall, he raced on, scattering some enemy light armoured vehicles on the way.

Shortly before sunset, the column reached the village of Rochehaut, and began looking for a bridge to cross the River Semois. Early the next morning, the river bank to the south was explored, but enemy troops high on the opposite bank opened fire with a machine gun, so it was decided to head north and try to cross at Mouzaive. The column came under artillery fire, but it arrived, unscathed, at a fordable section of river. Its anti-aircraft guns fired at French aircraft overhead, while its motorcycle troops crossed along a narrow bridge. The river was just a little over two feet deep at this point, and the tanks were able to drive through the water.

The column headed south again to Ban d'Alle, and soon it had entered the supposedly impenetrable Ardennes forest. Passing abandoned equipment and immobilised vehicles, it seemed clear that enemy troops had run terrified into the undergrowth at the approach of the Germans. Along a winding road, the column approached the French border. It had covered 137 miles since leaving Germany, and it now reached a sign pointing to Sedan. The first great German objective was close – and Carganico and his colleagues were confident.

The phoney war was over for the British troops. As John Williams later said:

The Phoney War was a dream time. I don't know what we expected. We were in an innocent state. We were doing what we were told, and we had our officers, and we knew all our lads, and we thought all was right with the world. When I look back now, I shudder. I could almost burst into tears.

Four

High Hopes

William L. Shirer, an American journalist in Berlin, was an observer of the everyday workings of Nazi Germany. In the days leading to Blitzkrieg, he noted a radio broadcast by Bernard Rust, the Nazi Minister of Education, preparing German schoolchildren for the coming attack: 'The German people under Hitler did not take to arms to break into foreign lands and make other people serve them. They were forced to take to arms by states which blocked their way to bread and union.'

German children were not being raised to believe in a world of tolerance and acceptance. According to Rust, 'God created the world as a place for work and battle. Whoever doesn't understand the laws of life's battles will be counted out, as in the boxing ring. All the good things on this earth are trophy cups. The strong win them. The weak lose them.'

This mentality was the distilled essence of Nazism. Describing it as Europe's greatest problem, Shirer wrote about it in his diary on the eve of Blitzkrieg. A fellow American war correspondent, Webb Miller, had died in a rail accident, and the German press was full of stories that he had been killed by the British secret service. 'What happens,' writes Shirer, 'to the inner fabric of a people when they are fed lies like this daily?' It is a question as important today as it was when posed on 9 May 1940.

The following day, Shirer was read a memorandum by Joachim von Ribbentrop, the Reich Minister for Foreign Affairs, announcing that Britain and France were about to attack Germany through the Low Countries and that Germany, desperate to safeguard their neutrality, had no option but to send its troops into Belgium and Holland. 'It sets up a new record,' writes Shirer, 'for cynicism and downright impudence.' Unsurprisingly, the German censors would not allow Shirer to describe the German attack as 'an invasion', though he *was* allowed to announce to Americans that the Germans had 'marched in' to Belgium and Holland. 'And anyway,' Shirer writes, 'America knew an invasion when it happened.'

Throughout this period, Hitler had been desperate to launch his attack, held up only by weather forecasts. He was finally given the meteorological go-ahead on the night of 9 May. Heinz Guderian, the author of a book entitled *Achtung! Panzer!* and, together with Manstein, the chief proponent of mobile warfare, was in command of XIX Panzer Corps, made up of almost sixty thousand men and twenty-two thousand vehicles. Known as *schneller Heinz* (speedy Heinz), he oversaw three Panzer tank divisions, one of which would be racing towards Sedan on 10 May. Guderian would later explain his belief that a 'determined and forcibly led attack' through Sedan and Amiens towards the coast, hitting the advancing Allied forces in the flank, had a 'great chance of succeeding'.

Attacking across the River Meuse at Sedan, supported by continuous raids from bombers and dive bombers (rather than concentrated raids which gave the defenders a chance to regroup), Guderian intended to disprove the Allies' belief that the French had the equipment and manpower to cope with any German effort to bypass the Maginot line.

On the face of it, Guderian's plan was hopelessly ambitious. He intended his three Panzer divisions to break through an area little more than three miles wide between the villages of Donchery and Wadelincourt. Surely his men could not force their way through such a tight bottleneck? Particularly as the French defenders had three times as much artillery as he had?

In fact, the Luftwaffe's rolling air raids proved to be the decisive factor. In the ninety minutes before the river crossing on the morning of 13 May, 750 aircraft, many of them Junkers Ju 87 dive bombers, rained bombs on the defenders. Commonly known as Stukas, the dive bombers were interesting aircraft. Inherently slow with a limited range, they would play very little part in the Battle of Britain, so vulnerable were they to fighter attack. But at this stage of the war, supporting ground forces and encountering few fighters, they were a formidable and terrifying weapon.

The Stuka's mode of attack made it an accurate bomber. With its distinctive kinked wings, it could dive near-vertically at a speed of 370 miles per hour from a height of 15,000 feet. A wing of Stukas might take turns diving at a target, peeling off one by one like angry seagulls, dropping their bomb at 1,500 feet before pulling up sharply and machine-gunning as they climbed away. A button on the pilot's control column automatically pulled the Stuka out of its dive; this was a crucial feature as the pilot (and his backward-facing gunner) were exposed to blackout-inducing forces of 6 or 7G.

Stukas would usually carry a central 250kg bomb and four 50kg bombs, two under each wing. Some Stukas were fitted with 'Trumpets of Jericho' (wailing sirens operated by small propellers fitted to the legs that became louder with speed), while the central bomb had cardboard sirens fitted to its fins, each tuned to a different pitch. The hellish screams these sirens created were the Stukas' greatest weapon, far beyond actual bomb damage, causing intense terror to soldiers and civilians. Rather as fear of Panzer tanks sometimes caused troops to panic and vacate their positions without the tanks even needing to be present, so the sound of a Stuka could often clear an enemy position without an attack having to be imminent or direct. As a French officer wrote, 'The noise from the siren of the diving aircraft drills into your ear and tears at your nerves. You feel as if you want to scream and roar.'

British officer Anthony Irwin of the Essex Regiment was left with an even more primal exhaustion after being attacked by six Stukas near Lens. 'As the bastards swept over my head,' he wrote, 'I could actually see the pilot of one, his head strained back against gravity, eyes shut and mouth wide open, and he seemed to be laughing at *me*.' After all six Stukas had moved on, Anthony lay where he was, shattered and gratified, as though recovering from an intense sexual experience. 'I sweated,' he says, 'and wanted more.'

Perhaps surprisingly, many Ju 87 units had actually removed their sirens by May 1940. This was done for a number of reasons; the sirens slowed the aircraft down in level flight, they alerted the enemy to the aircraft's presence when they failed to disengage, and having to listen to them for extended periods drove the crew mad. Yet it is very rare to read an account of German dive bombing by a British, French or Belgian soldier (or civilian) that does not include a description of the sirens. Perhaps the reputation of the Stuka was such that soldiers and civilians imagined the siren even when it was absent, or perhaps an aircraft diving almost vertically at 370mph could achieve a scream akin to a siren.

Supported by the aircraft, Guderian's tanks had a huge advantage. But a close examination of the celebrated German breakthrough offer some surprises. 1st Panzer Division, led by 1st Rifle Regiment and the Großdeutschland Regiment, constituted the central thrust of the attack. The Großdeutschland Regiment would attempt to cross the river at the northern edge of Sedan across the Pont Neuf Bridge; the orders given were simple: 'The 2nd Battalion will spearhead the regiment's crossing of the Meuse, break through the Maginot Line, and secure Point 247.'

For two sweaty and sweary hours, 6 and 7 Companies marched across six miles of no-man's-land towards the river, carrying ammunition, machine guns and mortars. They marched through the town of Floing, destroyed and empty save for cats and dogs. Beyond the town was the Meuse. Assault boats were called up, and when the French began firing from bunkers, anti-aircraft guns silenced them.

After a while, the first platoon of 6 Company crossed the river in the assault boats. It was followed by a machine-gun team. The rest of the company was covering them on the river bank when French rifle and machine-gun fire opened up from a previously unseen position; the Germans moved within charging distance, hurled in hand grenades and, yelling, stormed the position. The French defenders were taken prisoner, happy, according to their captors, to have escaped with their lives.

Once the majority of the company was across the river, it moved forward towards its objective – Hill 247, a strategically important piece of high ground. Soldiers passed through a suburban estate, fighting from house to house, taking prisoners who were passed backwards. Shots rang out from a wrecked factory, acrid smoke pouring from its windows. More prisoners were taken.

The attackers crossed the railway line running between Sedan and Donchery to the west. There they confronted sections of 7 Company, and learned that several large bunkers of French defenders were preventing them from making progress. A quick conference led to a decision: 6 Company would attack the bunkers. The attacks started straight away. The main body of the company ran towards the first pillbox through an orchard, while a sergeant and two men crept up on the left through a clump of trees, taking the occupants by surprise. A hand grenade was tossed into the pillbox, and the French came out surrendering.

As the company approached the second bunker, resistance started to increase; machine-gun fire opened up from the village of Frenois, artillery fire seemed to be intensifying, and an anti-tank gun began firing repeatedly – though from where was not clear. Men were falling and shouting for medical help. One man died as he gave his platoon leader a last message for his mother. Finally, it was realised that the firing was coming from a barn standing on a suspicious green base – which was really a gun emplacement. This was quickly put out of action, and when the second bunker was taken, dozens of bottles of water were found inside to slake the soldiers' raging thirst.

Joining up (by chance) with a machine-gun crew of 1st Rifle Regiment, advancing to the right, the company entered the last phase of its attack on the slopes of Hill 247 where the French defenders were waiting for them. As they approached, the Germans opened up with light mortars and machine guns. The French replied and several men fell. As the Germans came closer, they threw hand grenades, trying to ignore the French fire. And finally, as the first few Germans reached the position, they flew into close combat as the chaos of hand-to-hand fighting took over. 'We are all pulled forward in one great surge,' said Oberleutnant von Courbiere, commander of 6 Company, who realised that 'Point 247 is in our hands! The way to the south lies open!'

The theory of Blitzkrieg, as proposed by Manstein and Guderian, was, of course, formulated around the speed and mobility of the Panzer divisions. And received wisdom has long told us that the Panzer tanks forced the extraordinary breakthrough at Sedan that led to the events of May and June 1940. But when examined closely, it is clear that the initial success was really achieved by small assault teams who crossed the river with the help of engineers and aerial support. It was not achieved by the celebrated tanks at all. And it happened while the tanks were still carrying out maintenance in advance of their assault.

The tanks of 1st Panzer Division began to cross the river, on a bridge constructed by engineers during the night, on 14 May. Guderian quickly launched his tanks towards the Channel coast, leaving the infantry far behind. Yet though the image of the Panzers surging for the coast is more familiar than that of a small number of foot soldiers fighting their way across a river, the fact is that the initial breakthrough was made with the loss of little more than a hundred men. When compared with the tens of thousands lost searching for a breakthrough on a single day on the Somme twenty-four years previously, and given the pains that France had recently taken to keep the Germans from invading, it seems an extraordinary achievement.

To an observer, the speed and success of the armoured attack might have seemed an unmitigated triumph. Yet some foresaw problems. On 15 May, Guderian's superior, Paul von Kleist, ordered an immediate halt to the tanks' advance. Guderian was furious; he telephoned Kleist and voices were raised. Kleist backed down, and agreed to the advance continuing.

Yet the next day, 16 May, it became clear that both General Gerd von Rundstedt, commander of Army Group A, and Hitler himself shared Kleist's concerns. Just as the Allies began to sense impending defeat, so German fears grew that the French, attacking from the south, could overwhelm the Panzers. The motorised divisions must be halted, Rundstedt believed, until a 'pearl necklace' of infantry divisions could catch up to protect their flanks. Hitler quickly confirmed the order.

Franz Halder, Chief of Staff of German Army High Command, could see no such danger. He agreed with Guderian that the advance should be continued as vigorously as possible. Of Hitler, he wrote: 'The Führer is terribly nervous. Frightened by his own success, he is afraid to take any chance and so would rather pull the reins on us. Puts forward the excuse that it is all because of his concern for the left flank!'

This was only the first halt order to be confirmed by Hitler over the coming days. Halder was probably right; Hitler had been hoping to avoid a repeat of the last war's attrition by sending the armoured divisions through the Ardennes, but he had not anticipated such an easy passage. The fearless leader was scared by his own success.

By the following day, however, Hitler had changed his mind. He allowed the attack to continue. As Walter Warlimont (who was in daily contact with Hitler) notes, the Führer had given himself total power which he was determined to wield, but without knowledge or experience, his moods and emotions swayed him from one extreme to the other.

If the Germans were struggling with a capricious leader, the British had just acquired their own. When, on 7 May, the British Parliament had debated the recent Norway campaign, the country's leader was Neville Chamberlain. Most members of Parliament understood that the debate would be impassioned, perhaps bad tempered, but few would have expected it to end with a new Prime Minister. And fewer still would have expected their new Prime Minister to be that troublesome old adventurer Winston Churchill.

In the event, the debate turned from a discussion on Norway into an assessment of the administration's overall performance, its relationship with its citizens, and its ability to fight the war. One interested party, sitting in the public gallery, was the United States ambassador, Joseph Kennedy, who had just told Lord Halifax, the Foreign Secretary, that he was disgusted with Britain's performance. Britain would, Kennedy was quite sure, lose the war.

Chamberlain opened the debate with a weak defence of the government's Norway performance. He was heckled from the back benches, and forced into an embarrassing justification of his suggestion, made in early April, that Hitler had 'missed the bus'. The first speech to attract attention was from Admiral of the Fleet (and Conservative member for Portsmouth North) Sir Roger Keyes, who stood up, in full uniform with medals, to speak on behalf of 'some officers and men of the fighting sea-going Navy who are very unhappy'.

They were unhappy, he explained, because of the actions of the Admiralty and the War Cabinet which had brought about the Norway fiasco. Yet he exempted the First Lord of the Admiralty – Winston Churchill – from criticism. The House listened carefully as Keyes expressed his 'affection and admiration' for Churchill, adding that he was longing 'to see proper use made of his great abilities'.

That evening, King George VI attempted to meddle on behalf of his old friend, Chamberlain.* He offered to telephone Clement Attlee, leader of the Labour Party, to urge him and his socialist colleagues to 'pull their weight' and join a National Government under Chamberlain. The Prime Minister refused the King's offer; he did not think he needed royal assistance. But while he was at Buckingham Palace, Leo Amery, the Conservative member for Birmingham Sparkbrook, began speaking in the Commons. Amery was anti-Chamberlain and pro-Churchill, and his speech amounted to a rallying cry to others who felt the same. He finished in spectacular style, hurling at Chamberlain the words of Oliver Cromwell (or an approximation of them) delivered 287 years previously: 'You have sat too long here for any good you have been doing. Depart, I say, and let us have done with you. In the name of God, go!'

The following afternoon, the debate continued with a speech by Herbert Morrison, the member for Hackney South and one of the most respected Labour Party figures. In the course of his speech, Morrison called for a division; this amounted, in effect, to a vote of confidence in the government. And this suited Conservative rebels, such as Amery,

---

* George VI and Chamberlain were such close friends that the King had given Chamberlain a key to Buckingham Palace Gardens, providing the Prime Minister with a short-cut between his Belgravia home and Westminster.

who could watch others slit their leader's throat as they stood by.

The climax of an already surprising debate was a speech by Churchill in which he stoutly defended the government (and himself) whilst fully aware that his only chance of finally becoming Prime Minister depended on a defeat for the government (and himself). In fact, a telling exchange had taken place earlier when Churchill had said that he must take his full share of responsibility for the Norway campaign. 'The Right Honourable gentleman must not allow himself to be converted into an air-raid shelter to keep the splinters from hitting his colleagues,' said former Prime Minister David Lloyd George. If others were prepared to defend Churchill from himself, he might yet become Prime Minister.

Parliamentary voting is, and was, a theatrical affair. Members walk through a corridor (known as a lobby) either to the left, or to the right, of the chamber, depending on how they are voting. On the evening of 8 May, the two groups shouted schoolboy names at each other. 'Rats!' yelled one side, 'Yes-men!' the other. Many Conservatives, some serving officers in uniform, joined the opposition parties in the 'no' lobby. One of the rebels, a long-time supporter of Chamberlain, entered the lobby in tears.

The result was inconclusive, however. The government gained 281 votes, the opposition 200, and Chamberlain believed that this was sufficient for him to remain Prime Minister. The following day, his hopes were briefly raised, as the Conservative rebels let it be known that they would support him so long as his Cabinet included Labour and Liberal ministers. But his hopes were dashed again when the Labour Party decided that its ministers would not serve under him. He had no choice but to resign.

But who would take over? There were two candidates: Churchill and the Foreign Secretary, Lord Halifax. Churchill had enemies. Many in the Conservative Party disapproved of him and his circle for a supposed lack of decency. 'All we are fighting to uphold will go out of public life,' predicted Nancy Dugdale of a Churchill-led administration. Chamberlain preferred Halifax; so did the King. Yet Halifax placed himself out of the running. His peerage, he told Chamberlain and Churchill, would make the job impossible.

In reality, this was unlikely. During such a time of crisis, a constitutional exception would surely have been made. Perhaps the sheer weight of the job and the possibility of failure intimidated Halifax. Or perhaps he preferred to stay in the background, steadying Churchill's excesses, ready to pick up the pieces should he fail. (And he probably expected Churchill to fail; 'I don't think WSC will be a very good PM,' he wrote to Lady Alexandra Metcalfe on 13 May.) But for whatever reason, Halifax turned the job down.

On 10 May, the Nazi invasion of the Low Countries began. Chamberlain's instinct, in view of the expanding crisis, was to remain Prime Minister. But his close friend, Kingsley Wood, disagreed, telling him that a National Government was needed to confront the new situation. Chamberlain took the advice and tendered his resignation to the King.

Two small events that fateful day give a sense of contemporary British attitudes. Jeffrey Quill was the chief Spitfire test pilot, working for Vickers Supermarine. Early on the morning of 10 May, he called in to see an elderly couple, old friends of his parents, and casually said, 'I wouldn't be surprised if old Churchill doesn't get into power.' 'Good heavens, I hope not!' exclaimed the husband. 'It made me realise,' says Quill, 'how greatly his generation of Englishmen distrusted Churchill. In their eyes, he was a wild man politically.' And later that day, once the British public had learned of the German advance, Conservative politician Henry 'Chips' Channon, an American with a cut-glass British accent, wrote in his acidic diary: 'Another of Hitler's brilliantly conceived coups, and of course he seized on the psychological moment when England is politically divided, and the ruling caste riddled with dissension and anger ...' Here are the widespread views of Churchill as a liability, and of Hitler as the ultra-human genius, the sorcerer divining Britain's weakness from afar.

With Chamberlain's resignation, the path was now open for Churchill. When he arrived at Buckingham Palace later the same day, some banter played out between the King and his new First Minister. 'I suppose you don't know why I have sent for you?' asked the King.

'Sir, I simply couldn't imagine why.'

The King laughed and said he wanted Churchill to form a government.

There was less humour in an exchange between Churchill and his bodyguard, Walter Thompson, as they drove away from the Palace. 'I only wish,' said Thompson, 'that the position had come to you in better times for you have an enormous task.'

Tears welled up in Churchill's eyes. 'God alone knows how great it is,' he said. 'I hope that it is not too late. I am very much afraid that it is. We can only do our best ...'*

At the age of sixty-five, Churchill had the job that he had long coveted, and which his father had never attained. And

---

* This story is Thompson's own account from *Sixty Minutes with Winston Churchill* (1953).

though Thompson was right about the task ahead, it is hard to imagine it being offered to Churchill in any other circumstances.

It was the British soldiers, currently in France but about to move to prearranged positions in Belgium, on whom the responsibility would fall. Second Lieutenant Jimmy Langley of the Coldstream Guards, stationed near Lille, was woken as usual on the morning of 10 May by his chatty batman who handed him his tea, reported on the weather, informed him that his bath was ready, and mentioned, in passing, that the Germans had invaded France, Belgium and Holland.

Further west at Bailleul-lès-Pernes, Second Lieutenant Peter Hadley of the Royal Sussex Regiment began hearing a vague but very persistent rumour that the Germans had invaded. When he discovered that it was true, he had a sense of relief coupled with a sinking feeling; what, after all, would the future hold? But his men were given a sense of purpose, and the area was soon humming with excitement and anticipation.

The BEF's advance into Belgium was led by 12th Lancers' armoured cars. On 11 May, the River Dyle was reached, and thousands of men began digging new positions on the twenty-two miles of land between Louvain and Wavre. The purpose of holding this stretch was to keep the overall front short and to use as few divisions as possible. Lieutenant General Alan Brooke's II Corps held the left of the line, with its 3rd Division in front and 4th Division in reserve, while Lieutenant General Barker's I Corps held the right, with its 1st and 2nd Divisions in the front line and 48th Division in reserve. To the British left were the Belgians and to the right were the French, holding a line from Wavre to Namur then along the River Meuse, passing through the fateful town of Sedan.

Royal Engineers officer Anthony Rhodes remembers the welcome from Belgian civilians while the BEF was moving forward. As a member of the British army – and an officer – he was feted. Inside a café, he was mobbed by a cheering crowd, offered cigars and bought drinks. 'The good old Tommies!' someone shouted. 'They'll win the war!'

Rhodes's unit medical officer, elsewhere in the café, was being treated even better. A young woman was being ordered to kiss him by a young man, who told her that she should be happy to kiss one of her country's saviours. Eventually the woman did as she was told – at which point the young man insisted that she spend the night with the doctor. He assured the doctor that he would enjoy the young woman, and he ought to know; he was her husband. The doctor was very keen to accept the offer. It might be considered rude, after all, to spurn such hospitality. But Rhodes pulled him away. There was, after all, a war to fight.

Shortly afterwards, the same doctor believed that he had caught a spy – a Belgian fifth columnist, a concealed supporter of the Germans.* A local newspaper seller, who had somehow managed to get hold of copies of the *Daily Mail*, said in passing that he had lived for two years in Lincoln. The doctor, a Lincolnshire man, grew suspicious, and asked the paper seller about a particular Lincoln street. The seller replied that he had never heard of it. With an air of triumph, the doctor announced that the seller was lying, that he must be a spy. The seller might have been handed to the army's Field Security

---

* The expression 'Fifth Column' was probably coined during the Spanish Civil War by General Mola. As the Nationalists besieged Madrid with four columns of troops, Mola claimed that a 'fifth column' existed within the city, made up of Nationalist supporters waiting to rise when the time came.

Police for examination, had it not been discovered that he was telling the truth. He *had* lived in Lincoln: Lincoln, Nebraska.

In fact, spy paranoia was as rife in the BEF as it would become in Britain in the coming months. Rhodes attended an examination of suspected spies by the divisional Field Security Police. One officer and ten NCOs had the job of interviewing hundreds of suspects. The first suspect was a deserter from the Belgian army. An old woman said that she had seen him entering a house with a box containing a portable wireless set. No, said the man, the box contained food – some of which the old woman had eaten. (Doubtless numerous private grudges were elevated to fresh heights during this period.) Instead of releasing the man, the Field Security officer ordered that he be handed over to the local police – who would give him a few minutes to prove that he was not a spy before executing him.

It was not just the Field Security wing who dealt with alleged spies. The Provost wing, the red-capped military police, also dealt with the problem. Rhodes recalls hearing of a dinner conversation between his adjutant and the divisional provost officer, which left him at once disturbed and reassured:

'Do you really shoot spies?' asked the adjutant.

'Of course,' said the provost officer.

'And do you do it entirely on your own? I mean the trial and all that sort of thing?'

'Of course.'

'But I suppose you take good care that they really *are* spies, don't you? I mean, it's an absolute power of attorney, isn't it?'

'It's *absolute*, all right,' said the provost officer, grinning.

Spies were arrested on the flimsiest of evidence. Leon Wilson was a member of a French heavy artillery regiment.

Near Armentières, he saw a man ploughing a field in a particular direction, and concluded that arrows were being drawn 'to show the Stukas where we were'. The man was arrested and led away. And justice could be even more summary. Private Edgar Rabbets of the Northamptonshire Regiment remembers, 'If I noticed anybody ploughing wrongly, he got shot. I shot two men who were doing that. They knew what they were doing, and I knew what they were doing – so there was no need for discussion.'

Mistakes were made, of course. Two spies dressed as Jesuit priests were about to be shot by British gunners when their regimental padre intervened. He quizzed the spies in Latin – and discovered that they were perfectly genuine priests. And it was not just local people who came under false suspicion; on 23 May, an RAF pilot who had bailed out of his aircraft was captured and shot by French soldiers as a spy.

The British arrival on the Dyle went smoothly – for the most part. 3rd Division found its proposed position already occupied by a Belgian division, and a standoff occurred between Major General Bernard Montgomery and his Belgian counterpart, until German shelling began, at which point Monty's troops were allowed to take over.

On 14 May, a sunny late spring day, British troops made their first contact with the enemy. In 3rd Division's sector, Captain Humphrey Bredin, a Royal Ulster Rifles company commander, was sitting on the far side of the river reading a newspaper. A cavalry colonel came past with the news that the Germans were approaching. He wished Bredin good luck; Bredin thanked him and carried on reading his paper.

A while later, Bredin's batman said, 'Can you see? I think there's somebody coming!' Through his binoculars, Bredin saw a German motorcycle and sidecar coming up the road.

He waited for a few moments before ordering the batman and another soldier to open fire. The three then crossed the river to their platoon position, where Bredin told a Royal Engineers NCO to blow the already-primed bridge.

For three days, the Germans tried to break the line. They seemed well trained, says Bredin, but predictable. There was a four-storey building to the front right of the Rifles' position, about a hundred yards away, which the Germans wanted to take. But to get there, they began advancing across open allotments, dotted with wooden sheds. Bredin's men were expert marksmen, they had recently been issued with Bren guns, and they had little difficulty picking off the Germans in their polished helmets as they ran in ones and twos towards the building. Some took shelter behind the sheds – but .303 bullets were not stopped by wooden planks, and the Germans suffered heavy casualties.

Bredin's men were suffering as well, however. The Germans were using a heavy machine gun that made an alarming *g'doonk g'doonk g'doonk* noise as it fired. Enemy soldiers began reaching the four-storey house, and snipers took position on its roof with its clear view of the Rifles' position. A number of riflemen were picked off – including Bredin's batman, shot through the head – as the Germans consolidated the position.

The following day, the Germans mounted a charge that was knocked back, almost single-handedly, by a corporal firing magazine after magazine of Bren gun rounds. This charge was only a prelude, however. The Germans were clearly preparing for a major assault. Bredin's position was connected to divisional headquarters by cable, and he telephoned to say, 'Please bring down an uncle target onto a spot approximately a hundred yards in front of our position.'

An 'uncle target' was an emergency call for all the division's guns to fire at a single spot for two or three minutes; Bredin was directing them to fire at the house. He realised that some of the shells were likely to fall short, but, he says, 'we reckoned that it was better to be killed by our own shells than to be overrun by the enemy.' In the event, a couple of shells fell behind, none fell on the Rifles' position, and the house was obliterated. The rest of the day was quiet.

The following day, the Germans tried to steal through an imagined gap between the Rifles and a Grenadier Guards position to the right, but the Guards forced them back. Then, despite having successfully resisted the German attacks, Bredin received the surprising order to withdraw.

Subaltern Anthony Irwin of 2nd Battalion, Essex Regiment (nicknamed 'the Pompadours'),* was arriving back from leave when the Germans attacked. He spent several days, with one of his sergeants, trying to catch up with the rest of the battalion. As the pair drove towards Brussels, Irwin and his sergeant noted the large numbers of Belgian civilians – and Belgian soldiers – moving the other way. 'Look at them,' said the sergeant, 'it ain't bloody right!'

Approaching the city, looking for his battalion, Irwin stopped at an army control centre. An officer inside would surely have the latest order of battle. And a friendly and helpful captain did indeed show him the battalion's latest position on a map. Irwin thanked the captain before drawing his pistol and asking him whether he'd like to be shot, or to see Irwin's pass – one of the two. 'I'm awfully sorry, dear boy,'

---

* The regiment's predecessor had once worn purple uniforms. Purple had been the favourite colour of Madame de Pompadour, the mistress of Louis XV. Hence 'the Pompadours'.

said the captain, acknowledging how 'silly' he would have looked had Irwin turned out to be a German spy.

After another hour's driving, Irwin reached the small village where the battalion was billeted, and found his 'C' Company commander. The battalion, he was told, was to defend bridges along the Charleroi Canal in a suburb of Brussels, slightly behind the Dyle. These bridges, he was ominously told, must not fall; they must be defended to the last man.

Irwin found his platoon drinking in a local bar, where, he was pleased to see, they were sticking to beer and avoiding the Dubonnet and anise. They were not, however, avoiding a young woman who announced that she was giving her body to the brave British Tommies fighting for her land. Three members of the platoon took her up on her offer. That night, the battalion was seen off by almost the entire village as it moved to the canal, and the bridges it would defend.

As soon as the battalion arrived, the bridges were prepared for demolition by French engineers, and Irwin watched with fascination as they did their work. The blowing of the bridge in his own sector caused particular problems; it was a large structure, carrying four railway tracks across the canal, and three tons of explosives were placed at the base of its two main supports. But the engineers found that they had only enough flex to stretch thirty yards from the firing box to the charge. The French sapper detonating the charge must have known that he could not survive the blast at that distance – but he dutifully pushed the plunger, destroying both the bridge and himself.

Irwin was five hundred yards away at the time. He watched the railway lines rise into the air noiselessly, slowly, before the explosion sounded, smoke blanketed everything, stone and metal rained down around him, buildings shook and glass shattered. Irwin buried himself into the soil as deeply as he could.

He then watched the next bridge being blown, this time by British engineers. But the charge was accidentally detonated while the bridge was still being used by Belgian refugees heading for France. Imprinted in Irwin's mind was the snapshot of a cyclist, sitting on his bicycle, still pedalling, forty feet in the air, his clothes blown off.

Later that evening, Irwin led a patrol into the centre of Brussels. He returned to his position just in time. Despite the fact that he had not seen a German, orders had come through in his absence to begin withdrawing.

Humphrey Bredin and Anthony Irwin were both surprised by the order to withdraw. Two days earlier, on 14 May, Winston Churchill had been just as surprised to receive a telephone call from French Prime Minister Paul Reynaud informing him of the cause of these withdrawals – the German breakthrough. A diary entry on this day by Lieutenant General Henry Pownall, the BEF chief of staff, is telling. He wrote, 'The Germans, inexplicably, have got across the Meuse.' The word 'inexplicably' is key. Pownall and his commander-in-chief, Lord Gort, could not explain the breakthrough and had little idea how it was being countered. This was the alarming consequence of the BEF's subordinate status and its inability to monitor its ally.

The following morning, Churchill was woken by another call from Reynaud, this time panic-stricken. The road to Paris was open, said the French leader, the battle was lost, and France would have to give up. Churchill tried to calm him down. But on the same day, Holland surrendered. Her army was overwhelmed, and an intense Luftwaffe raid over

Rotterdam had killed almost a thousand people in just a few minutes. 'There was no chance that she would hold on for long, but five days is a bit short,' wrote Pownall.

On 16 May, the commander of French Army Group One, General Gaston Billotte (who was, in theory, responsible for ensuring that the BEF was kept informed), ordered the French, British and Belgian forces to withdraw in order to avoid being outflanked by the Panzer breakthrough at Sedan. These were the orders that surprised Bredin and Irwin. But when Churchill was informed, he was deeply unhappy; he could not understand why a hundred German tanks breaking through the line at Sedan should force the British to withdraw. It would surely expose the BEF to great risk.

Churchill decided to travel to Paris with his chief of staff, Major General Hastings Ismay, and the vice-chief of the Imperial General Staff, General Sir John Dill. They flew from Hendon to Le Bourget in Flamingo airliners, and they were taken first to the British embassy and then to the French Foreign Ministry on the Quai d'Orsay. There he met General Maurice Gamelin, the overall commander-in-chief of the Allies, Édouard Daladier, the defence minister, and Reynaud.

Gamelin began the meeting by explaining the situation. In front of him was a map of the Allied front resting on an easel. The clearest feature on the map was a small but heavily outlined black bulge representing the German advance. When Gamelin finished speaking, Churchill asked, '*Où est la masse de manoeuvre?*' Where is the strategic reserve? Gamelin shook his head, shrugged and said, '*Aucune.*' There is none.

Churchill was dumbfounded. Where was the rest of the mighty French army? How could the commanders fail to place a reserve behind a vulnerable point in the front line?

'The situation,' wrote Churchill after the war, 'was incomparably worse than we had imagined.' So bad was it that a French request for six further RAF fighter squadrons was granted, despite severe misgivings that their loss would severely compromise the defence of Britain. After this meeting, Churchill flew home, acknowledging the need for the BEF to withdraw in order to maintain a continuous line. (In fact, the following day he asked Chamberlain – who remained in his War Cabinet – to study the feasibility of withdrawing the BEF from France altogether, possibly 'by the Belgian and Channel ports'. As early as 17 May, an evacuation was being hesitantly mooted.)

The withdrawal began during the night of 16 May, and would conclude on the night of 18 May defending a line along the River Escaut. It was carried out brigade by brigade. Almost to a man, the soldiers could see no reason to retreat. Some wondered whether their unit was being sent rearwards as punishment for a misdemeanour, while others speculated that the enemy had made localised advances causing the line to be readjusted. Only when rumours began to circulate did any suspect that the Germans were close to outflanking the entire British army and cutting off its supply lines.

A few British units fell into disarray on the retreat, an early taste of what was to come for many others; as they retreated through the Forêt de Soignes, an artillery unit became disjointed, eventually arriving at the positions of 2nd East Yorkshire Regiment 'in a state of considerable shock and alarm'.

The Belgians who had welcomed the British as honoured guests were bitterly disappointed to see their guests moving backwards so quickly. 'How can the French armies to the south possibly be expected to hold if the British keep retreating like this?' Anthony Rhodes was asked. He in turn spoke to a local brothel keeper, who told him that she would get by perfectly well. 'The Germans,' she said, 'are very good customers. They are the best of all. I ought to know because I was here in the last war.' As 1st Battalion, South Lancashire Regiment retreated near Brussels, they were fired on by a Belgian unit which mistook them for Germans. A fierce fire fight took place, resulting in far more Belgian casualties than British. 'It was regrettable but we were rather pleased,' says one South Lancs soldier. 'That was our first action at close quarters, and we had come out of it well.'

Almost all the British troops were struck by the hordes of Belgian refugees streaming away from the German border, hour upon hour, day after day. Near Antwerp, Peter Hadley compared the scene to the road leading from Wembley Stadium ten minutes after the end of a cup final. They came in cars or horse-drawn carts and on bicycles, but most trundled on foot with bundles on their shoulders and suitcases in their hands.

One of these refugees was thirteen-year-old Louis van Leemput. On 10 May, in bed at home near Antwerp, he was woken by the sound of German aircraft swooping low over the house. The radio soon told the family what was happening, and Louis's father, who worked for the Belgian Military Arsenal, had to leave immediately. The rest of the family, Louis, his mother and his seven-year-old brother, packed a few things, locked the front door and set off towards Ypres, together with their neighbours. Like everybody else on the road, they were trying to get away from the Germans, and they carried their meagre belongings on a cart pulled along the cobbled roads by one of the neighbours while the others pushed from behind.

'It was just terrible walking to Ypres,' says Louis. The journey took a week. Food had to be found every day, usually bought from farms. The refugees were scared, says Louis, and there was little conversation; just pleasantries about where people were from. He saw no trouble, though if they had been on the road for much longer, he believes, fighting for food and water would probably have broken out, so scarce were both.

Hortense Daman, meanwhile, was a young Belgian girl whose family would later work for the Belgian Resistance. Betrayed by an informer in 1944, Hortense would be sent to Ravensbrück concentration camp, to become the subject of Nazi medical experiments. But on 10 May 1940 in Louvain, she can remember seeing a German aeroplane falling out of the sky. As it screamed towards the ground, her friends cheered its imminent demise – until it released a bomb and soared upwards again. It was a Stuka. At that moment a man came along, picked Hortense up under one arm, her sister under the other, and started to run. All was chaos, and half of the street was flattened by bombs.

'We thought the war wouldn't last long and we'd defeat them,' says Hortense. She, her mother, father, grandfather and two aunts left their house that day, and began walking, like Louis van Leemput's family, away from the German border. After a while, someone observed that they had brought nothing with them – no food, no clothes, no blankets – so her father and grandfather headed home to fetch things while the women waited in a field. But even when the men returned, they had forgotten to bring any money. Her mother was furious.

Hortense remembers confrontation on the roads. 'The panic was terrific,' she says. 'The panic and the fighting and the screaming! You couldn't believe your eyes!' She can remember cows screaming in the fields, and her grandmother stopping to milk them to relieve their pain. And she remembers a young man in British military uniform being badly beaten after someone shouted that he was a spy. The police took him away – but Hortense thinks that the man was a genuine soldier, a victim of spy hysteria.

Louis van Leemput has bitter memories of German attacks from the air. Every time an aeroplane appeared, his group would dive into a ditch by the side of the road. He remembers the *tuck, tuck, tuck* sound made by bullets on cobblestones. Each evening, Louis's group found a farm where they could sleep, on straw or hay. One night, they were chased away by equally tired Belgian soldiers, and they walked on until daylight. 'That day,' says Louis, 'I was so exhausted, I fell down at the side of the road and had to lie there. I didn't have the strength any more.'

Eventually, they settled down for a week on a farm near Ypres with other refugees. Louis was in the outhouse one day when he saw a flock of birds coming towards them. As the flock increased in size, he realised that they were Stukas. He leapt to his feet, pulled up his trousers in a hurry, and ran into the barn shouting 'Stukas!' But by then, they were already diving: 'The sound alone scares the hell out of you, and then you hear the bombs screaming, and you hear the people screaming – and we were so lucky. The bombs missed our farm and exploded next to it. So as soon as we could, we wrapped up our things and got back on the road with the horse cart.'

British civilians were experiencing a different war. A Mass Observation report compiled on 14 May noted 'a heavy increase in disquiet', particularly marked in London, but widely observed. Attitudes ranged from: 'He's [Hitler's] having a great smash up, isn't he? If we can only hold him for a little time it will be all right. If he can't get through he'll be done for,' to: 'Nobody could think anything but bad. My opinion is, it's the worst thing that's happened in history.'

Yet the increased unease had a positive corollary, as a tidal wave of volunteerism swept the nation. People started giving their time and energy in a communal drive to boost Britain's ability to defend and organise itself. Myriad organisations came to the fore. Among them were the Women's Institute with its jam making and rosehip collecting, the Women's Voluntary Service with its mobile canteens and evacuation assistance, and the Citizens' Advice Bureau with its welfare guidance. But on 14 May, the Secretary of State for War, Anthony Eden, announced the formation of a voluntary organisation for men aged seventeen to sixty-five – the Local Defence Volunteers – that was intended to serve as a civilian army to resist any future German invasion.

The name 'Local Defence Volunteers' did not survive very long. In July, Churchill insisted it be changed to the more punchy 'Home Guard'. But whatever the name, the organisation served a series of important roles, and its instant popularity – a quarter of a million men signed up in the first week – reflected people's desire to work together, and to resist the Nazi enemy.

Two early volunteers give a sense of the LDV's eccentric diversity. Private Standish Vereker was the brother of Lord Gort, the commander-in-chief of the BEF. Private Gebuza Mungu, meanwhile, was the son of Umundela Mungu, a Zulu commander at Rorke's Drift. Mungu had been a circus lion-tamer for eight years, before moving to south Wales to become a steel worker. Despite being sixty-three years old, he was said never to miss an LDV parade. (And he claimed the odd 'distinction' of having once been horsewhipped by General Smuts's father.)

In this early stage of its life, the LDV's military role was negligible. Members had armbands instead of uniforms, no pips or chevrons, they drilled with broom handles, and they carried out plenty of spurious guard duty, with mixed results. When one officer challenged a private on guard duty, they shared the following exchange:

'What is your job?'
'Don't know, sir.'
'Who is your platoon sergeant?'
'Don't know, sir.'
'Who is your platoon officer?'
'Don't know, sir.'
'Who is your company commander?'
'Don't know, sir.'
'Who am I?'
'Don't know, sir.'
'How long have you been in the company?'
'Three months.'
'How often do you parade?'
'Five nights a week, sir.'

The private was subsequently discharged as mentally deficient. But for all its early military limitations, the LDV had an important propaganda role to play. Not only would it offer citizens a sense of useful involvement, it could also calm the growing fear of airborne invasion. Most of Anthony Eden's speech focused on German parachute troops, and the role that the new organisation could play in countering them. 'We are going to ask you to help us,' Eden told the public, pre-empting John F. Kennedy – in polite English fashion – by over twenty years.

Over the months and years to come, the LDV (and Home Guard) would become more professional, better organised and far better funded, but in its earliest days it was a home-spun organisation, in which most developments came from members rather than the authorities. Antiques (including an ancient Chinese bronze cannon) were removed from museums to supplement arsenals, while many units made their own Molotov cocktails. Bexley LDV collected old whisky and soft drink bottles (beer bottles were considered too thick), before filling them with a blend of tar and petrol that had been care-fully heated to allow the ingredients to mix, and then placing them in specially made canvas holders. Each member could then defend the Kentish border armed with twelve cocktails.

One LDV unit that stands out during these early days was the Upper Thames Patrol. Operating on the non-tidal waters of the River Thames between Teddington and Lechlade, a distance of 125 miles, the patrol consisted of owners of motor launches charged with guarding the river and its banks, and with protecting its bridges, locks and weirs from sabotage. In the event of invasion, the patrol would be responsible for blowing up the bridges. Three of the patrol's boats – *Constant Nymph*, *Surrey* and *Bobell* – were to play a significant part in the Dunkirk evacuation.

Another notable unit (although not formed until early July) was the First American Motorised Squadron. Made up of United States citizens living in Britain, mainly businessmen and professionals, the squadron was created by Charles Sweeny, a wealthy financier and society figure, who wired his even wealthier father in the States of the need for weapons and ammunition. One hundred Tommy guns and 100,000 rounds of ammunition were promptly delivered. With its dozens of well-connected members, their fashionable American cars repainted in military colours, and a brigadier general in command who had served under General Pershing in the last war, the squadron was a uniquely well-equipped and well-organised unit, able to hold its own in manoeuvres against elite British army units.

Churchill, keen to entice America into the war, took a special interest in the squadron – while, tellingly, Joseph Kennedy, United States ambassador, disapproved of its formation. It stands as confirmation, though, that some Americans at least were committed to the war effort long before December 1941.

The sheer number and enthusiasm of Local Defence Volunteers, in the meantime, stands as evidence that British volunteerism, in its many guises, was keeping the nation busy and involved, a crucial tool in the government's struggle against civilian complacency and dissatisfaction.

Across the Channel, meanwhile, the BEF's withdrawal to the line of the River Escaut was complete by the night of 19 May. But Lord Gort realised the growing danger that the Germans would outflank this position, so he began creating emergency forces, amalgamations of existing units, to move into vulnerable areas. Macforce – made up chiefly of 127th Infantry Brigade – was sent to guard the BEF's southern flank along the River Scarpe between Râche and St Amand. In effect, Macforce was insurance against the collapse of General Blanchard's French First Army, a prospect that now seemed eminently possible. Petreforce, meanwhile, consisted mainly of untrained digging battalions (as well as an elite battalion of Welsh Guards), which were moved into position to defend Arras.

Gort has received heavy criticism over the years for his conduct of the campaign. Some of the most damning came from Montgomery, lightly sprinkled though it was with the faintest of praise. Monty described Gort as a most delightful person and a warm-hearted friend who was not clever, did not bother about administration, and should never have received the job in the first place. 'He knew everything there was to know about the soldier, his clothing and boots,' wrote Monty, but 'the job was above his ceiling.'

Monty's biggest complaint concerned the state of confusion at Gort's headquarters. 'It was difficult to know where anyone was,' he wrote. The problem stemmed from Gort's desire to be close to the action, causing him to divide GHQ into three echelons rather than the usual two. The result was an exasperating communications breakdown. 'Communications would be established only to find that the officer or branch required was at one of the other places,' wrote a member of I Corps staff.

In his role not only as commander-in-chief of the BEF, but also as an army commander answerable to several layers of French authority, Gort's job was huge and complex; efficient communications were crucial, both for the performance of the BEF and in order to monitor French actions and intentions. Nevertheless, Gort's creation of his improvised forces demonstrated his willingness to react to situations; the movement of troops south would prove important in the days to come. And during discussions with Pownall on 19 May, an idea arose whose consequences remain with us even today.

As Gort saw it, the BEF had three options. It could take part in a counter-attack launched simultaneously from the north and the south to cut off the advancing Germans and maintain a defensive line. It could attempt to withdraw to the line of the River Somme, keeping its supply lines open. Or it could take the third, apparently most drastic but probably only sensible option. It could head north-west, protected by canal and river lines, towards Dunkirk where it could be evacuated back to Britain.

Such an audacious move would almost certainly mean leaving most of the BEF's weapons and equipment in France. It might well be viewed as treachery by the French and Belgian allies. And it would probably be resisted by those at home who did not appreciate the severity of the BEF's plight. Sure enough, when Pownall telephoned the War Office to inform the Director of Military Operations of the plan, the response he received was 'stupid and unhelpful'.

All the same, with his determination that Britain be protected at all costs, his force's administrative shortcomings, and his lack of faith in the French to resist the armoured divisions, Gort and his staff began planning for a retreat to Dunkirk.

Five

Fighting Back

Winston Churchill's doctor, Lord Moran, once wrote of his patient that 'without that feeling for words he might have made little enough of life.' Perhaps, but Churchill's instinctive ability to enthuse beleaguered minds was badly needed when he made his first broadcast to the nation as Prime Minister on 19 May:

> ... the British and French peoples have advanced to rescue not only Europe but mankind from the foulest and most soul-destroying tyranny which has ever darkened and stained the pages of history. Behind them – behind us – behind the Armies and Fleets of Britain and France – gather a group of shattered States and bludgeoned races: the Czechs, the Poles, the Norwegians, the Danes, the Dutch, the Belgians – upon all of whom the long night of barbarism will descend, unbroken even by a star of hope, unless we conquer, as conquer we must; as conquer we shall.

The response was positive. 'You have never done anything as good or as great,' wrote Anthony Eden. 'Thank you, and thank God for you.'

Behind the scenes, however, Churchill could not afford much confidence. In a telegram sent later that night to United States President Franklin Roosevelt, he made an implicit threat; if America failed to assist Britain, and she was forced to surrender, then the Royal Navy would pass into German hands. The consequences of this were left for Roosevelt to ponder, as Churchill signed off with the words, 'Once more thanking you for your goodwill.'

That evening, Anthony Irwin's Pompadours reached the village of Belleghem, behind the River Escaut. The previous days had consisted of endless marching without sleep, punctuated by dreamlike incidents. Some machine guns had opened up on them south of Brussels. As red-hot tracers flashed past their heads, Irwin and his men threw themselves down and opened fire with Bren guns. 'Cease fire!' yelled a voice eventually, and somebody arrived announcing that the 'enemy' was actually a Middlesex Regiment machine-gun platoon. By that time, two Pompadours, one a company sergeant major, had been wounded.

Shortly afterwards, Irwin's company was dispersed around the edge of an orchard when the members became emotionally involved in a one-sided aerial battle between a virtually defenceless RAF Lysander,* with a top speed of 212mph, and six heavily armed Messerschmitt Bf 109s with top speeds of 350mph. The company watched as the 109s took turns in diving at the Lysander and pulling up to attack

---

* Of the 175 Lysander army co-operation aircraft deployed in France and Belgium, 118 were lost. This episode perhaps explains why.

her again on the way back up. Each time this happened, the Lysander throttled back and jinked, and every 109 overshot her. As the final attack missed her, one watching soldier burst into tears. And then, when the 109s changed their tactics and attacked her simultaneously from different directions, the Lysander went into a deliberate spin before straightening up low over the company. The 109s were not giving up, however. They chased her down – but as they flew low towards Irwin's company, every Bren gun on the ground opened fire.

The first 109 hit the ground in flames, and the other five pulled up and flew away. But they soon flew back in formation, looking to take revenge on the company with their machine guns. At that moment, however, three RAF Hurricanes appeared and chased them away. All the while, the Lysander flew serenely on.

A rather more mundane incident occurred shortly afterwards, Irwin and a fellow officer (and good friend) threatening each other with pistols as their platoons tried to take up the same position. Both were too tired to think about moving to another spot. In the end, Irwin lost the position on the toss of a coin.

Shortly before reaching Belleghem, Irwin's platoon passed a gingerbread factory. Some troops had already broken in; Irwin's men – most of whom had last eaten some days ago – followed. Soon they were sharing crates of gingerbread cakes. And an hour later they were squatting by the side of the road, sharing diarrhoea.

At Belleghem, behind the Escaut, the battalion was expecting to mount a stand. But on the afternoon of 20 May, they withdrew again. This time, however, they understood why; news of the Panzers' advance had reached them.

Twenty miles away in the village of Froidmont, 2nd Battalion, Royal Norfolk Regiment, was preparing to travel the short distance to the Escaut. That night, the battalion moved to a spot near Calonne, where it relieved the Royal Berkshires. 'A' Company took the central position, its front stretching for nearly eight hundred yards; this left the men far too strung out for comfort. Nevertheless, the company commander, Captain Peter Barclay, spent the night making sure that every man had a solid defensive position.

The river was twenty yards wide, giving a measure of protection. All along the company's front were buildings; one section established itself in a cellar, another behind a garden wall, and a third, on the extreme left, in an old cement factory. Here, Private Ernie Leggett and his comrades had placed themselves on the upper floor. Over to the right was company headquarters, comprising Barclay, Sergeant Major George Gristock and others. A problem faced by the entire company was a long, thin wood on the far side; it offered the enemy some – though by no means total – concealment.

As dawn broke with no Germans in sight, Barclay – a member of the banking family – decided to take a little time off. His batman had spotted rabbits in the grounds of the nearby Château Carbonelle, and had somehow also discovered hounds and ferrets locked up in the chateau's stables. For an hour and a half Barclay and his fellow officers played at being country gentlemen, until the Germans started sending shells over. Then, says Barclay, he thought he'd better 'deal with the other situation'.

For some time, all remained reasonably quiet until some Germans appeared on the far side of the river. Barclay instructed his men not to fire until he had blown the hunting horn he liked to keep with him. The Germans wandered off into the wood and started to cut down trees. They were going to try to build a simple pedestrian bridge using concrete blocks that were already sitting in the river. All the while, the Norfolks kept quiet, and as the minutes passed, more soldiers arrived on the far bank, including a black-helmeted SS man. Relaxed, unaware they were being watched, they began putting the bridge together, before crossing over to the Norfolks' side. There was utterly no sense of urgency – until Barclay blew his horn and the Norfolks opened fire. Every German, on both sides of the river, was killed.

In their cement factory, Ernie Leggett's section had positioned themselves on the upper floor where they could look out over the wood. Now, 150 yards away, the enemy was advancing with light tanks. A ferocious fire fight began, Leggett hammering away with his Bren gun. The Germans managed to reach the river bank before retreating. They came again, this time advancing over their own dead. Twice more they were beaten off – but Leggett and his comrades were now also under mortar fire, with its tell-tale 'pump' followed by a brief but agonising wait for an explosion.

Further along, the headquarters too was coming under shell and mortar fire. Seeing Captain Barclay wounded in his stomach, arm and back, and with all the stretchers already in use, Barclay's batman improvised by ripping a door from its hinges. Barclay continued giving orders as four men carried him around on the door.

Problems were now developing to the right. On the immediate right flank, the Germans had somehow captured a friendly position, while on the far bank an enemy machine-gun post had appeared. Barclay delegated his sergeant major, George Gristock, to capture both positions, with the assistance of a motley group including a company clerk and a radio operator.

Seconds later, Ernie Leggett looked out from his factory position on the left, to see Gristock crawling on his knees and elbows, inching towards a German machine-gun nest on the Norfolks' side of the river that had – so far – failed to spot him.

Suddenly, a previously hidden machine gun, with a flank view of Gristock, opened up, raking his legs and smashing his knees. But he continued advancing until he was twenty yards from the first enemy position; there, he leaned back and began tossing grenades, before turning over and firing his Tommy gun. He made sure that all four Germans were dead before dragging himself back to where he started.

At this point, Barclay passed out. Waking up some time later in the chateau, now transformed into a regimental aid post, he found himself lying next to Gristock. In the meantime, Leggett remained at his post. Of the twenty-five members of his section who had begun the morning in the factory, only four remained. There were no wounded; all the others were dead. And as Leggett crossed the floor, preparing to look out to the left for Germans, he received a shock:

The next thing I knew I'd hit the ceiling, and then I heard a loud bang. I came down and hit the floor. I realised that I'd been hit. It was one of those blasted three-inch mortars and I'd been hit. My left leg was absolutely numb, my back was numb from the waist down, I couldn't move my legs, and all I saw was blood all over the floor. Two others ran across to me, and one said, 'Bloody hell, Ernie! You've had it!'

Leggett was half-carried, half-dragged down the stairs where he was laid down beside a six-inch-high railway line. Naked except for his underpants, he began to pull himself agonisingly along the railway line, sheltered by the rails from gunfire, covered by earth from shellfire, his hands bleeding from the effort of dragging himself along. Hundreds of yards later, he reached the company headquarters where he was placed on a stretcher. He remembers being inside a truck, and a nun leaning over him with a flowery wimple, and a medical officer saying, 'Just a prick, old boy.'

Despite the ferocious fighting, and two German breakthroughs that were reversed, the battalion held its position. That evening, orders came to withdraw, first to Bachy and then to the Bethune sector – where it was to experience further horror.

A while later, in hospital in England, Ernie Leggett was told that he was going to be all right, despite various wounds including one caused by a piece of shrapnel that grazed his femoral artery before exiting through his groin. And in the next ward was George Gristock, whose legs had been amputated from the hip. Every day, Leggett was wheeled in to see his sergeant major – who was allowed to drink as much beer as he liked. 'Beautiful!' he would say as he supped it from a little teapot.

Leggett told Gristock that he had seen what happened to him. 'Bastards!' said George. 'But I wiped them out!' Every day, they talked about the old days in the regiment, and the early months of the war. 'And then,' says Ernie, 'that horrible morning came when they didn't come and get me, and I said to the nurse, "Take me through to see my sergeant major," and she said, "No. Sorry." He had died.'

George Gristock was awarded the Victoria Cross for his

action; it is on public display at the Royal Norfolk Regiment Museum in Norwich.

On 20 May, Lance Sergeant Cyril Roberts* was at Vauchelles, south of the Somme. His unit, 2/7th Battalion, Queen's Own Royal Regiment, had been brought to France to carry out labour duties, spending the first half of May working under the direction of French engineers at Abancourt, between Amiens and Dieppe. They had not been expecting to fight, having received virtually no training in England over the winter, and none at all in France. They were badly equipped, with just three Bren guns for the entire battalion, not a single mortar or carrier, and only fourteen trucks and one car. And they were almost devoid of communications equipment and trained signallers. But they were soldiers – and with the BEF in crisis, they had been ordered forward.

On 18 May, they were ordered first to Abbeville, and from there to Lens, where their train was bombed and machine-gunned from the air. Eight men of another battalion were wounded, but none of Roberts' comrades were hurt. Very soon afterwards, however, it was realised that a mistake had been made. The battalion should have stayed in Abbeville, so everybody boarded another train and headed back; this was where, on 20 May, the men found themselves, in a small nearby village named Vauchelles, as the Panzer divisions swept towards them. Hitler's vacillations had not yet significantly affected German progress, and allowed off the leash once more, the tanks raced forward. Cyril's battalion found itself in the eye of their storm. The result was chaos.

Heinz Guderian's orders were for 2nd Panzer Division to hold the ground between Abbeville and Flixecourt, clearing

---

* See Chapter Three.

the sector of British and French resistance. 1st Panzer Division would take the area between Flixecourt and the river east of Amiens, while 10th Panzer Division would hold the ground further east to Peronne.

On 20 May, once 1st Panzer Division had captured Amiens, Guderian had a walk around the city. The cathedral was beautiful, he decided, but he could not stay long. Moving eastwards, he passed his advancing columns – and spotted a number of British vehicles in their midst, trying to blend in, hoping for a chance to break for the south. 'I thus quickly captured fifteen Englishmen,' he wrote.

That morning, Oberleutnant Dietz of 2nd Panzer Division had set out at dawn from the village of Sorrell. His entire battle group was moving forward – the tank brigade, two infantry battalions, tank destroyers and armoured pioneers (engineers in fighting vehicles). They were heading for Abbeville and the sea, and they encountered little resistance on the way. Twelve miles from the town, the giant winding snake halted. All around were the carts and detritus of refugees, mostly Belgians. To Dietz these were men, women and children forced out of their homes by the French and left to their fate. He could neither accept nor imagine any German responsibility for their plight.

For the time being, the tanks remained where they were; they had finally run short of fuel. The infantry now drove forward to capture Abbeville's western defences. Soldiers fought their way from house to house, supported by the pioneers' armoured vehicles. The town, like others before it, erupted into flames, and it soon came under German control. The race to the coast, it seemed, was complete – until a message arrived that the Luftwaffe had ordered a Stuka strike on the Abbeville bridges.

To the battle group's HQ staff, this seemed madness. The bridges had already been secured at some cost; there was no need for any further action. And a retreat would open the town again to the enemy. But when a further message came through that the Stukas were on their way, orders were quickly given to withdraw all men and machines from the town to a distance of several miles.

Orderly officers and dispatch riders hurried through Abbeville shouting the order to move out to the countryside. Tanks – which had now reached the town – roared into life. Their sound was magnified in the tight urban confines. Not unlike the British on the River Dyle, German soldiers who had spent ten days focused on reaching the Channel coast were now being told to retreat away from it. But not everybody was going to withdraw. The bridges would remain occupied by German troops, and the headquarters staff would be staying where they were. The town would not simply be handed back to the enemy – whatever the cost in lives.

At staff headquarters, officers tried to sleep aware of their almost certain fate. But the Stukas never came. Their attack was called off without any message reaching the battle group, and by seven o'clock the next morning, most of the town's positions had been retaken. During that day, several thousand prisoners – mostly British – were rounded up and sent to the rear.

The decisive phase of the Manstein Plan, crossing the River Meuse, pushing through the area around Sedan and surging north-west for the coast, was now complete. The British army, the Belgian army and the French First and Seventh Armies were trapped in a pocket 120 miles deep and 80 miles wide, all of them cut off from the remainder of the French army to the south. And they would now be facing attacks from every direction. The only reassurance to the British was that the Germans had not yet taken the Channel ports. Until this was done, and the British army had been captured, the war was not lost.

On the morning of 20 May, a platoon of Cyril Roberts' battalion was on duty guarding bridges in Abbeville. As refugees streamed into the town, the platoon headed out to rejoin the rest of the battalion. Setting out eastwards, progress was slow, and eventually the party was forced to stop, halted by burning air-raid debris. They turned back, trying to find another route.

Passing a farmhouse, they noticed refugees reacting to something, and, a moment later, a machine gun opened up. Some of the party jumped into a ditch, while others stayed on the road. The men in the ditch, thinking the machine gun was in the farmhouse, began to fire at it. At this point, a German armoured column came up the road, led by a tank. One of the men in the ditch, Private Jakeman, watched as his comrades on the road were taken prisoner. Meanwhile another armoured vehicle came up behind him and his colleagues in the ditch. As Germans jumped out with revolvers and submachine guns, Jakeman and friends threw up their hands and surrendered.

The group was sent walking down the road. They were unescorted – but German motor vehicles and sentries were stationed at frequent intervals to prevent their escape. After a mile, the road passed a wood, and Jakeman, sensing a momentary absence of cars and sentries, dodged behind a tree, scaled a fence and ran into the wood. He carried on across country, stopping when he reached a thick copse.

All that day, he lay hidden. He could hear a German anti-aircraft battery firing to the north, and a great deal of gunfire all around him. That night, he carried on moving south-east, until he reached the heights above the Somme. He climbed down, swam across the river, and crossed some marshland, a road and a railway line. At one point, he was fired at, so he hurried on, running into some parked German vehicles. As he fled, dawn was beginning to break. He found another wood, and hid there throughout a wet and miserable day.

That evening, he knocked on the door of a farmhouse in Bettencourt; the family allowed him to stay the night, telling him that the Germans had recently passed through the village. The next day, they warned him that door-to-door searches for Allied soldiers had begun, and the only safe direction for him to travel was south. So he set off, avoiding towns and villages, until he reached Selincourt, where he was told by civilians that the French still held Harnoy, a few miles further on. At Harnoy he was questioned by French officers at a road barrier. He passed their scrutiny, and was soon whisked off in a British vehicle, before finally being transferred to British Northern Command at Rouen.

Private Jakeman may not have been taken off into captivity, but most other members of his battalion – including Cyril Roberts – were not so fortunate. As German air attacks on Abbeville began to strengthen on the morning of 20 May, the battalion came under intense bombardment. They were in open country, with barely any anti-tank weapons or Bren guns; the commanding officer gave the order to withdraw towards Épagne-Épagnette and across the Somme. He wanted to place the river between his men and 2nd Panzer Division. Though these orders were delivered to HQ Company and part of 'D' Company, they never reached the other companies.

Major Adams of HQ Company managed to guide a group (consisting of two officers and about sixty men) across the Somme to Blangy. From here, he was able to reach brigade headquarters, and finally Northern Command at Rouen. The battalion commander, Lieutenant Colonel Girling, meanwhile, led a group for nearly three days on a trek from the outskirts of Abbeville through the abandoned village of Hamicourt and across the River Bresle, to St Pierre-en-Val. The group split up under machine-gun attack, but all its members finally reached Rouen.

Most of the remainder of the battalion, however, including Cyril Roberts, remained in position at Vauchelles. No orders had been received, and when two officers headed off to gather information and failed to return, confusion reigned. Early on the morning of 21 May, a large formation of German tanks arrived at their exposed position. At a stroke, several hundred men of 2/7th Battalion, Queen's Own Royal Regiment were taken prisoner.

As the Panzers were arriving at Abbeville, General Edmund 'Tiny' Ironside, Chief of the Imperial General Staff, was arriving at Gort's headquarters with a directive that the BEF attack south-west across the Somme in order to join up with the French in the south. Pownall was furious at the suggestion, sensing Churchill's hand behind it – 'a scandalous (i.e. Winstonian) thing to do and, in fact, quite impossible to carry out', he wrote in his diary.

Gort patiently explained to Ironside that, first, he did not have the troops to do it (it would involve the disengagement of seven divisions currently fighting for their lives on the Escaut), and second, the Germans were now holding the line of the Somme. In short, the attack would leave the seven British divisions fighting desperate rearguard actions at the same time as they went into battle with strong Panzer formations – all the while having to guard their flanks.

Yet while this was a clear impossibility, Gort offered Ironside an alternative. He could mount a limited attack in a southerly direction, carried out by 5th and 50th Divisions, the only reserve divisions available to him. Ironside relayed this to War Secretary Anthony Eden, whose report was duly read to the War Cabinet in London. Yet Churchill's instinctive optimism remained; he continued believing in the feasibility of a massive southerly attack by the BEF. (Although reality was clearly biting at some level: at the same meeting, Churchill told the War Cabinet that he had asked the chiefs of staff to prepare a study of possible operations if it 'became necessary to withdraw the British Expeditionary Force from France'.)

Later that day, Ironside and Pownall met with Blanchard and Billotte. The latter was trembling and emotional, yelling that his infantry could not withstand any sort of attack at all. Ironside, whose nickname 'Tiny' was an ironic reference to his huge physical presence, could not bear the self-pity. He grabbed Billotte by the lapels and shook him. This seemed to have an effect; Billotte calmed down, and agreed as the British generals urged him to mount an attack towards Cambrai, and to contribute two divisions to the British attack.

Even if Churchill's favoured attack was not feasible, the British commanders understood that some form of action must be mounted. An Allied attack had been feared by the Germans – not least of all Hitler – for some days. And with good reason: as the Panzers pushed to the coast, the more stretched and vulnerable their flanks became. With its infantry lagging far behind its motorised formations, the German thrust could be compared, as Churchill wrote, to a tortoise whose head had protruded far from its shell. And if the Allies did not mount a substantial attack soon, the head would be drawn in, and the shell would remain impervious.

There was, meanwhile, a new French Supreme Commander; General Maxime Weygand had taken over from Gamelin, and he assured Ironside that the Germans could be halted by simultaneous attacks from the north and south. (This – 'the Weygand Plan' – was substantially identical to the existing plan.) But Ironside had grown privately disillusioned with his ally. 'God help the BEF,' he wrote in his diary, 'brought to this state by the incompetence of the French command.' And on the same day, disappointment began to emerge publicly as the usually impeccably courteous Gort harangued the French liaison officer about the quality of the French army and its desire to fight. If the French would not fight, Gort threatened, the British would have to evacuate.

Despite Billotte's assurances, the forthcoming British attack would have to go ahead without the two promised divisions. The French corps commander reported that his troops simply refused to take part – though a French light mechanised division would, ultimately, assist the British force.

The attack would focus on the BEF's only current cause for hope: its continued possession of the town of Arras. The plan was to reinforce the town's garrison, to hold the line of the River Scarpe, and to take the area south of the town, cutting the Panzers off from their communications. The attacking force would be split into two mobile columns. Each column would have an infantry battalion, a motorcycle company, a battery of anti-tank guns, a field artillery battery and a tank battalion. Of the eighty-eight British tanks available, fifty-eight would be Matilda Mark Is (slow and armed only with machine guns), sixteen would be Mark IIs (far quicker and armed with 2-pounder guns), and fourteen would be light tanks.

While this British force was not strong, the Germans' nervous anticipation meant that they risked treating it as something far greater than it was. But if the Germans were overestimating the British, it seems that the British were underestimating the Germans, entirely unaware of the presence of Generalmajor Erwin Rommel's 7th Panzer Division in the sector.

The British columns set off on the left and right. On the left, the motorcyclists of 4th Battalion, Royal Northumberland Fusiliers went forward alongside a scout platoon in Daimler Dingo cars. Behind were the tanks of 4th Battalion, Royal Tank Regiment, one of which – a light tank – contained Second Lieutenant Peter Vaux, the battalion reconnaissance officer. Behind them were the soldiers of 6th Battalion, Durham Light Infantry.

Coordination of the tank squadrons was extremely difficult without wireless communication – and the tank crews had been ordered to maintain silence. There was also little coordination between the tanks and the infantry, and an almost total lack of orders and advanced information. So when Vaux's tank climbed a crest at Dainville on the southern outskirts of Arras, he was astonished to drive into the flanks of Rommel's 7th Panzer Division and the SS Totenkopf Division. Neither the Germans nor the British had any knowledge of the other's existence – but the Royal Tank Regiment had the upper hand in the exchange. British tanks opened fire on motorcycles, lorries and half-tracks towing anti-tank guns, and the German machines burst into flames. A motorcyclist in front of Vaux was desperately trying to kick-start his engine, but could not get it going. 'My gunner was laughing so much,' says Vaux, 'that he couldn't shoot the gun. Eventually the German threw the motorcycle into a ditch and ran away. We hadn't fired on him at all!'

The chance success of this section of the advance was extremely significant. The headquarters of 7th Panzer Division began receiving terrified radio messages – 'Strong enemy tank attack from Arras. Help, help.' German gunners were unable to penetrate the armour of either mark of Matilda, and the tanks started to gain for themselves, for the division, even for the BEF, a lofty reputation among the enemy.

The tanks' advance continued. Vaux soon arrived at a crossroads where he noticed a lorry with a large 'G' painted on the door. As his mind played little games with itself (he imagined the 'G' standing for German), the lorry's driver suddenly jumped out wearing an enemy uniform. 'Shoot!' yelled the suddenly focused Vaux, and his gunner fired at the lorry. The terrified lorry driver ran down the street, the gunner firing, tracer bullets zipping past him. He jumped into a garden, managing to get away – at which point a woman who had been waiting patiently for the excitement to stop, calmly stepped out of her house and emptied a bucket into a dustbin.

A while later, Vaux's tank was shot by 'some wretched small weapon' which missed him and his gunner by inches and made a hole in either side of their turret. Without a word, the gunner reached into his pack and fetched out a pair of socks. A sock was stuffed into each hole. 'It seemed somehow a bit better that way,' says Vaux.

Between Beaurains and Mercatel, the battalion was ambushed by several batteries firing at once; twenty tanks were destroyed. Among those killed were the battalion's commanding officer, Lieutenant Colonel Fitzmaurice, and a squadron commander, forty-seven-year-old Major Gerald Hedderwick, who had fought the Germans over the same ground twenty-three years earlier. Shortly afterwards, Vaux drove through this valley of death, without realising at first that the tanks were knocked out. Only as he drew closer did he notice men lying next to their machines and hanging out of their turrets. Vaux stood up in his seat, shouting instructions to his driver and gunner – unaware that a German soldier was on the ground nearby, lining up a shot at his head. Vaux's life was saved by his adjutant, Captain Robert Cracroft, who spotted the man and shot him dead.

Shortly afterwards, having taken some revenge on nearby batteries, the tanks fell back to Achincourt. There were good reasons for this; the infantry was still a long way behind, and forward units of 5th Panzer Division were beginning to arrive on the scene. The tanks withdrew to act as a rearguard alongside the motorcycles and Daimler Dingos of the Royal Northumberland Fusiliers.

John Brown was guarding a crossroads in his Dingo when a tank appeared along the road. Some of Brown's comrades opened fire with their Bren guns until others started shouting; the tank, it turned out, was British, and the men stopped firing before any damage was done. When another tank followed, the men opened fire again. There was more yelling, and the firing stopped once more. But this time, the tank was German. Stopping at the crossroads, it opened fire in turn. 'The first shot got my mate,' says Brown, 'and he blew up.'

At another crossroads nearby, Peter Vaux, Robert Cracroft and every surviving member of the battalion gathered. A

Matilda Mark II had broken down some way ahead, and could now be heard clattering towards them in the gloom. Cracroft walked up to the Matilda and waved some maps in front of the driver's visor. The hatch opened, and enemy heads popped out. It was another German tank. Cracroft shouted a warning and raced 250 yards back to his tank – while several German tanks lined up along the road and began firing. After almost ten minutes of heavy but futile firing by both sides in near darkness, the Germans withdrew.

During the fire fight, Vaux had run out of ammunition, and pulled out. With him were his driver, Corporal Burroughs, and Major Stuart Fernie (the battalion commander following the death of Lieutenant Colonel Fitzmaurice), who had replaced his gunner. As Vaux drove, he passed through a scene of spectacular confusion. British Bren carriers and German motorcyclists mingled on the road without any apparent idea where they were going or what they were meant to be doing. He turned off onto an unfamiliar road and soon found himself passing a steady stream of German traffic – none of which recognised him for what he was. He finally ran out of petrol in a small village forty miles west of Arras. Vaux, Burroughs and Fernie quickly found an empty house and spent the next night and day inside.

Despite the haphazard nature of 4th Battalion's advance, it had unsettled German troops with little experience of armoured warfare. And the tanks of 7th Battalion, Royal Tank Regiment on the right were having the same effect – even though their advance was even more chaotic. They lost their way repeatedly, first drifting too far west, then too far east, bypassing Warlus, one of their objectives, where they would have encountered 25th Panzer Regiment, one of

Rommel's units.* Instead, they wandered off in three separate directions.

Two of the groups, mainly Matilda Mark Is, began moving towards the village of Wailly from the north and the west. Wailly was defended by the tanks of 25th Panzer Division – all of which were currently carrying out an attack elsewhere. This left the village defended by a few infantry platoons, and some anti-tank and anti-aircraft guns. Tom Craig, advancing in his Matilda Mark II, was fired on by an armoured car, but the shell made no impact. When he fired back, the car burst into flames.

With the British tanks about to overwhelm his position (and compromise his growing reputation), Rommel took personal control of the defence from a nearby hill. He brought every gun, anti-tank and anti-aircraft, into action, giving each gun a target and orders to fire as rapidly as possible. Gun commanders who complained that the range was too short were overruled. And he called up a secondary line of heavy guns from divisional headquarters.

In this fashion, Rommel saved the position, although he was almost killed twice, once when his aide, Leutnant Most, was shot dead standing next to him, and again when he and his telegraphist were trapped by a British tank, only for the crew to surrender rather than shoot him or take him prisoner.

And it is worth considering what might have happened had the position not been saved. The breakthrough of the tanks at Arras might have joined the breakthrough at Sedan

---

* It was the RNF's unfortunate Daimler Dingos who met the Panzers instead. More than half of 12 platoon's scout cars were destroyed in the action.

as the twin turning points in the campaign. With the Allies pouring through a breach in the German line, Guderian and his forces would have been trapped in a pocket by the sea, praying for an evacuation. In this parallel world, however, it is hard to see where the German evacuation fleet would have sailed from.

Such an outcome was not to be, however, despite further heroics by two Matilda Mark IIs, commanded by Major John King and Sergeant Ben Doyle. Operating entirely on their own at Mercatel, they drove through enemy territory firing at anything that moved.

As they charged on, they were fired at by three or four anti-tank guns. Rather than firing back, they simply drove over them. For ten minutes, machine guns popped up and fired at them; each was silenced in turn. When two German tanks swung their guns round to fire at them, the shells bounced off – but their guns destroyed the German tanks.

Driving deeper into enemy territory, breaking through roadblocks, they encountered a convoy of tanks and put at least five out of action. (They lost count.) Even when King's tank caught fire, he carried on for another hour. 'We just kept on, letting them have it,' says Doyle. Eventually, like so many other members of the tank battalions, he and King were both taken prisoner. They had finally been stopped by 88mm flak guns. The remainder of 7th Battalion, Royal Tank Regiment, just like the remainder of 4th Battalion, was ordered to withdraw. Between them, they had lost a large number of their Matilda Mark Is and all but two of their Mark IIs.

Put simply, the Arras counter-attack was a British failure. A brave failure, certainly, given that the attacking force was facing five times as many infantry soldiers and ten times as many tanks. But a failure nonetheless. None of the original objectives were achieved. The attackers ended the day exactly where they had begun – and the Germans were not cut off from their communications. Rommel's 7th Panzer Division suffered heavy casualties, but so did the BEF – and the German war machine could replace its losses far more easily. From a British perspective, such losses put an end to the prospect of another substantial attack.

Yet the Germans, usually so keen to claim victory, were not treating Arras as a British defeat. A study of German war diaries for 21 May makes interesting reading. The 6th Panzer Division diary records a 'strong enemy force' making an 'armoured breakthrough from Arras to Doullens', while Guderian's XIX Corps notes that 'Numerous individual reports about the breakthrough of the English tanks are further received – which has apparently caused nervousness throughout the entire Kleist Group area.'

So nervous was Kleist that he ordered 6th and 8th Panzer Divisions to move east to counter the danger of a British breakthrough – long after any danger had passed. And on 22 May, the day after the counter-attack, Rundstedt vowed to deal with the 'situation at Arras' before allowing Guderian's Panzers to move on to the Channel ports. In his post-war evidence at Nuremberg, Rundstedt admitted fearing 'that our armoured divisions would be cut off before the infantry divisions could come up to support them'. Even after the counter-attack was over, German commanders still feared that it would defeat Blitzkrieg.

The counter-attack certainly gave the Germans their first genuine fright. Had it been better organised, had more divisions and more tanks been employed, then it might have broken through the German lines. As it was, Rommel's division suffered over four hundred casualties, and the elite SS Totenkopf Division lost hundreds of men to captivity. But it was not nearly as successful as the German commanders believed. So why were their reactions so extreme?

Partly it was because the German thrust had created a vulnerable extended limb that the Allies ought to have been able to pierce. The longer the limb grew, the more vulnerable it became, and the more apprehensive the generals – and Hitler – grew. And as Halder noted, Hitler was becoming increasingly scared by his own success.

But there was another reason. In his reports of the fighting, Rommel exaggerated British strength and numbers. The attack was made, he claimed, by five divisions and hundreds of tanks. Yet as well as bolstering his reputation, Rommel's embroidery also served to confirm senior generals' fears about the vulnerability of Blitzkrieg. It seems little wonder, in all the circumstances, that the attack on the Channel ports was delayed, that Guderian's 10th Panzer Division was not allowed to advance on Dunkirk (a crucial misjudgement), and that the Arras sector was heavily fortified by troops who might have been better deployed elsewhere.

The manner of defeat was, ultimately, a blessing for the BEF. Its commanders had already lost faith in their French counterparts. Now they were clear that they could not fight their way out of their predicament. They had insufficient strength to force a breakthrough to the south. Only one real-istic alternative to surrender remained – evacuation. For this to be achieved, more time was needed. And thanks to the counter-attack at Arras, more time was bought.

Six

Halting the Panzers

On 21 May, the War Office issued a memo concerning the possible emergency evacuation 'of very large forces' across the Channel. It drew up a list of ferries and transportation ships available to sail at short notice, and noted that smaller ships – Thames barges and Dutch schuits (coastal vessels) – were currently being collected together by the Ministry of Shipping.

The memo calculated that thirty thousand troops might be evacuated over a twenty-four-hour period from three French ports – presumably Calais, Boulogne and Dunkirk. No mention was made of possible beach evacuations but smaller ships, it was proposed, could be used to ferry soldiers to larger ships anchored outside the ports.

'It will be realised,' the memo warned, 'that these notes provide for an emergency which may arise only in certain circumstances.' Yet even this was a significant change of tone from a note made the previous day which considered a large-scale evacuation 'unlikely'. It was starting to dawn on all concerned that an evacuation might actually be necessary.

On the same day, General Weygand called a meeting of Allied commanders at Ypres town hall to discuss his plan

– an attack south by all available British and French forces, while the French forces in the south simultaneously attacked northwards. Unfortunately, Gort – the victim of habitual organisational difficulties – did not initially show up at the meeting, so it went ahead without a crucial participant. Only after Weygand had left did Gort finally arrive.

At the meeting, it was agreed that the British would retreat from the River Escaut to precisely the same line on the French-Belgian border that they had occupied before 10 May. This was a practical necessity – the three British corps commanders were in agreement that a shorter front line would free up divisions to be used when necessary. They were – in theory – available to take part in Weygand's attack. Yet in spite of Gort's belief that the attack could no longer succeed, he did not make his views known. He simply pointed out that the BEF could not contribute its most effective fighting formations to the attack. Had he taken a firmer stance, and vetoed the attack at this moment, the evacuation of the BEF might have begun sooner.

As it was, Churchill arrived back in France the next day. He met Weygand, who assured him that the attack would go ahead the following day with eight divisions. On his return to London, Churchill was in good spirits as he passed on this news to the War Cabinet. If an attack was mounted, after all, victory seemed possible. Without it, he felt, defeat was surely certain.

At Gort's headquarters, meanwhile, the mood was far from buoyant. Pownall wrote in his diary:

Here are Winston's plans again ... How does he think we are to collect eight divisions and attack as he suggests? Have we no front to hold (which if it cracked would let in the flood)? He can have no conception of our situation and condition … The man's mad.

On 22 May, it became clear that the Germans had cut the BEF's lines of communication – meaning that supplies would now have to be brought from the Channel ports. Confident that the German advance would move along the coast, Gort rearranged his forces. The new BEF front along the French-Belgian border was now defended by four divisions (42nd, 1st, 3rd and 4th). The area running north from Arras along the canal line to La Bassée was protected by a further two divisions (2nd and 48th). And the area to the north of this, all the way to the sea, was defended by four patchwork forces, each a collage of smaller, often untrained units. There were two significant consequences. First, the weakest British forces would be confronted by the German armoured divisions while the strongest forces would face only infantry. And second, Gort would be extremely hard pressed to set aside units for Weygand's attack, an operation with which he fervently disagreed.

In the meantime, nine Panzer divisions were advancing into threatening positions on the La Bassée canal line. Anthony Irwin of the Essex Regiment was on the other side of the line. He remembers 'being dumped in a little village by a canal'. The village was named Pont à Vendin, south of La Bassée, and it was here that his company was given three bridges over a 2,500-yard front to defend. As his Pompadours were digging in, Irwin shouted over to a French soldier on the far bank of the canal, asking who he was. The soldier spat defiantly in response before tossing his rifle and ammunition pouches into the canal. When he started to shout abuse, Irwin ordered a sergeant to shoot him dead.

By this time, Irwin's battalion was desperately short of supplies. Second Lieutenant Patrick Barrass remembers his quartermaster raiding abandoned dumps and NAAFI canteens to keep the men fed. Irwin recalls two warrant officers finding chickens from goodness-knows-where, while a fellow officer managed to get hold of an eighteen-gallon cask of beer from a nearby bar. But difficult as conditions were for the soldiers, they were worse still for the Belgian refugees crossing the canal in swarms. When Irwin pulled out a handful of sweets to hand to a refugee child, he was swamped by adults trying to grab one.

Orders were given to the battalion to destroy the barges on the far side of the canal that might be used by enemy troops (and *were* being used by refugees). Many barges were burned, others were sunk by opening their sea-cocks, and a few were shot at close range by a howitzer. Then, one afternoon, three unmarked armoured cars drove up to the far side of the canal in Irwin's sector. Two officers jumped out and shouted, 'Hi, you bastards, come over and give us a hand, we've had a bit of trouble!' The section commander moved forward to help when somebody noticed a black cross on the side of one of the cars. The Germans were on a reconnaissance assignment, and they were posing as British soldiers, trying to lure Irwin and his men into a trap. A fierce fire fight broke out across the canal. One of the Germans was shot dead on the bank before the armoured cars sped away.

As they went, a man fell from one of the cars, jumped to his feet and started running back towards the canal. Fired at by one of Irwin's soldiers, he fell again, before picking himself up and running closer. He was, it transpired, a Cameron Highlander who had been captured by the Germans and kept in the armoured car for three days. Despite being shot twice, his injuries were not serious and he was sent to the rear, after telling how the Germans parked their cars every night and slept in local houses – ideally with young French women.

The following day, the bridges were blown – to Irwin's relief – as they threatened to funnel an entire Panzer army directly towards his men. And they were blown just in time, because the Germans returned shortly afterwards. At first, several motorcycle combinations rode forward. One was destroyed, its crew of three killed. A second was put out of action. And a third stopped, its crew jumping out to set up a machine gun. Their bullets struck the wall behind Irwin's head; a second later a British anti-tank shell removed the gunner's head.

Irwin asked for volunteers. Two soldiers spoke up, both of them, according to Irwin, men with grubby crime sheets and the hearts of lions. The three Pompadours rowed across the canal; one grabbed the machine gun, while Irwin ran to the motorcycle where he found two German maps. Under fire, the men returned to their side of the river, before a tank rolled towards them pushing forward an anti-tank gun manned by a gunner. British and German shells and bullets crossed; a German shell hit the wall between Irwin and his corporal as a British bullet killed the German gunner, and machine-gun fire smashed the tank driver's face through his narrow visor. Once the tank had stopped, Irwin's men were able to fire repeatedly into it. By the end of the action, one tank, one large gun, two motorcycles and several German soldiers had been 'dealt with' to varying degrees, while the British had suffered no casualties. Irwin earned a Military Cross for his part in the action.

This had not been a serious German effort to cross the canal, just a flank reconnaissance as their divisions moved towards the coast. In fact, the Germans would mount no concerted push to cross the canal line, even though such an attempt, made at this stage by combined divisions, would have cut off almost the entire BEF from the coast.

But Heinz Guderian, whose Panzer corps was at the forefront of the German advance, was not overly interested in this kind of thrust. As his corps diary of 23 May noted, 'the essential thing seems to the Corps now to be the push to Dunkirk, the last major harbour; with the fall of this the encirclement would be complete.' Dunkirk was the Panzer generals' glimmering objective, and it was within their reach, not much more than a stone's throw from the most advanced German units. On capturing the town, and assuming that they could hold it, the war would effectively be over. The British army would be captured, or killed trying to resist, and the Germans could attack the demoralised French to the south of the Somme.

On 23 May, the German army and army group commanders-in-chief, Kluge and Rundstedt, met to discuss their concerns about a potential Allied attack across the Somme. Greatly alarmed as they already were by the Arras counter-attack and its apparent success against Kleist's Panzer group, they were now concerned about an Allied attack while the Panzer divisions remained stretched out. A temporary halt, they believed, would allow the lagging infantry to close up, concentrating the formations and strengthening the flanks. By advancing too quickly on the Marne in 1914, after all, the Germans had cost themselves a quick victory.

From Rundstedt's perspective, a halt made sense for other reasons too. Kleist was reporting that over half of his Panzer group's tanks were out of action, and a halt would give him a chance to refurbish this force for the forthcoming fight against the still substantial French army south of the Somme. Fighting over the marshy, canal-covered ground and then inside the confines of Dunkirk would put the Panzers at risk and leave them possible prey to the impressive British Matilda Mark IIs. Why risk the armoured divisions in these circumstances against an already beaten enemy when a far more pressing challenge remained to the south? Paris, after all, had still to be taken.

To Franz Halder, Chief of Staff of German Army High Command, this decision made no sense. The tanks of Army Group A were on the verge of encircling the BEF, and encountering little resistance. Yet they were being stopped, while the infantry of Army Group B, encountering far greater resistance head on, was expected to push the BEF into submission.

On 24 May, Hitler confirmed Rundstedt's existing order – but with different motivation. When Hermann Goering, the Luftwaffe commander-in-chief, had learned that British forces were almost surrounded, he sensed an opportunity to win glory for his air force and for himself. Goering telephoned Hitler, imploring him to allow the Luftwaffe to finish off the BEF. Goering was close to Hitler, an ally from the early days of the Nazi Party. He understood that Hitler mistrusted the majority of his army generals. They were conservatives, not loyal Nazis. Goering warned that if the generals were to achieve the final victory over the British, their success would earn them a prestige with the German people that would threaten Hitler's position. If, on the other hand, Goering's loyal Luftwaffe won the victory, it would be a triumph for Hitler and National Socialism.

Hitler was receptive, particularly when, visiting Rundstedt's headquarters the next morning, he discovered that Army

High Command (made up of the very generals he distrusted) had just ordered that the Panzer divisions be removed from Rundstedt's control. A furious Hitler reversed the order and confirmed Rundstedt's halt order. He would not allow his authority, and that of the trusted Rundstedt, to be undermined by jealous men of dubious loyalty. Had he not authorised Blitzkrieg when his generals had urged against it? Now he would halt it while they strained at the leash.

This is not the whole story; Hitler agreed with Rundstedt that the armoured divisions ought to close up, and that the tanks should be conserved for the coming battle against the French. He had grown, as Franz Halder previously noted, scared of his own success. But he also felt very strongly that his generals needed to be taught a lesson. The halt order was to be that lesson.

It has been argued, down the years, that Hitler's chief motivation for halting the Panzers was to provide the BEF with a 'golden bridge' to return safely to England. That he was keen, in other words, to let the BEF escape. No one argued this more insistently than Hitler himself, after most of the British had already escaped. Rundstedt's chief of staff also made this claim after the war. They both had their reasons; Hitler in order to justify his error of judgement, and Rundstedt's aide in order to excuse himself and his boss.

There was no golden bridge. The explanation sometimes heard is that Hitler had great respect for the British, that he saw them as equals in a world of inferior races, and that he had no designs on their empire. He did not want to have to defeat them, merely sign a peace treaty with them. While there is truth to this, it does not follow that he allowed the BEF its freedom.

For one thing, Hitler's Führer Directive No. 13, issued on 24 May, states: 'The next objective of our operations is to annihilate the French, British and Belgian forces.' For another, some Panzers were actually allowed to ignore the halt order; the tanks of 1st and 2nd Panzer Divisions carried on moving towards Boulogne and Calais, in order to cut off British supplies. And of the roughly nine hundred ships and boats involved in the eventual evacuation, well over a third were sunk or badly damaged by bombs, mines, torpedoes or shells. Similarly, around 3,500 British soldiers, sailors and civilians were killed at sea or on the beaches between 26 May and 4 June. Many more soldiers were killed on the Dunkirk perimeter by Hitler's troops – who attacked them ferociously. What better way to force Britain to the negotiating table, after all, than to destroy her army? None of these factors suggests the existence of a golden bridge.

Hitler finally allowed the Panzer divisions to move again on the afternoon of 26 May, although they would not advance until the following morning. And by this time it was more difficult to secure a great German victory. The BEF had moved north, the perimeter around Dunkirk was developing, a rescue fleet was forming, and evacuations had already begun. Through a combination of Hitler's fear and pride, Rundstedt's timidity and Goering's ambition, the BEF was offered a chance of survival.

That chance was still extremely slim, however. As 2nd Panzer Division moved on Boulogne, two battalions of Irish and Welsh Guards prepared to defend a ten-thousand-yard perimeter around the town. The war diary of XIX Corps reported that its attack on the city and the citadel was meeting violent resistance from the British defenders, adding that Luftwaffe support was inadequate and the attack was progressing slowly. In the event, it took the Germans three days to capture Boulogne, and the majority of the Guards were able to escape back to Britain, having spent an exceptionally difficult long weekend in France.

On the afternoon of 23 May, meanwhile, officers and men of the Rifle Brigade and the King's Royal Rifles stepped onto the dock at Calais to join members of the Royal Tank Regiment and Queen Victoria's Rifles who had previously arrived. Collectively they would serve as the Calais Garrison under Brigadier Claude Nicholson; their job was to defend the town against 10th Panzer Division, commanded by General Ferdinand Schaal.

According to Major Bill Reeves of the Royal Tank Regiment, Calais was an eerie, sinister place at this time. Houses had been knocked down, streets were full of rubble, and the few remaining civilians appeared drunk on looted wine. Considering the town difficult to hold, Nicholson sent a patrol of four tanks, led by Major Reeves in his cruiser tank, to Dunkirk to ascertain whether the path was clear.

Having passed through a roadblock, Reeves's patrol drove past a Panzer unit that had stopped by the side of the road for the night. Mistaking the Panzers for French tanks, an officer leaned out of his turret and began addressing the Germans in French. Reeves quickly drove up alongside him and shut him up. 'For God's sake,' Reeves said, 'move on as fast as you bloody well can!' The patrol moved a mile further, passing a procession of Germans on both sides of the road. Trying to avoid suspicion, they waved occasionally. After a while, a dispatch rider came up behind Reeves and shone a torch on his number plate, before driving away again. They now expected an attack from the rear – but none came, and they drove on.

As they approached a canal bridge at Marck, Reeves spotted mines along the bridge. The patrol was stuck – so a sergeant volunteered to attach his tank's tow rope to the mines, and drag them slowly and carefully over to the side of the road. This courageous act enabled the tanks to start crossing the bridge, but they found the other end choked with anti-tank wire which needed cutting, forcing them all to sit stationary and vulnerable for half an hour. Eventually, they moved on to reach Gravelines, on the edge of Dunkirk.

There, the French commander asked Reeves to assist in the coming battle with the German Panzers. Reeves agreed, and took up position covering the main bridge over the River Aa, while the rest of his tanks covered the other bridges. When a German armoured car appeared three hundred yards away on the other side of the river, Reeves opened fire with his 2-pounder gun and blew the vehicle up. Seeing the crew escape into a blockhouse, Reeves fired again and knocked it down. As he sat and waited, two more tanks appeared, and Reeves scored direct hits on them both. He was soon coming under mortar and shell fire, so he withdrew to a spot in the town where he had an angled but clear view of the same bridge. From there he shot two more armoured vehicles and five more tanks as they attempted to cross.

By midday, not a single German tank had managed to cross the bridge – though Reeves's tank had been the victim of friendly fire, shot by a British anti-tank gun. By evening, all was quiet. The German halt order had come into force, and there would be no more attacks for three days. But Reeves's adventure demonstrates just how close the Germans came to taking Dunkirk, and how significant the halt order was. In fact, had Reeves's patrol not been sent from Calais, the Germans could conceivably have entered Dunkirk before the halt order had even been issued.

Back in Calais, meanwhile, Brigadier Nicholson had received a telegram from the War Office informing him that the town was to be evacuated. As he was surrounded by a much stronger enemy, and defending a huge perimeter with limited resources, Nicholson was relieved at the news. Hours later another War Office telegram announced that evacuation would be delayed by at least a day, and as Nicholson focused on the short-term defence of the town, the French commander scuppered his plans by complaining to his superiors about the British intention to evacuate. As a result, a further telegram from the War Office, received that night, stated that the evacuation was cancelled. This, Nicholson was told, was for the sake of Allied solidarity. He was to select his best position and fight on. So, the following morning, when General Schaal sent the (Jewish) mayor of Calais to ask Nicholson whether he would surrender, he replied that he would not. 'Tell the Germans,' he said, 'that if they want Calais they will have to fight for it.'

Yet even as Nicholson was speaking these words, French naval personnel had already put their guns out of action and evacuated on their own ships. Nicholson was receiving little moral support from London either. Woefully underestimating the strength of the German forces besieging Calais, Winston Churchill sent a succession of messages to his chief of staff asking why the garrison was failing to attack the Germans. 'If one side fights and the other does not, the war is apt to become somewhat unequal,' he said.

By now, the garrison had been fighting a fierce action for a day – and the fighting continued over the following day as fierce German attacks were supported by artillery and Stuka raids. Again, the German commander called upon Nicholson to surrender, and again he refused. 'It is the British army's duty to fight,' he wrote in a message delivered to Schaal, 'as well as it is the German's.'

Inside the town, Second Lieutenant Philip Pardoe of the King's Royal Rifles had no thought of surrendering. 'The prospects,' he says, 'were that either we should be reinforced and we would break through the German lines, or if the worst came to the worst, we would be evacuated.'

Lance Corporal Edward Doe, of the same regiment, remembers being driven back towards the canal as the Germans pushed in on all sides. He fired his Boys anti-tank rifle for the first time at a tank fifty yards away crossing a canal bridge. The shell hit the tank – and did little more than dent its paintwork. 'It just bounced off,' he says, 'and made a noise like a ping-pong ball.' William Harding, the gunner who had fallen for a French girl in Nantes during the phoney war, witnessed sights he would never forget, such as a sobbing soldier dragging himself along by the elbows, leaving two red trails behind him. The man's feet had been blown off.

Bugler Edward Watson of Queen Victoria's Rifles remembers watching a sergeant major yelling at a man with a large hole in his back. The man was flat on the ground crying as the sergeant major screamed at him to get up. And, to Watson's amazement, the man did as he was told: 'I thought this sergeant major was a rotten sod – but he really made the fellow move!'

Along with a small group of riflemen, Philip Pardoe walked into a square – where he came upon a large group of Germans with armoured vehicles. Both groups spotted each other at the same time, leaving the riflemen to run down a street as the Germans jumped into their vehicles. Pardoe and his men quickly dived into the cellar of a house – but instead of staying there, they climbed up to the first floor and lay down in a bedroom. 'Don't ask me why,' says Pardoe, 'we just did.' Moments later Pardoe heard one of the German vehicles coming down the road. It stopped at every house and opened up with machine guns. When it arrived at Pardoe's house, the cellar was machine-gunned, and then the ground floor. Upstairs, Pardoe waited for his turn – but nothing came. The vehicle moved on to the next house, and started firing again.

Edward Watson, meanwhile, was in the cellar of a house somewhere else, having his first taste of wine. He did not like it much, it was too bitter, so he was not too concerned when his officer said, 'You can drink as much as you like, but if you're drunk, I'm going to kill you.' But when Watson needed the toilet, things became trickier. He tried to hold it in, as it meant going outside, and mortar shells were coming down. After a while, when nature called too loudly, he ran as fast as he could to the outside toilet. But, opening the door, he found a dead Frenchman sitting on the seat. He ran back inside and did his business in the corner of a room.

After a while, Watson's group noticed a team of Germans a hundred yards away. They were coming round a street corner, carrying an anti-tank gun. Watson watched closely as the Germans set up the gun and began firing – unaware that they were observed.

'What do we do?' he asked.

'This is your job,' said the officer. 'But you must kill! There mustn't be any missing, because if you miss, they'll know where the shots are coming from.'

Watson rested his rifle on the window sill. It was set at a convenient height to allow him a good aim. Frightened at first, he relaxed into the job, and started to enjoy himself. 'After a while it felt quite fun just to kill them,' he says. Three, four, five men fell dead, and he vividly remembers the looks on the faces of the living who could not work out where his shots were coming from, but feared they were next. Eventually they moved around the street corner out of Watson's sight.

Soon, however, when Germans started running up the street in numbers, the officer gave the order that it was every man for himself – except for Watson, whom the officer wanted to accompany him.

'No!' said Watson. 'I want to go on my own!'

'You come with me!' insisted the officer, and together they ran out of the back door of the house, while snipers fired at them. Running into another house, they saw a German sniper at a window with his back to them. The officer shot him straight away. 'I'd never seen it before at such close quarters,' says Watson. 'There were no questions. No "What are you doing?" Just – BANG!'

On the night of 25 May, a War Cabinet Defence Committee meeting took place in London, discussing whether to attempt a last-minute evacuation of Calais or instead to order the troops to hold on at all costs – on the understanding that this would mean the loss of the entire garrison. The latter course of action was agreed upon. The troops would hold Calais to the very end. 'If we attempted to withdraw our garrison from Calais,' the meeting's minutes surmised, 'the German troops in Calais would immediately march on Dunkirk.'

This was a decision that found favour with Churchill. Earlier that day, when shown the initial War Office telegram informing Brigadier Nicholson of the impending evacuation, he had reacted furiously. 'This is no way to encourage men to fight to the end!' he wrote to Anthony Eden, adding, 'Are you sure there is no streak of defeatist opinion in the General Staff?'

The following day, as the garrison's defence continued, Guderian, commander of XIX Panzer Corps, became impatient with Schaal, commander of his 10th Division, asking him whether Calais should now be left to the Luftwaffe. Schaal argued that this would be counterproductive; bombs, he said, would not be effective against the thick walls and earthworks of the medieval fortifications, and an air assault would necessitate the withdrawal of German troops from advanced positions which would then have to be retaken. Guderian accepted the arguments – and that afternoon, the garrison finally surrendered. Almost four thousand British prisoners were taken.

Second Lieutenant Philip Pardoe was one of the prisoners. He and his men had sat in their bedroom for half an hour, waiting for darkness before heading out. But before they could move, they heard German shouts, and realised that a party of Germans was searching the next-door house. 'This was,' he says, 'the worst decision I'd ever had to make in my life.' He could kill the leader when he came in. But what good would it do? Was it worth sacrificing the lives of his three men – who would do whatever he told them – just in order to kill a German or two? In the end, he told his men to put away their weapons, and when the Germans opened the front door, he went downstairs with his hands up. His men followed. 'This was, to me, the most dreadfully shaming moment in my life.'

Edward Watson was also taken prisoner inside a house. German soldiers stood in the street yelling and throwing grenades. 'Tommy, for you the war is over,' they shouted, satisfying a stereotype. 'They must have been taught to say this,' says Watson.

It is worth asking whether Philip Pardoe, Edward Watson and so many others were sacrificed to any purpose. Winston Churchill was clear that the sacrifice was worthwhile. In the second volume of his history of the Second World War, he would write:

> Calais was the crux. Many other causes might have prevented the deliverance of Dunkirk, but it is certain that the three days gained by the defence of Calais enabled the Gravelines waterline to be held, and that without this, even in spite of Hitler's vacillations and Rundstedt's orders, all would have been cut off and lost.

Perhaps Churchill's sentimental attachment to historical events led him to attach greater significance to Calais than it deserved. It was, after all, England's final possession in France, lost in 1558, its name engraved on Mary I's heart. And it is not entirely clear why Brigadier Nicholson's garrison had to be sacrificed in order to achieve the aim of holding up 10th Panzer Division. Had it been evacuated on the night of 25–26 May, its influence on subsequent events would hardly have been lessened. Certainly Heinz Guderian did not agree with Churchill's analysis, writing that, although he considered the defence of Calais heroic, it did not influence the progress of events around Dunkirk.

This assertion seems logical. Guderian was, after all, intending to attack Dunkirk with a different division from the one attacking Calais. Yet had 10th Panzer Division achieved a quick victory at Calais, surely it could have moved quickly along the coast to assist 1st Panzer Division, thus having considerable influence on 'events outside Dunkirk'.

In the end, given that Guderian's Panzers were already at

the gates of Dunkirk when they were stopped by Rundstedt and Hitler, the halt order seems to have exerted a greater influence on the salvation of the British Army than the defence of Calais. All the same, Guderian cannot be correct when he writes that the defence had *no* influence on events.

There is a sad postscript to the tale of Calais. On 26 June 1943, Brigadier Claude Nicholson committed suicide in his prisoner-of-war camp in Rotenberg. It seems that he had long suffered from depression intensified by a feeling of responsibility for the loss of Calais. Yet whatever Brigadier Nicholson told himself in his darkest moments, it is abundantly clear that he behaved honourably and courageously throughout the defence. He is one of the heroes of our story.

The public mood in Britain, meanwhile, as gauged by Mass Observation on 25 May, was one of confusion and growing pessimism. Even the strongest optimists (generally working-class males) were beginning to express doubts about the future. Confusion was chiefly expressed as a failure to understand why the Germans were relentlessly advancing and the British retreating. Perhaps, some wondered hopefully, this was part of a preconceived British strategy.

Pessimism chiefly took the form of fatalism, as though people were increasingly prepared for any bad news. 'The whole structure of national belief would seem to be rocking gently,' notes MO's daily report. But not everybody felt this way. In rural areas, the mood was lighter. A gardener in East Sussex, for example, a soldier of the last war, was recorded as saying, 'A feller from London was down here last week and he asked me if we weren't afraid of being invaded. I said that's an insult to the British Navy!'

One frequently discussed topic on this day was a speech given by King George VI to mark Empire Day. 'The decisive struggle is now upon us,' he told his subjects, adding that the enemy was seeking 'the overthrow, complete and final, of this Empire, of everything for which it stands, and after that the conquest of the world'. The King, with the help of his speech therapist, Lionel Logue, had been rehearsing his words for days, and was pleased with his performance. The British people seem to have agreed, many commenting on the improvement in his delivery. They were generally less impressed with his content, however. It was too much of a sermon, said some, while others complained that it did not say very much that they did not already know.

An interesting perspective comes from British photographer and costume designer Cecil Beaton. He was due to sail from Britain on 22 May to fulfil a work contract in the United States – but felt reluctant to go. To leave careworn Britain for the untroubled New World, he fretted, would surely be wrong. He asked a friend, Viscount Cranborne, for advice. 'Well, the news is howwid,' said Cranborne, 'but ... I should go, as by the time you come back the news will still be howwid.' So he went.

In New York, the disconnect between the relaxed luxury of Fifth Avenue and the bleak news reports coming from Europe was unsettling to Beaton. 'Nowhere could one find solace from the prevalent gloom,' he writes. 'One's worst fears were confirmed each hour by friend and news bulletin.' When the time came to return to Britain, well-meaning American friends tried to persuade him to stay. 'What are you going back to?' they asked. But Beaton was impatient to return to desperate Blighty.

As his liner pulled out of New York, it passed a pleasure cruiser manned by a German crew – who grinned happily as they poked their thumbs down at the liner's passengers.

Beaton said that his spirits soared on arrival at his Wiltshire home. 'The future might well be gruesome,' he wrote, 'but, somehow, to be in the midst of this maelstrom was far less painful than to hear it from afar.'

On 25 May, in the midst of the maelstrom, the British received a stroke of fortune. In a village along the River Lys, a sergeant of the Middlesex Regiment opened fire on a large blue car containing two German officers. As one of the officers, Eberhard Kinzel, ran away, he left behind a briefcase containing two documents, along with a boot jack. On examination by II Corps' senior intelligence officer, the documents were found to include details of the German order of battle, as well as plans for an imminent attack on the Ypres–Comines front.

At first, Lieutenant General Alan Brooke was concerned that the papers might be a plant, an attempt to deceive the BEF into expecting an attack that would in reality never come. But Brooke soon decided that the plans were genuine (the presence of an incongruous boot jack seems to have convinced him). Unfortunately, there was only one brigade defending the Ypres–Comines canal, and a gap seemed to be growing on the BEF's left where the Belgians were losing cohesion. All this meant that if the German attack were to succeed, it would cut off the BEF from the sea.

These facts finally killed off the Weygand Plan as a rational possibility in Lord Gort's mind (although Weygand himself would not give up on it; two days later, he was still sending messages urging strong British participation in his forthcoming attack). This meant that 5th Division, which Gort had unwillingly earmarked for the attack, could now be sent to defend the Ypres–Comines front, and 50th Division to defend the area around Ypres itself. The next morning, Gort visited General Georges Blanchard in his headquarters. Blanchard was now commander of the French First Army, after Billotte's death in a road accident, and the two men agreed that an attack southwards was impossible. Instead, a further withdrawal was necessary.

While Gort and Blanchard may have seemed to be in agreement, they were actually thinking differently. For Blanchard, a withdrawal meant a retreat to a safer position. But for Gort, it represented the start of an evacuation. Without the approval of the politicians in London or of his French and Belgian allies, Gort was deciding to retreat to Dunkirk – the only Channel port still in Allied hands – in the hope of bringing as many of his troops as possible back to Britain across the Channel. Perhaps his leadership style was disorganised. Perhaps the evacuation could have started sooner. And perhaps a number of stars had collided to ensure that an escape route remained. But on 25 May 1940, Lord Gort made an exceptionally courageous decision, with consequences that endure to this day.

As 1st Battalion, Oxfordshire and Buckinghamshire Light Infantry moved towards the Ypres–Comines line, it had to struggle through 'a traffic jam of vast proportions' to reach its destination. Lance Corporal John Linton had marched nearly sixty miles over the previous week, and he was exhausted. His latest defensive position was a dry canal that did not look difficult to cross. He lay across a railway line, men on either side, waiting for the enemy to attack. Just as Major Bill Reeves and his men had held up Army Group A moving towards Dunkirk from the west, so now Lance Corporal Linton and his comrades had to block Army Group B as it attempted to force its way through to Ypres and on to Dunkirk.

Tired, unshaven and hungry, Linton had eaten only a few pieces of dried fruit that day. He and those alongside him were responsible for holding the line while tens of thousands of soldiers streamed towards the coast behind them. Yet Linton was desperately short of ammunition – with only six rounds in his rifle. 'What are we going to do when the Germans come?' he wondered. 'Bite them?'

Elsewhere along the front, the Germans were gaining the upper hand, but 50th Division was finally arriving to take its position to the north around Ypres. As dawn broke, Linton could hear the battle raging nearby. Later in the day, as the valley grew quieter, he watched as a small German patrol moved slowly towards him through tall grass. He had been told that his company was expected to fight to the last man, but he could not afford to waste ammunition, so he waited before firing. Suddenly, German artillery opened up. At first the shells exploded to the rear, but Linton felt a shock running through his body. He had been hit by a piece of shrapnel.

The next thing Linton knew, he was being carried along by two privates. They were taking him to the regimental aid post. But then an officer ordered them to put him down and return to their positions. The brigade, it seems, was being outflanked by the enemy, and wounded men were not a priority.

In the meantime, Brooke had visited General Alexander at 1st Division HQ. Alexander came to his assistance with three battalions, a yeomanry regiment and a number of tanks, all of which were put to work reinforcing the canal line and gaining back ground that was being lost to the enemy. Help had arrived for 5th Infantry Division – if not yet for Lance Corporal Linton.

One of these battalions, marching ten miles to the rescue, was Lord Gort's old unit of Grenadier Guards. For a night and a day, the guardsmen fought courageously in an attempt to win back ground. In the late evening of 27 May, they mounted an attack. For half an hour resistance was mild, but it grew steadily heavier until the guardsmen reached their objective, the canal. The Germans soon countered ferociously, and they began pushing the Guards back – until a company commander, Captain Stanton Starkey, came up with a plan.

Opening one of the battalion's final ammunition boxes, Captain Starkey had been devastated to find that it contained not bullets but flare cartridges. A supply error had been made. But rather than bemoan his luck, Captain Starkey thought laterally. The enemy's effective mortar fire, he had noticed, was always signalled by a red-white-red pattern of flares. After a while, this would be replaced by a white-red-white pattern, signalling the mortar fire to stop and the infantry to attack.

Captain Starkey, with his huge supply of coloured flares, waited for the German infantry to advance before firing a red-white-red pattern over their heads. German mortars duly opened fire, hitting their own men. The Germans quickly fired off a white-red-white configuration to rectify the situation. The mortars stopped and the surviving infantrymen moved forward. Captain Starkey waited a moment before sending up another red-white-red pattern. The mortars opened fire once more, and the infantrymen were again bombarded. The chaos continued to grow until the mortars ceased firing and the infantry stopped advancing. Cunning had overcome strength.

By now, ferocious struggles were taking place up and down the front, until the two brigades of 5th Division had been reduced to a fraction of their fighting strength. But by the evening of 28 May, the Ypres–Comines line had been held, protecting countless soldiers as they retreated north towards Dunkirk.

The remains of 5th Division would eventually withdraw to the line of the River Yser, just west of the French-Belgian border. In the meantime, however, Brooke had ordered Montgomery's 3rd Division to carry out an extremely difficult night-time move in an attempt to fill a gap along the canal to their north. Starting from the area around Roubaix, 3rd Division crossed the River Lys near Armentières, moved north through Ploegsteert, and slid into position north of Ypres before daybreak. Even though the entire formation was moving within a few thousand yards of a battle front, the Germans had no suspicion that it was there. 'The division was like a fine piece of steel,' wrote Monty, who showed great pride in his men. If the move had been suggested by a student at staff college, he added, the man would have been considered mad. The retreat was encouraging a great deal of improvisation.

The reason for 3rd Division's move was the difficulty in which the Belgian forces found themselves, leading on the night of 27–28 May to the nation's surrender (or 'capitulation', as it was pejoratively described in Britain). And while the story of the surrender is barely remembered today outside Belgium, within the country it remains a contentious topic – particularly to those who believe that Belgian King Leopold III was the victim of 'a great and scandalous lie' perpetrated by Winston Churchill. This strange story is worth exploring as a study in the relationship between politics and war, and as an example of how an accepted history is created.

Belgium is a divided country with a short and troubled history. Created in 1830 out of two distinct, mistrustful communities (the French-speaking Walloons and the Dutch-speaking Flemish), the First World War had turned it into a battleground for its foreign neighbours. 'We suffered so hard,' says Louis van Leemput, 'and the Germans were brutal. It was a disaster. Ruins all over the country.' Having experienced this horror so recently, Belgians were unusually united in the desire to prevent a repeat – but they understood the reality.

This is why King Leopold and his government had chosen a stance of 'armed neutrality'. Despite Churchill's description of Belgium feeding the German crocodile in the hope that she would be eaten last, the Belgians clearly faced a dilemma. While there was no question in their minds that Germany would be the aggressor, by allying themselves with France and Britain they would simply be inviting the Germans to invade. By staying neutral there was at least a small chance that a repeat of the country's destruction could be avoided. They therefore agreed to share military information with the Allies while preventing them from entering Belgium until an invasion came.

When Germany's advance began on 10 May, Belgium became an ally of Britain and France. 'At the last moment, when Belgium was already invaded, King Leopold called upon us to come to his aid, and even at the last moment we came,' writes Churchill.

While relations were cloudy between Leopold and his allies, they were to grow positively frigid between Leopold and his own government. As the Germans advanced and the Allies retreated, the Belgian Prime Minister, Hubert Pierlot, urged Leopold to leave the country, both to escape capture and to lead Belgian resistance from abroad. But this was not Leopold's intention. He intended, he said, to stay in Belgium and share the same fate as his troops.

At a final meeting with his ministers, Leopold declared that the military situation was growing hopeless, and that Belgium would have to surrender. The ministers, frustrated by the King's apparent disregard for the constitution, pointed out that surrender could not be decided by the monarch alone. And once again, when they urged the King to leave the country, he refused.

Leopold had a number of reasons for acting as he did. For one thing, he was not merely the monarch but also the commander-in-chief of the Belgian armed forces, and he felt that an honourable commander did not abandon his troops. Second, he believed that Belgium's own interests were supreme, and that once the battle was lost, no moral obligation remained to the Allies simply because they had come to Belgium's assistance. But most importantly, Leopold felt that staying with his people was the right thing to do. He trusted his own sense of justice above the law.

So Leopold confirmed to his ministers that he intended to stay in Belgium. He did not intend to set up a new government to achieve advantageous terms with Germany. He had no desire to become a Nazi puppet. But this is what Pierlot and his ministers feared, and they made it clear that they deplored his actions. Nor were they alone in trying to dissuade Leopold from his stance. Sir Roger Keyes, the admiral who had taken Churchill's part so effectively during the Norway debate, and an old friend of the King's, was now British liaison officer to Leopold. He suggested that the King take refuge in Britain – and he, too, was rebuffed.

On 25 May, the day that the Belgian government went to France, Leopold wrote to King George VI confirming that Belgium's surrender was inevitable and that he would stay with his people. He added that his entire army was fully engaged and that 'Whatever trials Belgium may have to face in the future, I am convinced that I can help my people better by remaining with them, rather than by attempting to act from outside, especially with regard to the hardships of foreign occupation, the menace of forced labour or deportation, and the difficulty of food supply.'

In his reply, George VI disagreed with Leopold's course and said that no monarch should fall into the hands of the Nazis:

> In taking this decision your Majesty will not have overlooked the extreme importance of establishing a united Belgian Government with full authority outside territory occupied by the enemy … It seems to me that Your Majesty must consider the possibility, even probability of your being taken prisoner, perhaps carried off to Germany, and almost certainly deprived of all communication with the outside world.

Between 24 and 27 May, the Belgian army was fighting desperately on the River Lys. Thousands of men were lost to the Germans, who eventually succeeded in crossing the river, and more than a million refugees were wandering through the towns and cities. At 12.30 p.m. on 27 May, Sir Roger Keyes, who was with Leopold, sent a cable to Gort, informing him that the moment was coming when the Belgian army, having fought continuously for four days, would no longer be able to continue. '[Leopold] wishes you to realise,' wrote Keyes, 'that he will be obliged to surrender.' Two hours later, the French authorities were similarly informed that resistance had reached its limits. And at 5 p.m., Leopold sent an envoy to the Germans requesting terms for a ceasefire.

An hour after that, Lieutenant Colonel George Davy, the War Office's representative at Belgian army headquarters, reported the ceasefire request to Gort – although his message was not received. Churchill certainly discovered the fact, however, because at 7 p.m. he told a meeting of the Defence Committee of 'disturbing news' that the Belgians had asked for an armistice. Half an hour later, a Belgian emissary was received by the Germans and an unconditional surrender came into effect later that night.

Meanwhile, thirteen-year-old Louis van Leemput was sheltering in the house of strangers near Ypres with his mother and brother. He remembers being woken early the following morning by people crying in the street, 'The Germans are here!' He is grateful to Leopold for ending the war. 'He saved my life and the lives of my mother and my brother,' says Louis.

That day, Sir Roger Keyes arrived in London to speak to the War Cabinet. He was sharply defensive of Leopold, reporting that 'only the King's personality had held the Belgian army together for the last four days'. Once Keyes had gone, Churchill was relatively mild in his attitude towards the King, pronouncing that history would doubtless criticise Leopold for having involved Britain and France in Belgium's ruin, 'but it was not for us to pass judgment on him'. Shortly afterwards, Lieutenant Colonel Davy joined the meeting, giving an account of the bravery of the Belgian troops.

Later in the day, however, the international mood began to turn against Leopold; the received wisdom painting him as a defeatist who betrayed the Allies was already falling into place. The French Prime Minister, Paul Reynaud, made a radio broadcast describing the Belgian surrender as secret and treacherous: 'In the middle of the battle, without any consideration and without any notice to his British and French allies, King Leopold III of the Belgians laid down his arms.' Reynaud was followed on air by Belgian Prime

Minister Pierlot, now in exile, who said that the King's actions had no 'legal validity' and accused him 'of separate negotiations with the enemy'.

The ferocity of these words is explained by a telegram sent on 29 May by Sir Ronald Campbell, the British ambassador to France, to Winston Churchill, warning that the French Minister for Information had urgently appealed to Campbell 'to do everything possible to prevent prominence being given in the British Press and radio, and to omit any reference whatever in BBC news transmissions in French, to Admiral Keyes' statements ... urging the suspension of judgement on King Leopold'. The reason for this is revealed as the message continues. If Leopold's surrender was condoned, this would encourage defeatism in France 'at the moment when French opinion has been roused to anger (with consequent improvement of morale) by disgust at the apparent treachery ...'

A similar message was sent to Churchill, on the same day, by General Edward Spears, the War Office's liaison officer at the French War Ministry. Spears' message read: 'The fact that a very mild attitude towards the King of the Belgians is being taken in London is causing considerable concern here ... a very great deal depends as far as morale here is concerned upon making him out to be the villain he certainly appears to be.' In other words, in order to keep French morale from sinking further, and to deflect blame away from the French commanders and the French army, a scapegoat was needed – and King Leopold came along at just the right (or wrong) moment.*

---

* A scapegoat was probably also desirable to deter the French from accusing the British of betrayal – since the evacuation of British troops from Dunkirk had already begun without the knowledge of the French.

Thus is history made. On 4 June, Churchill told the House of Commons: 'Suddenly, without prior consultation, with the least possible notice, without the advice of his ministers and upon his own personal act, he [Leopold] sent a plenipotentiary to the German Command, surrendered his army, and exposed our whole flank and means of retreat.' Churchill, after all, was desperate to keep France in the war, and the reputation of King Leopold III of Belgium was a small thing to sacrifice in order to do so. Perhaps the greater shame is that the Belgian army's brave efforts to resist the Germans have been overshadowed – and sometimes denied – by the politics at play in late May and early June 1940, and again, several years later within Belgium when Leopold briefly returned to the throne before being forced to abdicate. A number of factors – from the halt order to the Arras counter-attack to Gort's decision of 25 May – made the British evacuation possible, and we will encounter others. But an important factor that should no longer be overlooked was the contribution of the Belgian army.

It is certainly possible to argue that Leopold hampered the Allies' preparations for war with his policy of armed neutrality. One can criticise him for self-importance, for unconstitutional attitudes towards kingship, for a lack of gratitude to his allies. But Belgium's surrender was militarily unavoidable. King Leopold did not enforce or manufacture it. And it is clear that he made efforts to keep the British and French informed of his army's true situation, and of its inevitable fate. Indeed, if any information was being withheld on 27 May, it was that the British had begun to evacuate their army – and it was being kept from her allies.

In March 2017, the National Archives in Kew released a British Foreign Office file on the Belgian surrender that had been closed for many decades. Hidden in the midst of the file, among myriad documents concerning the surrender and its post-war Belgian consequences, is a small note written in 1949 by a junior diplomat named John Russell (later Sir John Russell, British ambassador to Brazil and Spain). He writes:

> From some 18 months' unhappy acquaintance with these files I have personally derived the impression that the surrender was inevitable from a military point of view: nor did it come as a surprise to us. However there is no point in going now into the rights and wrongs of this troubled story and I fully agree with [another diplomat] that we should in no event allow ourselves to be drawn into public argument.

In its unassuming way, this note encapsulates the sorry tale. The surrender was inevitable. The British knew it was coming. But neither of these things could be admitted; there were just too many sensibilities in the way.

Seven

Escape to Dunkirk

For those continuing to fight the Germans on 28 May, the Belgians were already a thing of the past. The chief consequence of Leopold's surrender was a twenty-mile gap that had opened up between the left of Montgomery's 3rd Division and the coastal town of Nieuport, only twenty miles east of Dunkirk. Monty's reaction was to call on 12th Royal Lancers, a venerable cavalry regiment equipped with Morris CS9 armoured cars, with orders to demolish every bridge over the Yser Canal from the division's flank to the sea.

This was a very timely intervention – only ten minutes after the crucial Dixmude–Furnes road bridge had been destroyed, the first party of enemy motorcyclists arrived, followed by infantry in lorries. The Germans were surprised to find the bridge blown, and more surprised to find the 12th Lancers' armoured cars lying in wait. All the motorcyclists and many of the soldiers were killed or wounded. Had 12th Lancers arrived any later, the Germans would have swept across the canal line towards Dunkirk.

In Nieuport, however, only one bridge had been destroyed, while the other was still intact. And as 12th Lancers' B Squadron fought an entire day to keep the Germans out of the town, no engineers could be found to blow the bridge. As darkness fell, an officer and two sergeants tried to destroy it with hand grenades, creeping as close as they dared. Just as they were about to throw their grenades, the Germans sent up a flare, and the three men became visible. They managed to hurl their grenades, but none of them damaged the bridge, and one of the sergeants was killed as the other two men ran for their lives. Before long, the town was on fire, and 12th Lancers were forced to withdraw. The way was worryingly open for the Germans to advance along the coast into Dunkirk.

12th Infantry Brigade was immediately sent to Nieuport to block the Germans' advance – but there was confusion in arranging their transport, and hours passed before they arrived. In the meantime, two field companies of the Royal Engineers were hurriedly sent to destroy the remaining bridges, and they managed to keep the Germans at bay until 12th Infantry Brigade finally arrived. And so, to the east of Dunkirk, the Germans had not yet broken through.

To the south-west, 2nd Infantry Division had the job of keeping the Germans back from a fifteen-mile stretch of La Bassée Canal. This was a crucial task, and a difficult one. The main British forces were retreating directly behind the canal, and an astonishing variety of German forces were trying to break through – including 3rd, 4th and 7th Panzer Divisions, and the SS Totenkopf Division. Now that the halt order had been lifted, the Panzers were aching to make up for lost time.

The town of St Venant, at the north of the canal line, held by the Royal Welch Fusiliers and the Durham Light Infantry, was attacked on the morning of 27 May by German tanks and infantry. Although the British battalions managed to hold the Germans off for much of the day, most of their men had been killed or captured by nightfall. A machine-gun battalion of Argyll and Sutherland Highlanders* failed in its attempt to reach Merville, while further south towards Bethune, 2nd Battalion, Royal Norfolk Regiment (with whom Peter Barclay, Ernie Leggett and George Gristock had fought so bravely on the River Escaut) was holding the line against a ferocious Stuka and Panzer assault.

Robert Brown was a soldier in the 2nd Royal Norfolks. On the morning of 27 May, he was keeping watch near a farmhouse when he saw behind him a machine gun mounted on a German motorcycle combination. He quickly returned to battalion headquarters with the unwelcome news that the enemy had stolen in behind. For most of the day, he and another soldier took up position in an outside toilet, knocking out bricks to make loopholes. Other members of the depleted battalion had done the same in nearby stables, cowsheds and barns. Overall the battalion had created a solid defence, and they spent most of the day fighting.

Late in the afternoon, the commanding officer came round asking for opinions: should they carry on or should they surrender? Some said surrender, but Brown opted to continue. 'Morale was so high,' he says, 'that I had no thought of being taken prisoner, or being killed or wounded. We were just firing, and making a joke out of it, really.' In the end, though, the officer ordered them to stop. But he said that if anybody thought that they could escape, they were entitled to try. Brown and two friends had noticed smoke billowing down a road, so they started walking in that direction, hoping to use the smoke as cover. But they were soon forced into a roadside

---

* In the film, shoulder titles worn by the character Alex show him to be a member of this battalion.

ditch, where they were spotted by German soldiers who shouted at them to put their hands up.

Brown stood with his hands in the air. As they reached him, he was immediately struck by their striking appearance, with their SS flashes, death's head badges and automatic rifles. 'But they treated us as reasonable as you'd treat an enemy,' he says, 'just the normal knocks and pushes and shouts.' The rest of Brown's battalion had been taken prisoner elsewhere – where their treatment would prove very different.

By the end of the fighting on La Bassée Canal, only about 10 per cent of the division's strength remained. Yet it had managed to protect the British army as it retreated, with the result that, by the night of 27–28 May, the bulk of the BEF was safely north of the River Lys.

Contemporaneous German reports of the fighting make interesting reading. XXXXI Panzer Corps' war diary for 27 May describes an enemy who 'fights tenaciously and stays at his post to the last man'. Indeed, so tenacious was this enemy that 'the Corps cannot gain ground to any extent worthy of mention eastwards or north eastwards.' And XXXIX Corps' diary records two important details. First it notes that the Germans 'suffered considerable casualties when attacking over the stubbornly defended La Bassée Canal', and second that 'the flow of Anglo-French troops' heading 'towards the Channel could no longer be intercepted in time and with sufficient effect'.

These are the sorts of reports one might expect to read after a German defeat – yet the Germans had virtually destroyed an entire British division. In fact, had the Germans mounted a concentrated attack on the flanks, they might well have broken through and ended the war. Even without a concentrated attack, a large part of the French First Army was now trapped to the south, under simultaneous attack from east and west, unable to reach the Lys.

After 2nd Division's heroic stand, its meagre remains joined the British exodus north, living to fight (and evacuate) another day. The majority of those captured were marched away. But for the surviving members of Robert Brown's battalion, captured by the SS Totenkopf Division, the day would end with horrifying abruptness. In a village with the ironic name of Le Paradis, the men were stripped to the waist, marched into a meadow, lined up against a barn and machine-gunned. Only two men out of ninety-nine, Signallers Bill O'Callaghan and Albert Pooley, survived. O'Callaghan was shot in the arm and Pooley in the leg, and they both lay, covered by the shattered bodies of their comrades, as SS men walked round finishing off anybody who moved or groaned.

Both O'Callaghan and Pooley survived the war and were called as witnesses at the 1948 war crimes trial of Fritz Knoechlein, the commander of the company responsible. Explanations for his men's behaviour have varied from a belief that the British had been using outlawed dum-dum bullets, to anger that the company had suffered heavy casualties during an earlier engagement with the Royal Scots. But no explanation could ever suffice. Knoechlein's men were responsible for the cold-blooded murder of their prisoners. Of several SS officers present at the time, only one raised any protest at the murders, and he was dismissed as a 'frightened rabbit' for demonstrating concern. Knoechlein was found guilty at his trial and executed in January 1949.

And this was not a lone incident. At Wormhoudt, the following day, men of the Royal Warwickshire and Cheshire

Regiments, as well as a number of artillerymen and French soldiers, were murdered at Wormhoudt by members of the Leibstandarte SS Adolf Hitler – though the company commander responsible, Wilhelm Mohnke, was never brought to justice, dying in 2001 aged ninety.

And while the German army cannot be blamed for these particular atrocities (the SS units responsible were Nazi Party organisations), the Wehrmacht was responsible for at least one massacre, at Vinkt near Ghent. Between 26 and 28 May, 337th Infantry Regiment murdered up to a hundred civilians. Some (including a man of eighty-nine) were shot dead while families and friends were made to watch. Others were used as human shields as the Germans crossed a bridge, before being executed at random. And even after the Belgian army had surrendered, some were shot dead after being made to dig their own graves.

These were dark times for the BEF. Retreating under almost irresistible pressure, its allies surrendering and fragmenting, every hour brought further difficulty and bad news. The song 'We're Going to Hang Out the Washing on the Siegfried Line', previously sung with hope, was now sung with dark irony. Yet as the days went by, the continued holding of certain key strongpoints, such as La Bassée, meant that the Allied corridor was strong enough for British troops to pass through German-held territory, like Israelites streaming across the Red Sea. And some of these strongpoints were growing stronger. Gravelines, the town blocked to the Germans on 24 May by Bill Reeves of the Royal Tank Regiment, was now defended in far more depth by the French 68th Division.

Another strongpoint was the town of Cassel. Members of 2nd Battalion, Gloucestershire Regiment and 4th Battalion,

Oxfordshire and Buckinghamshire Regiment, were ordered to hold the town – an elevated strategic point on the road to Dunkirk – against 6th Panzer Division. Companies of both battalions were scattered throughout Cassel, defending key points, and various platoons were stationed outside the town.

On 27 May, 8 platoon of the Glosters' 'A' Company, commanded by Second Lieutenant Roy Cresswell, moved into an unfinished concrete blockhouse north of the town. The blockhouse already contained Belgian and French refugees, and the platoon brought with them some biscuits, a nearly-full tin of meat paste and a few eggs. For the rest of the day, the soldiers turned the blockhouse into a defensible position, blocking up doorways with sandbags and creating firing slits for Bren guns and anti-tank rifles.

That evening, Germans were seen moving forwards about six hundred yards away – and the platoon opened fire. Several Germans were seen to go down. Later that night, the enemy came back in greater numbers. A shell suddenly exploded inside the blockhouse, wounding a lance corporal in the head and throat. An attacker got close enough to start hammering at the door before he was killed by a hand grenade. Eventually, the attack was forced back. And it had given the Glosters one advantage: German incendiary bullets had set light to a nearby haystack which burned brightly, allowing the platoon to keep a careful watch throughout the night.

On the morning of 28 May, the enemy attacked again. This assault too was resisted, but the number of casualties was growing, and most had now been painfully struck by metal shards and chips of concrete knocked from the walls by ricocheting bullets. In addition, food was running low, and with no new rations arriving, the platoon was living on rum and water (except for the wounded, who were denied the rum).

The next morning, a Royal Artillery prisoner was brought to the blockhouse by the Germans to persuade the platoon to surrender. The prisoner, Captain Derick Lorraine, having been wounded two days earlier, had been sent in an ambulance to a casualty clearing station with three other wounded men. On the way, the ambulance was captured by the Germans and the driver taken away. The four wounded men were left inside the ambulance without treatment or food for two days and nights. On the third day, Captain Lorraine was ordered out of the ambulance by German soldiers, brought to the Glosters' blockhouse, and told to walk around it and persuade the occupants to surrender. Captain Lorraine objected. His injured leg, he said, made walking impossible. But the Germans waved a gun in front of his face, making it clear what would happen if he refused.

And so the wounded and hungry Derick Lorraine hobbled slowly around the blockhouse with the help of a stick, shouting, 'Wounded British officer here!' Cresswell started to speak, but Lorraine quickly replied, 'Don't answer back!' in an undertone, before looking down at a dead German and saying, 'There are many English and Germans like that round here.' Halfway through the sentence, he raised his eyes meaningfully to stare at the roof.

Cresswell understood what Lorraine was trying to tell him. Germans had climbed onto the blockhouse roof. Once Lorraine had hobbled away, there was a sudden explosion, and the blockhouse filled with acrid smoke. The Germans on the roof were trying to smoke the platoon out by unblocking a concreted observation hole, filling it with straw, rubble and petrol, and firing it with hand grenades. Cresswell and his men had their gas masks; they quickly put them on, and blocked the gap in the roof with a quilt. The fire burned throughout the night, but the smoke was just about kept under control.

Aware that the occupants of the blockhouse would not give up easily, the Germans increased the scale of their attacks the following day. When the firing became so intense that bullets were flying through the gun slits, Cresswell told his men that they would try to make a break for Dunkirk after dark. By 5.30 p.m., however, it was clear that the blockhouse was heavily surrounded, and there would be no way through. Having had no food for three days, no medical aid, some rum but almost no water, the platoon finally surrendered.

In the town of Cassel, meanwhile, the garrison had managed to hold out until an order was received to join the retreat to Dunkirk. Wounded men, along with a stretcher bearer who volunteered to stay with them, were left in local houses with some food and the hope that the Germans would treat them well. Second Lieutenant Julian Fane was one of several hundred Glosters joining the retreat. At one point, his company was spotted by the Germans, who called out, 'Hitler is winning the war, you are beaten! Come out or we will shell you!' Fane, who had heard stories of the SS massacres, told his men of the treatment they might receive. The men, unsurprisingly, chose not to surrender. Instead, they waited – before suddenly charging across open ground towards a wood. Many of them were killed and wounded by machine-gun fire as they ran.

After four nights of retreat, Fane and his party, reduced to just nine men and himself, arrived in Dunkirk. He had watched an officer drown in his own blood, and an NCO explode when the rounds in his bandoleer were ignited by tracer bullets. He had eaten very little food, suffered agonising pain from his boots and received a wound to his arm. On one occasion, he had walked up to a German soldier, thinking him French, and asked him for directions. Yet he had survived.

As the corridor held, the motley procession filed along. Sergeant Leonard Howard of the Royal Engineers remembers walking and running for sixteen hours. His small, dishevelled group only stopped when they came under attack from Stukas, shells, machine-gun or small-arms fire. 'Survival,' he says, 'was the main object in everybody's mind.' And he remembers an experienced soldier, a warrant officer, walking along the road, tears streaming down his face, saying, 'I never thought I would see the British army like this!'

Private Fred Clapham of the Durham Light Infantry remembers a more prosaic problem. As he walked down the corridor, the early summer heat caused his woollen long johns to chafe his genitals. Officers and men were marching with their legs splayed as far apart as possible. 'It must have looked quite comical,' he says.

The Germans, meanwhile, were dropping propaganda leaflets onto the Allied troops, encouraging them to surrender. The most common displayed a surprisingly accurate map of the surrounded British forces, and some accompanying commentary in English and French. The English section read: 'British Soldiers! Look at this map: it gives your true situation! Your troops are entirely surrounded – stop fighting! Put down your arms!'

The leaflets were so widely circulated that most British soldiers can remember seeing them. They were dropped in huge cylinders, each carrying 12,500 leaflets and held together with long steel bands. Luftwaffe air crew would load these cylinders into a bomber through the bomb bay doors in the same way as they would load bombs. At a prearranged altitude, the aircraft would drop the cylinders, fitted with fuses set to explode a certain height above the ground, breaking the steel bands. The leaflets would then scatter, landing forty or fifty feet apart over a distance of two or three square miles – although sometimes closer together. British soldiers tended to use them as toilet paper – or as maps to guide them towards Dunkirk given the almost complete absence of official charts.

The Germans, meanwhile, were well aware that the British were trying to get away. As early as 26 May, only a day after Lord Gort had made his courageous decision, XIX Corps' war diary was speaking of 'the evacuation of English troops', noting that they were 'trying to escape in the direction of Dunkirk and that must be prevented'. Extraordinarily, the French had less knowledge of the coming evacuation than the Germans. General Blanchard, commander of the French First Army, was not officially informed of the British intention to evacuate its army until 28 May.*

Often, however, the last people to learn about the evacuation were the British soldiers themselves. Until very late, some had no idea why they were retreating – perhaps it was punishment for a misdemeanour, or possibly their unit was due a rest. Even when told that they were on their way to

---

* Much of the bad feeling between France and Britain over the last seventy-seven years can be traced to this act of supposed betrayal. While this is understandable, two points need to be added. First, retreat and evacuation were the only sensible courses of action in the circumstances. By keeping alive his impractical plan to attack southwards, Weygand was endangering both his and the British forces. Second, British ships were to evacuate huge numbers of French troops alongside British troops. The exodus from Dunkirk was a desperate effort to keep the war alive, not a sly British bid to cut and run.

Dunkirk, many soldiers had no idea what this meant. A few, particularly baffled, thought Dunkirk was in Scotland.

On 27 May, Anthony Rhodes of the Royal Engineers was astonished to hear from his colonel that his unit would be evacuating from Dunkirk. 'We are going to attempt something essentially British,' said the colonel. 'I daresay only the British would dare to attempt such a hare-brained scheme.' He did not inspire much confidence in his men by explaining that plans for the evacuation had not yet been made, and that they were just going to have to chance it.

Confusing to some and disheartening to others was the fact that they were told to ditch and destroy their vehicles and equipment. Five miles out of Dunkirk, Fred Carter and his party of Royal Engineers were told to leave their trucks behind and blow them up with hand grenades, and as Peter Hadley of the Royal Sussex Regiment retreated from Poperinghe, he walked past an unbroken line of shattered vehicles. Understanding *why* the vehicles had been destroyed (the Germans must not be allowed to use them), he was nonetheless stunned by the sacrifice of millions of pounds' worth of virtually unused equipment.

Working vehicles were now in short supply. On one occasion, a Bren gun carrier was stopped by soldiers asking for a lift down the corridor. When the officer in charge refused and the carrier drove away, one of the soldiers took a shot at it with his rifle. He hit the driver – who was left disabled for life.

The chaos grew so great at times that soldiers taken prisoner by the Germans managed to escape in the mayhem. One man did three days' kitchen fatigue as a German prisoner before slipping away. Those who remained free often went without sleep: a soldier found he could stay awake by rubbing coffee grounds in his eyes – though he might be considered lucky to have had coffee in the first place. And despite being warned to leave the wounded behind, men did not want to leave their friends, but nor did they have the strength to carry them for days. This explains why the wounded were often seen in wheelbarrows.

Drawing nearer to Dunkirk, congestion on the roads became appalling. Men, horses and vehicles came together in the dark to create one huge fleeing organism. Peter Hadley found that the only way to keep his men together was to make them hold on to the man in front, while regularly shouting the name of the unit to attract those who had wandered off. But by this time, many groups of men had lost their battalions altogether, and were moving on in smaller groups. One soldier thought he was walking with four friends – until he turned round to see twenty strangers close behind. In circumstances such as these, anyone displaying natural authority became a leader. Rank was losing its influence.

On entering Dunkirk on 27 May, Anthony Irwin of the Sussex Regiment stood on a ridge above the city and looked down at the docks, all but destroyed by Luftwaffe raids. As he hurried down the hill in the sunshine, he heard explosions, and minutes later arrived at their source. A convoy of ambulances, all displaying red crosses, was strewn across the road, mangled and burning. It had been bombed. Screams came from inside the ambulances, and bodies lay beside them, but there were already people helping, so Irwin moved on.

Anthony Rhodes entered Dunkirk on the same day across a bridge over the Bergues Canal. He spoke to French civilians who seemed perfectly aware that the British were evacuating. Most of the civilians were heading out of town, nervous that the Luftwaffe would soon flatten the entire city and everyone in it. And sure enough, within moments, the sun was blotted out by German bombers whose sound grew to a crescendo. 'A series of small earthquakes seemed to take place in succession all around us,' Rhodes remembers. The bridge had been hit, and two large lorries next to it had disappeared, reduced to nothing in thirty seconds.

Peter Hadley, meanwhile, arrived several miles to the east of Dunkirk, at a small village. From there he could see a strip of blue directly ahead. He halted his men, ordered them to close up, and marched them a few hundred yards in perfect order. The scene they encountered – at Bray Dunes – was striking. A sandy beach reached into the far distance to the left and right. Straight ahead was the sea, behind the beach were grassy dunes, and on it were the men of the British Expeditionary Force.

Some few miles to the east was La Panne, a seaside town where Lord Gort was setting up his latest (and final) headquarters. On 30 May, Frederic Wake-Walker, a naval officer on board HMS *Hebe*, surveyed the scene from La Panne westwards. It was, he said:

> One of the most astounding and pathetic sights I have ever seen. Almost the whole ten miles of beach was black from sand-dunes to waterline with tens of thousands of men. In places they stood up to their knees and waists in water waiting for their turn to get into the pitiable boats. It seemed impossible we should ever get more than a fraction of all these men away.

For the evacuation to have any chance at all, the perimeter around Dunkirk and the beaches would have to be defended to prevent the Germans from mopping up the soldiers who had entered down the corridor. The fighting was by no means over. Gort placed Lieutenant General Sir Robert Adam, commander of III Corps, in charge of the defences.

The perimeter would have to be large enough to protect Dunkirk, the beaches and the mass of humanity within. It would also have to be large enough to prevent the Germans from shelling the beaches with anything but their heaviest guns. Yet it would have to be small enough to allow it to be defended with limited numbers of soldiers. And it would have to take advantage of the canal lines which provided ready-made defensive obstacles.

To this end, the perimeter would be about twenty-five miles long and eight miles deep. It was agreed that French troops would man the sector from the port of Dunkirk to the west, while the British would defend the area from Dunkirk to Nieuport in the east. And the man given the critical tasks of, first, finding the troops to do the job, and then organising them, was Brigadier Edward Lawson, who in peacetime had been the general manager of the *Daily Telegraph* newspaper. The speed with which the perimeter forces were created and the tenacity with which the men defended their positions (in the full knowledge of the sacrifice they were likely making) are too often forgotten when the story of Dunkirk is told.

While retreating near Poperinghe, Second Lieutenant Jimmy Langley of the Coldstream Guards was approached by his brigadier. 'Marvellous news, Jimmy,' said the brigadier, 'the best ever!' Langley wondered what could be so marvellous, short of an immediate German surrender. The answer was that the battalion had been chosen to man a section of the perimeter along the Bergues–Hondschoote Canal.

Arriving on 29 May, Langley's No. 3 Company dug in along the canal close to a large cottage which would house the company's headquarters. The company had already been reduced by fighting to thirty-seven men, but by helping themselves to the contents of British lorries by the side of the road, they increased their arsenal, picking up twelve Bren guns, three old Lewis machine guns, an anti-tank rifle and thirty thousand rounds of ammunition. Langley also found some new battledress, a compass, a radio and five hundred very welcome cigarettes.

Over the next two days, Langley and his men watched as a continuous procession of British and French soldiers crossed the canal and moved on to Dunkirk. The men ranged from pristine Welsh Guardsmen who had been fighting at Arras, to disillusioned Frenchmen, to bedraggled British odds and ends. One corporal carrying two Bren guns whose straps had cut through to his collar bones particularly impressed Langley. When he had tried to requisition the guns, the corporal refused to part with them. His dead major, he said, had ordered him to take them back to England, where they would soon be needed. Langley poured some whisky into the corporal's tea, put dressings under his straps, and wished him the best of luck.

Soldiers may have been pouring past Langley, but only one aeroplane flew overhead, and he fired furiously at it. Fortunately, it passed serenely on; it was a British Lysander giving Lord Gort a tour of the perimeter line.

Once Gort had moved out of range, and the stream of retreating men had reduced to a trickle, the Germans were spotted. Some of Langley's men were positioned in the attic of the cottage, where they had removed roof tiles and created Bren gun nests. The Germans, standing in a field six hundred yards away, were easy targets. The result was, according to Langley, a massacre, and it made him feel sick.

Later that afternoon the battle began in earnest, with a German attack to the right of the cottage, a position held partly by No. 1 Company and partly by a Border Regiment company. As Langley's Bren guns kept up a constant fire, trying to assist the neighbouring companies, the Germans wheeled up a large anti-tank gun and pointed it at the cottage. For a while nothing happened – until Langley heard a tremendous crash and a brightly coloured object started bouncing around the attic, stopping by the chimney stack. It was an incendiary anti-tank shell, and the attic occupants grabbed their guns and ran downstairs as four more shells were fired into the attic.

The German attack was growing more intense, and while Langley was seeking orders from Major Angus McCorquodale, the pair were approached by the captain in command of the Border Regiment company on the right. The captain said that the Germans were massing for an attack, and he was proposing to withdraw.

McCorquodale ordered him to stay put and fight, but the captain said this overrode his own colonel's orders to withdraw when able. McCorquodale pointed to a large poplar tree further down the road, saying, 'The moment you or any of your men go back beyond that tree, we will shoot you.'

The captain began to argue, but was interrupted by McCorquodale. 'Get back,' he said, 'or I will shoot you now and send one of my officers to take command.'

The captain walked towards his company position in silence. McCorquodale picked up a rifle and told Langley to get one for himself. 'Sights at two-fifty,' McCorquodale said. 'You will shoot to kill the moment he passes that tree. Are you clear?'

Very soon the captain appeared, accompanied by two men. They stood by the tree for a while as Langley and

McCorquodale took aim. Then the captain walked beyond it. The Guards officers fired simultaneously, the captain fell, and his companions ran in the other direction. The Border Regiment battalion stayed where it was.

Shortly afterwards, artillery opened up across the length of the Guards' position, and an attack followed – but was halted. When all had become quiet, the officers of No. 2 Company on the left came over for a visit. McCorquodale ordered his batman to fetch a bottle of sherry, glasses, and a table from the cottage. In the middle of a battlefield, four officers, three of whom would be dead within twenty-four hours, stood and toasted 'the gallant and competent enemy'. And when firing started again, they returned to their positions and recommenced battle.

Later that afternoon, the officer in charge of No. 1 Company was killed trying to retrieve a Bren gun from an exposed position. There was now just one officer remaining on the right, Second Lieutenant Ronald Speed, who had only joined the battalion a few weeks earlier. Langley told McCorquodale that Speed wanted to withdraw to No. 3 Company's position.

McCorquodale gave Langley his flask and told him to make Speed drink all of it. 'If he won't or still talks of retiring, shoot him and take command of the company,' said McCorquodale quietly. 'They are not to retire.'

Langley walked back to Speed's position, handed him the flask and advised him to drink it. Fortunately, he did. Langley told him he was not to retire.

Speed nodded. He was killed half an hour later.

The next few hours were something of a blur for Langley. He remembers eating a chicken stew, allowing an old woman to take refuge in the cottage, delivering a furious rant at the

Germans for taking over other people's countries, setting three German tanks on fire with Bren guns – and crouching over Major McCorquodale as he died. 'I am tired, so very tired,' said the major, before smiling and ordering Langley back to the cottage with his last breath.

As he and his men made a last stand in the cottage, Langley was shot in the arm. The limb hung uselessly at his side, the wound leaving blood all over his battledress. He was brought downstairs and bundled into a wheelbarrow. He felt no pain, only thirst, as he was transferred into an ambulance, driven to the beach and then carried to the water's edge on a stretcher. But unable to stand up, he was not allowed onto a boat. A stretcher would take the space of four fit men, he was told, and only the walking wounded were now being evacuated. Instead, he was brought to a casualty clearing station on the edge of Dunkirk. There, when the Germans finally arrived, Jimmy Langley was taken prisoner.*

Yet for all the Coldstream Guards' efforts, and those of officers and men up and down the perimeter, there was a danger that political discussions taking place in London would leave them counting for nothing. On 28 May, Winston Churchill had spoken to Sir Roger Keyes, telling him that Lord Gort did not 'rate very highly' the BEF's chances of survival. He had then spoken to Parliament, saying that the situation was 'extremely grave' but that Britain should remain confident in her power to make her way 'through disaster and through grief to the ultimate defeat of her

---

* But not for long. Langley escaped from hospital a month later and made his way to Marseille in the Vichy 'free zone', where he worked for an escape network. Arriving back in England in 1941, he joined MI6, working to facilitate escape lines on the continent.

enemies'. From the chamber he went directly into meetings, first with his War Cabinet and then his wider Cabinet. It would be no exaggeration to describe these meetings as the most important political discussions to take place in Britain over the last hundred years.

With the War Cabinet, Churchill discussed Italy's desire to act as broker in peace negotiations between Britain and Germany. Lord Halifax, the Foreign Secretary and Churchill's recent prime ministerial rival, believed that Britain ought to consider making concessions which did not compromise her independence. This, he felt, was common sense. Britain would receive better terms negotiating now than she would in three months' time when her situation might have worsened. No, said Churchill. Hitler's peace terms would put Britain completely at his mercy – whenever they were offered.

Neville Chamberlain now spoke up to say that he could not see what was so wrong with making it clear that, while Britain would fight to the end to preserve her independence, she would consider decent terms if they were offered.

The first response was pure Churchill. Nations that went down fighting rose again, he said, but those that surrendered tamely were finished. The second response, from Deputy Prime Minister Clement Attlee, was more practical. Once negotiations began, he said, it would be impossible to rally the morale of the British people.

Churchill's style of oratory, usually pitched somewhere between Edward Gibbon and Shakespeare's Henry V, could sometimes seem masterful and sometimes hollow. But nowhere was it ever used to better effect than in the meeting that followed with twenty-five members of his full Cabinet. Many of these men did not share Churchill's views on peacetime issues. Some, such as committed socialists Herbert

Morrison and Ernest Bevin, could never have imagined serving under him. But all now listened as Churchill set out the situation in France, and the likelihood that the Germans would attempt an invasion of Britain. They listened as he admitted having considered the possibility of negotiating with Hitler, whom he described as 'That Man'. And they listened as he warned that any peace would turn Britain into a slave state. 'I am convinced,' he told his rapt audience, 'that every man of you would rise up and tear me down from my place if I were for one moment to contemplate parley or surrender. If this long island history of ours is to end at last, let it end only when each of us is choking in his own blood upon the ground.'

The attitudes in Churchill's rarefied War Cabinet were one thing. But in his full Cabinet, a better microcosm of the country, he could begin to gauge the reaction his words would receive in British pubs and living rooms. And the ministers loved what they heard. 'There were loud cries of approval all round the table,' wrote Hugh Dalton, the Labour Minister of Economic Warfare, adding that 'no one expressed even the faintest glimmer of dissent.' Churchill was able to return to the smaller War Cabinet later that evening to inform them emphatically that there would be no surrender. The fight would continue. The war was not over.

Had these meetings ended differently, had Britain decided to speak to 'That Man', the sacrifices made by the men of the British, French and Belgian armies would have amounted to little – because the war would almost certainly have come to an end shortly afterwards. We forget nowadays how close Britain came to making peace with Hitler, how close she came to a puppet government, to round-ups of Jews, dissidents and anybody else who displeased the authorities, to the suppression of ideas and dissent, to the implementation of the kinds of laws described in a previous chapter of this book.

For Lord Halifax, Britain was a geographical entity, a place of hills, dales, moors and tors, an H. E. Bates world durable enough to resist whatever brutal regime was in effective charge. For Churchill, Britain was more than this. It was the original model of liberty, a land whose existence depended on freedom and the rule of law. If these were extinguished, her survival meant nothing. And while both views were rosy and sentimental in their different ways, the latter was closer to the truth – and a great deal more humane.

Eight

No Sign of a Miracle

In the opening scene of Chris Nolan's film, *Dunkirk*, we see Tommy entering Dunkirk through a section of the perimeter held by French troops. Once inside, he finds himself in the Dunkirk bubble, a world of misrule populated by the men (and, occasionally, women) we have met in the pages of this book, whose initial goal has been to reach Dunkirk, but who, once there, are desperate to leave again. Wandering down onto a beach, Tommy is confronted by queues of soldiers leading to the water. They are hoping to be picked up by a small ship which will take them offshore to a bigger ship, which in turn will take them back to England. Tommy is turned away from the first queue he attempts to join, before teaming up with another soldier and becoming an ad hoc stretcher bearer. He has already been papered with enemy propaganda leaflets, helped the other soldier to bury a body, been attacked by a Stuka, and tried to relieve himself on several occasions.* These were the sorts of incidents experienced inside the perimeter by hundreds of thousands of people over the days of the evacuation.

---

* A regular (or irregular) occurrence that often caused problems; remember Edward Watson in Calais.

It can hardly be overemphasised how the experiences of these people varied. A private of the Royal Warwickshire Regiment arrived on the beach only to be turned away from several queues, like Tommy, by men saying, 'Find your own unit, chum! Not here!' Other soldiers, in contrast, were able to join the first queue they saw, while others still were so appalled by the length of the queues that they settled down in the sand. Some saw no queues at all.

Some veterans will set aside their pride and tell you how they went to the toilet. But another told me vehemently that nobody had eaten anything for days, so there was absolutely no need for anybody to do so. Captain Humphrey Bredin of the Royal Ulster Rifles, whom we last met fighting doggedly on the River Dyle, speaks of small groups of British soldiers sitting on the beach playing cards in the sun as though at a holiday resort. Others tell of impromptu cricket matches, Royal Engineers stunting on motorcycles in the sand, and an ex-circus performer doing tricks on the back of a horse as soldiers watched appreciatively.

Sub-Lieutenant John Crosby came ashore at La Panne on Wednesday 29 May from a Clyde paddle steamer. With his ship grounded by the tide for most of the day, he made his way to the Hotel Splendide, where he sat lazily with a bottle of wine alongside two British soldiers who were drinking lemonade because, they complained, there was no beer left in the town. There were, however, brothels, and men could be seen waiting patiently in queues – a peculiar parallel of those on the beach – to receive a last taste of the continent.

It was here, too, that Fred Carter of the Royal Engineers had his first taste of champagne. Having dug a foxhole in the sand dunes with his hands, Fred and his friends decided to visit an estaminet a little way away. They 'had a good feed', spending all of their remaining cash. Fred decided to try some champagne to see what all the fuss was about. It was, he discovered, 'glorious'.

Yet men were simultaneously arriving in Dunkirk so shattered, bloodied and demoralised that the offer of a quick one before Blighty would have been meaningless. One soldier describes his uniform as being so battered and dirty that it had lost its colour, while his socks and feet had merged into a single bloody, woolly mess. An officer who jumped from the mole onto a ship crumpled in a heap on landing. When his boots were removed, the bones of his feet were visible. Vic Viner, a beachmaster responsible for order and discipline, recalls experienced NCOs breaking down in tears in front of him. 'It's hard to express how gruesome it was,' he says.

Elsewhere, a platoon found a tin of baked beans and shared it; they ended up with three beans each. Several men, meanwhile, were seen sitting in a circle on the sand, maddened by days without food, pretending to eat a meal. They mimed the use of knives and forks, and chewed imaginary food. Another man was seen trying to eat the leather strap of his helmet. Robert Halliday of the Royal Engineers scoured Dunkirk for food, entering one house after another. He found nothing at all – and his search was interrupted by a falling bomb that tossed him fifty yards down the road, blowing out both of his eardrums.

After this, Halliday and fifty other Royal Engineers built a raft on the beach at Bray Dunes. Made from the floorboards of lorries and buoyant petrol tins, it was held together by scavenged rope. The plan was that one member of the team would swim out to contact a boat, while the non-swimmers were placed on the raft and pushed towards the boat by those who could swim. The men spent two busy days building the raft before a naval officer ordered them to stop immediately. 'What I want you to do,' the officer said, 'is to file straight out into the sea as far as you can go and stay there.'

While Halliday and his friends were working in vain, countless others lay around on the sand doing nothing, or burying themselves in sandy trenches. 'Blimey, he's dug himself in well,' said one joker, staring at a helmet sitting on the beach.

Here are just a few tastes of Dunkirk's messy paradox. Life is always complex, nuanced and contradictory. We instinctively know this. But too many modern politicians and media sources would have us believe that it is straightforward and monochrome. If one thing alone is remembered about Dunkirk, then it should be this: there was no single story. And this is a theme reinforced by Chris Nolan's film, which takes place in three realms: land, sea and air. In each of these realms, people were having very different experiences. And they are all equally valid.*

The evacuation, as we have seen, was being tentatively contemplated as early (in relative terms) as 17 May. And two days later, the sending home of the 'useless mouths' had begun. This was the unflattering description given of anybody considered peripheral to the essential running of the British Expeditionary Force. By the end of 26 May, almost twenty-eight thousand butchers, bakers and candlestick makers had been sent from Dunkirk home to England. But now, the real evacuation – of as many soldiers as possible – was to start.

---

* Not only does the film show differing experiences, it also shows the same action experienced differently from multiple viewpoints.

On 26 May, Lord Gort received two telegrams, one from Anthony Eden, another from the War Office. The first warned him that evacuation might prove necessary, the second confirmed that it *was* now necessary. In overall charge of the evacuation would be a fifty-seven-year-old vice-admiral, Bertram Ramsay, a meticulous and impatient man who had only recently been persuaded by his friend, Winston Churchill, to return to the Royal Navy.

Ramsay's headquarters would be in Dover Castle's Dynamo Room. Once the home of the castle's lighting generator, it now lent its name to the daunting effort of organisation, improvisation and willpower that lay ahead. The evacuation of the British Expeditionary Force began a few minutes before seven o'clock in the evening of Sunday 26 May with a signal sent by the Admiralty: 'Operation Dynamo is to commence.'

The first ship to sail after the signal was sent was the Isle of Man steam packet *Mona's Isle*, which embarked 1,420 troops from the harbour; twenty-three of them were killed on the voyage home by artillery fired from the shore at Gravelines and a machine-gun attack from the air. This set the tone for the days to come – but *Mona's Isle*, which eventually arrived back in Dover at noon the following day, was not the first ship to sail on 26 May. Even before the sounding of the signal, a number of other passenger ships had set off for Dunkirk. These included ships with soon-to-be-familiar names such as *Mona's Queen*, *King Orry* and *Maid of Orleans*, which would each bring many thousands of men to safety over the next nine days.

At the start of the evacuation, British expectations were low. The Allies were trapped in a narrow pocket, fighting for their lives against stronger forces. The Germans were ten miles from Dunkirk and victory. Winston Churchill believed that thirty thousand troops might be rescued, while Ramsay hoped for forty-five thousand. But this would depend on many variables. How many troops could reach Dunkirk? How long could the French and British soldiers hold out on the perimeter? How effectively could the Luftwaffe neutralise soldiers, ships and equipment within the perimeter, at sea, and perhaps at receiving ports in England? Would a truly effective means of evacuation be found, allowing large numbers to be evacuated every day? Would the weather favour the evacuees or the attackers? On the evening of 26 May, nobody knew the answers.

At 1 a.m. on Monday 27 May, Major Philip Newman, a surgical specialist with 12th Casualty Clearing Station, arrived in Dunkirk. With him were forty men in three lorries, and they had come to open a front-line medical unit in a chateau alongside a French field ambulance. Newman, until recently a surgeon at the Middlesex Hospital in London, was resigned to the fact that while everybody else would now be going home, he and his colleagues would not. 'There was an awful languid feeling among all of us,' he writes, 'in having to open up again and hold the baby.'

His first impression of Dunkirk was of blazing buildings and exploding bombs. The Luftwaffe had already been bombing the town and the port for some time, but this was the day when they would be pulverised by continuous large raids. Newman settled down that night in an empty, but still beautifully furnished, terraced house, and at dawn moved to the chateau. There he began setting up his operating theatre in a room on the ground floor with large windows, good artificial lighting, and parking space outside for an X-ray van. Within minutes, ambulances full of wounded men began arriving.

Anthony Rhodes arrived in Dunkirk at about six o'clock that morning. He remembered it from peacetime as a pleasant place, full of nice restaurants and shops to buy foreign gifts for friends. Now, the first thing he saw was the huge pall of smoke from the burning oil tanks that would characterise the evacuation, and which is recreated in the film. Like many of those who arrived in Dunkirk at the start of Operation Dynamo, he found a cellar near the harbour in which to shelter from the bombing. That harbour, after all, was the obvious point of evacuation.

Rhodes believed that a cellar was the safest possible place to shelter from a Luftwaffe raid. Bombs would surely explode on the upper floors, leaving the basement untouched, and as he was beneath a three-storey house, he felt secure. But he felt less secure when he came out at the end of the first raid to find that an identical building opposite had been reduced to a pile of rubble. Anybody in its cellar would clearly have been buried alive.

Norman Prior of the Lancashire Fusiliers also moved into a cellar on arrival. He took his boots off for the first time in a fortnight, lay down – and felt a small movement. When he looked up, he saw a Frenchman trying to steal the boots. 'I just blasted him with a mouthful of whatever,' he says, 'it didn't come to fisticuffs.' He kept them on at all times after that.

Many of those arriving in Dunkirk on that day, before the British authorities had taken proper control of the town, witnessed an anarchy inspired by fear and relief. Ernest Holdsworth, a lifelong teetotaller, found himself in a hotel cellar, drinking a mixture of rum, whisky and brandy. It was a nightmarish scenario – British, French and Senegalese soldiers, all together, singing, vomiting and passing out.

On that day, Captain William Tennant, chief staff officer to the First Sea Lord, was sent to Dunkirk to assume the position of Senior Naval Officer Dunkirk. A navigational expert, diffident by nature, Tennant would be responsible for organising the distribution of ships and the embarkation of soldiers. He was encountered by a snarling mob of British soldiers, ready to challenge his authority. And he met soldiers smeared with lipstick and a drunk sergeant wearing a feather boa.

Carrying on to Bastion 32,* the headquarters of Admiral Abrial (the commander of French forces at Dunkirk), Tennant met two senior British army officers and a naval commander, who informed him that the harbour was too badly damaged, and too vulnerable to air attack, to be used for Operation Dynamo. All embarkations would have to be made from the beaches. They also told him that the Germans would arrive in Dunkirk in twenty-four to thirty-six hours' time. Faced with the reality that large ships could not come near the shore, and with the almost total lack of small boats to ferry the men from the beaches to these ships, his job appeared impossible. Churchill's aim of rescuing thirty thousand troops seemed hopelessly ambitious.

From Bastion 32, Tennant started sending wireless messages to Ramsay in Dover Castle. He asked for every available craft to be dispatched immediately to the beaches. In the Dynamo Room, all ships on their way to the harbour were correspondingly diverted. Tennant's naval party, in the meantime, started rounding up the soldiers in cellars around the harbour and sending them to the beaches.

---

* Adjacent to the present-day (and extremely atmospheric) Dunkirk 1940 Museum.

One of these men was Anthony Rhodes. By now, air raids were coming every half-hour, and, apart from a brief and unsuccessful trip to find another shelter further out of town, Rhodes had spent all day in his cellar. It was far too dangerous, he decided, to be outside. But that afternoon, he heard a cry from the street for 'Officers!' Heading up to find out more, he was informed that no more evacuations would be made from the harbour, and was told politely to collect as many men as possible and escort them to the beaches. And so Rhodes – and almost everybody else in the town of Dunkirk – headed eastwards.

The resulting crocodile of troops was duly attacked from the air. As the bombs fell, Rhodes flattened himself, face down, on the ground. And when the aircraft came back to machine-gun the survivors, he did the same again, noting that two men who had stayed erect to fire a Bren gun at the attackers were riddled with bullets.

After the raid was over, Rhodes continued on to the beaches. Once there, he looked into the distance; he was impressed by the sight of so many thousands of men, some staring, some eating, some sleeping, waiting for the next ship or the next raid. He might be an officer, but army battledress was so generic that it was difficult for a stranger to distinguish him from the rank and file. It would be much easier, over the next few days, for naval officers, dressed in their striking blues, to assert their authority than it would be for men such as Rhodes. He walked a couple of miles, eventually settling down in the sand dunes at the beach's edge. His wait had begun, for the large ships that would anchor offshore – and the small boats to ferry him there.

The shortage of small vessels was a problem from the start of the evacuation. Not until 30 May did they begin to appear in any numbers. Until that time, the lifeboats and whalers of larger ships had to be used. But even when the boats were available, they suffered heavily. When the sea was at all rough, it was very difficult for soldiers to climb onto them from the shore. Beyond this, the boats were used so heavily that they became prone to mechanical breakdowns and the exhaustion of their crew. Indeed, many boats were requisitioned from their owners and operated by naval personnel who simply did not know how to handle them. And once a boat had been rowed out to a larger ship, it was often allowed to drift away rather than returning to shore to pick up more soldiers.

Late on the night of 27 May, Captain Tennant noticed that while the Luftwaffe had been exerting itself in an effort to destroy the main Dunkirk harbour, it was neglecting to bomb the outer harbour. The result was that two long breakwaters – the eastern and western moles – were intact. These were not piers or jetties; they were huge concrete arms protecting the harbour, and preventing it from silting up. Tennant quickly spotted the potential of the eastern mole. It stretched almost a mile out to sea, it had a wooden walkway on top that could accommodate four men walking abreast, and soldiers could be brought there relatively easily from the beaches. On the other hand, it had a fifteen-foot tidal drop and was subject to treacherous currents, while there was no obvious method of berthing ships alongside it. But, figured Tennant, there was little to lose. And so the first crucial improvisation of Operation Dynamo was put into practice.

A passenger ship – *Queen of the Channel* – was quickly diverted from the beach at Malo-les-Bains to the mole, and soldiers were brought alongside to clamber on board as best they could. At a little after four o'clock on the morning of

28 May, *Queen of the Channel* set out for Dover carrying 950 British troops. Tennant's idea was clearly workable, and other ships were ordered to the mole. If the troops defending the perimeter could hold the Germans off a little longer, if the weather remained good, if plenty of ships and boats could be pressed into service, if the Luftwaffe could be prevented from destroying those ships and boats – as well as the mole – then Churchill's ambitions *might* be met. By the end of Monday 27 May, 7,669 soldiers had been brought home, and the following day, it was hoped, many more would follow.

All the time, more and more soldiers were arriving inside the perimeter. Some, like the Guards battalion seen marching up the mole in perfect order, arrived as a unit, but many came in dribs and drabs. And many, despite the appalling experiences they had endured and the dismal conditions they continued to face, were keen to bring home souvenirs of their time abroad. These ranged from those with hundreds of cigarettes jammed into their haversacks, keen to avoid customs regulations, to a man holding a large model seaplane intended as a present for his son. One soldier brought a motorbike onto the mole. 'Can I get this on board your ship, mate?' he asked a sailor, adding – as though that might convince him – that it had only done 280 miles. Given that the aim of Operation Dynamo was to bring as many men home as possible to defend Britain, and to allow the war to continue, it is hardly surprising that the sailor said 'no'.

Yet it still seems harsh to discover the fate of the pets befriended by soldiers as they retreated. Able Seaman Ian Nethercott, a gunlayer on board HMS *Keith*, was surprised by the stream of dogs that men tried to bring on board, and appalled by what happened to most of them. 'As the men arrived with their dogs,' he says, 'the military police were shooting them and throwing them in the harbour.' Every time this happened, a loud 'boo' went up from soldiers and sailors. Not even the sight of a dachshund puppy's head poking from a haversack softened the military policemen's hearts.

Thankfully, however, not every dog was summarily executed. A terrier mongrel named Kirk (presumably after the port where he now found himself) came aboard HMS *Windsor* and was warmly welcomed by the crew. Kirk, who initially responded only to French commands, stayed with the ship throughout the evacuation, and was then placed in quarantine in England. At the end of his adventure, he was adopted by a country vicar, the father of a sub-lieutenant on the ship.

Other animals spotted included a caged canary balanced on a man's head as he queued in the water, and a black-and-white rabbit in a basket held by an inexplicably naked man. One soldier's kitbag was full of watches intended for sale in England; that of another, who hoped to open a barber's shop, was full of hair clippers. Many soldiers carried post-cards and photographs of their time in France, but one particularly grisly souvenir was eight bullets prised from the body of a man shot for spying. And one of the saddest was spotted spilling out of a man's tunic as he lay dead on the beach at Bray Dunes: several tiny dresses intended for his daughter.

As soldiers arrived in Dunkirk, they passed others, men such as Jimmy Langley, defending the perimeter against German units trying to break through. But the Germans were trying to frustrate the evacuation in other ways. Shells fired by German batteries were a constant danger to those inside the perimeter, and the further the Germans advanced, the heavier the shell fire became. It was a particular problem to ships crossing the Channel. The shortest crossing between Dover and Dunkirk, known as 'Route Z', involved sailing close to the French shore between Calais and Dunkirk – but this was far too dangerous in daylight due to the batteries of German guns positioned along the coast. As a result, a much more northerly 'Route Y' was introduced. It was initially safer, but it increased the round trip from 80 miles to 172 miles – and it, too, came within the range of German guns when Nieuport was captured. A compromise route, 'Route X', soon became the only safe method of crossing during the daytime. With a round trip of 108 miles, it was *relatively* short, and since it avoided exposing ships to the shore batteries, it was *relatively* safe.

Other methods of attack included motor torpedo boats and submarines which attacked ships as they crossed the Channel. (HMS *Grafton*, for example, was sunk by a U-boat.) And, of course, the Luftwaffe bombed and strafed soldiers on shore and ships at sea.

The ships did what they could to avoid attack. They kept a strict blackout at night, meaning that they had to sail without navigation lights. And onshore, there was very little anti-aircraft defence, short of a few Bofors guns close to the mole and the beaches.

The principal reason for the deficiency was the destruction of the heavy anti-aircraft guns defending Dunkirk – by the troops manning them. This extraordinary act had been the result of mistaken communication between two officers. The first officer had sent a message that wounded men should be taken to the beaches for evacuation. The message received by the second officer, however, was that *all* men should be taken to the beaches for evacuation. Believing that all his men were now returning to England, the second officer ordered that their guns be destroyed. Once this had been done, he marched up to Lieutenant General Adam, saluted, and proudly told him that all the BEF's heavy anti-aircraft guns had been spiked. Adam was appalled and very nearly speechless. 'You fool. Go away ...' he finally managed to say.

One of the Luftwaffe's most important – but lesser known – jobs was mine laying. Beginning seriously on the night of Tuesday 28 May, and focusing on points along Route X, mines were floated down into the sea by parachute. They might be buoyant contact mines, detonated by a ship pressing one of the mine's protruding horns, or the more insidious magnetic mines, which could destroy a ship without the need for contact. Lying deep in the water, these consisted of an explosive attached to a magnetic mechanism set to detonate when any steel-hulled ship passed overhead.

This potentially catastrophic weapon might have killed tens of thousands of soldiers during Operation Dynamo, and prevented tens of thousands of others from being rescued. It might, in fact, have changed the story of the evacuation. But, in the event, it sunk only two ships despite being heavily laid throughout the Channel.* The neutralising of the magnetic mine by a Canadian scientist working in London is one of the great – and least known – stories of Dunkirk.

Charles Goodeve became, in 1939, the deputy director of the Admiralty's Department of Miscellaneous Weapon Development, a coven of scientists and problem solvers known collectively as the 'Wheezers and Dodgers'. Goodeve shared a conviction with Winston Churchill, then First Lord of the Admiralty, that the application of science would have a huge impact on the war. Not everybody agreed. Arthur

---

* The two ships were *Mona's Queen* and *Grive*.

Harris, future chief of RAF Bomber Command, detested Churchill's reliance on science. 'Are we fighting this war with weapons or slide-rules?' he once asked furiously.

Churchill puffed his cigar calmly. 'That's a good idea,' he said. 'Let's try the slide-rule for a change.'

With Churchill's support, Goodeve began trying to find an effective means of countering magnetic mines. He first suggested an improved method of sweeping them. This involved two boats, sailing in parallel, towing long cables behind them. A current would be passed through the cables, creating a magnetic field between the ships that would detonate any mines within.

By chance, a magnetic mine had just been defused at Shoeburyness, allowing Goodeve the opportunity to examine its mechanism. As a result, he set up an elaborate experiment on a salt-water lake near Portsmouth. Acting as decoys, a number of sailors dragged model boats across the lake, watched by curious members of the public, as Goodeve and his assistants conducted the real experiment in a rowing boat. The electrical cables were submerged at the bottom of the lake while Goodeve sat in the boat with the mechanism from the defused mine. When a current was passed through the cables, creating a magnetic field, a dial on the mine's mechanism started to flicker: the mine would have detonated had it been active. The experiment was a success.

Known as the 'Double L Sweep', Goodeve's method of clearing magnetic mines came into use in February 1940, making nearly three hundred mines safe over the next three months. Had this been his most significant achievement, it would have been impressive, as the Double L Sweep kept Routes X, Y and Z clear of magnetic mines throughout the Dunkirk evacuation.

But Goodeve achieved far more. By blending expertise with creative thinking, he came up with a method of 'wiping' ships to make them impervious to magnetic mines. Once wiped, they could sail over the mines all day long and suffer no harmful consequences whatsoever.

The practice of 'coiling' already existed. It involved wrapping a ship's hull with live copper coils to counteract its magnetic field. But not only was this a time-consuming and expensive process, there was neither enough copper coil nor the fitting facilities to deal with the vast number of ships needing protection. Goodeve came up with a far superior solution. If a large electrical cable, with a current of 200 amps, was passed up and down the ship's sides, it had the same effect as coiling. But the procedure could be carried out cheaply and easily by the ship's own crew.

Goodeve suggested the idea to the Admiralty but received no response, so he decided to begin his own experiments. Starting with small boats, and progressing to larger ships, the experiments were successful, although it became clear that the altered magnetic field would be eroded very gradually by the vibrations of the ship's engines and by the pounding of the sea – meaning that the ship would need to be wiped every six months.

Goodeve called the process 'Degaussing', a name he came up with during a night of drinking; it paid homage to Carl Friedrich Gauss, the first calibrator of magnetic force – and it rhymed nicely with 'delousing'. In the immediate build-up to Operation Dynamo, a remarkable four hundred ships of all shapes and sizes were degaussed in just three days by teams working round the clock. Over subsequent days, another thousand ships were wiped. This, combined with the Double L Sweep, kept British ships astonishingly safe from mines throughout the evacuation. The miracle of Dunkirk owes much to Charles Goodeve and the fortunate timing of his work. As he said after the war: 'The battle of the magnetic mine was the first technical battle of the war and one in which Britain won a decisive and, to Germany, totally unexpected victory.' And it set the tone for a war fought not solely by guns and bravery, but also by amps and volts and Arthur Harris's beloved slide-rules.

But even if degaussing kept ships safe from the dreaded magnetic mines, they would still need somewhere to embark troops – and the most practical embarkation point, so long as it remained viable, was the mole, which at high water could fit sixteen good-sized ships. Queues from the mole often stretched far back into the town. Admiral Frederic Wake-Walker (sent to Dunkirk on Wednesday 29 May to work with Tennant as Senior Naval Officer afloat) remembers watching an unending stream of exhausted men moving forwards, lit up in silhouette by huge flames. Sometimes, he writes, they would break into a tired run, and sometimes they would 'just plod blindly on towards safety'. The distinctive noise that accompanied their progress was the muffled tramp of boots and the clatter of rifles.

Once on the mole, with the rise and fall of the tide, it proved difficult to board the ships. At low tide, the naval destroyers sat so low in the water that larger passenger ships sometimes lay up between them and the mole, acting as floating platforms. At other times, the men would lower themselves on ladders, walk gingerly across on planks, or – despite the risks of drowning, broken bones, and being crushed between ship and piles – would simply jump. And even when the tide was more accommodating, the wooden walkway's unbroken protective rail meant that everybody, even the stretcher cases, had to clear an obstacle before boarding.*

At eight o'clock on the morning of Wednesday 29 May, the Isle of Man steamer *Manxman* arrived at the mole to find it completely deserted of men. 'It was very eerie,' says a sailor on board, 'streaming in with not a soldier to be seen.' There was no one even to take *Manxman*'s ropes. But then, as the ship moved in closer, soldiers began to appear. An air raid had sent them hiding underneath the mole, desperately hugging and straddling the criss-cross piles, some chin-deep in the water. Once the bombing was over, they clambered back on top. This striking image is referenced in the film as Tommy and Gibson take shelter in the piling beneath the mole.

By Wednesday morning just over twenty-five thousand soldiers had been evacuated. Churchill's desired figure of thirty thousand had not yet been met, but embarkations from the mole onto passenger ships and destroyers offered hope. Even given its problems, the mole allowed about six hundred men to board a destroyer in just half an hour – an exceptional rate of evacuation.

Until that day, most attacks on the mole had come from heavy artillery about seven miles to the west. But on Wednesday, the heavy smoke over the town was cleared by a northerly wind. The result was consistent heavy raids on the mole by Stukas and other bombers as well as strafing raids from Messerschmitts.

That afternoon, *Crested Eagle* came alongside the mole. A Thames paddle steamer, she was originally fitted with a telescopic funnel that retracted whenever she passed under London Bridge. Her peacetime job was to take holidaymakers from London to the seaside resort of Southend and further

---

* At least until the railing was broken down in places to ease boarding.

along the coast to Clacton and Felixstowe. Fitted with two anti-aircraft guns, she was pressed into wartime service on the Thames, before receiving orders, on Tuesday afternoon, to join Operation Dynamo.

As she sat on the seaward side of the mole, a ferocious Stuka attack – the third of the day – began. The mole was crowded with passenger ships, destroyers and fishing trawlers. *Crested Eagle* was berthed directly behind another paddle steamer, *Fenella*, diagonally across from two destroyers, HMS *Grenade* and HMS *Jaguar*, and opposite six trawlers moored together. Behind the trawlers sat a large transport ship and a French destroyer.

Ordinarily the mole was difficult for an aeroplane to spot. It may have towered over ships at low tide, and appeared substantial when viewed from the side, but from the air it amounted to a barely visible sliver. On this afternoon, however, with no cloud or smoke cover, and with large ships moored down its length, it was a very clear and tempting target for bombers. Near misses on *Jaguar* put her out of action; her troops were transferred elsewhere. *Grenade* was hit by several bombs. She caught fire, and desperate efforts were made to cast her off to prevent her from sinking and blocking a section of the mole. She drifted into the harbour channel and was finally towed into open water by a trawler, where she sank.

One man who watched this happen was Vic Viner, a naval beachmaster at Bray Dunes. Viner's brother, Albert, was a leading telegraphist on *Grenade*, and Viner received permission to walk up to the harbour to greet him. Drawing near the mole, he witnessed the Stuka attack, and returning to Bray Dunes to continue his job, he had no way of knowing what had happened to his brother. In fact, Albert survived, and like many others from *Grenade*, he was moved onto *Crested Eagle*.

As the attack continued, a bomb landed directly on the mole, making a large hole. Almost immediately, another aircraft swooped low to machine-gun troops who had clambered onto the mole from *Grenade*. On the other side, meanwhile, *Fenella*, a mainly wooden paddle steamer of similar design to *Crested Eagle*, was hit on her promenade deck, before a near miss blew concrete from the mole through her hull. A third bomb blew out her engine room, and she sank at her berth.

Despite the chaos, the momentum of Operation Dynamo had to be maintained, and there were still undamaged ships beside the mole waiting to embark troops. Many men were now fleeing down the mole in panic, desperate to escape danger. In their way stood Commander James Clouston, a naval officer brought to Dunkirk to maintain order on the mole, and Lieutenant Robin Bill, responsible for the trawlers. Clouston and Bill, standing aloof in their naval blues and gold braid, were able to restore order – although they had to brandish their revolvers to do so.

'We have come to take you back to the UK,' said Clouston calmly to the mob of desperate soldiers. 'I have six shots here, and I'm not a bad shot. The lieutenant behind me is an even better one. So that makes twelve of you.' And then he raised his voice: 'Now get down onto those bloody ships!'*

Clouston's words seemed to calm the men down. Many of them turned around and boarded *Crested Eagle* – which throughout the chaos had not been hit.

---

* Clouston would be dead within a few days, drowned after his RAF boat was attacked by Stukas.

The minesweeper HMS *Pangbourne*, meanwhile, was nearing the beaches when she, too, was attacked by a swarm of Stukas. A sub-lieutenant on board remembers hearing a voice shouting 'Take cover!' – before realising that the voice was his own. Deciding that the advice was good, he threw himself down on the wooden deck. He could not distinguish the scream of the bombs from the scream of the diving plane. And in that instant the world went mad:

> I stagger to my feet and gaze at a picture of utter horror. Blood and flesh is everywhere; mutilated bodies that ten seconds ago were men I knew personally, are flung in grotesque heaps all about me ... I climb with difficulty to where the gun layer is lying, his neck and stomach torn open, and his hand blown away. He is still breathing and moaning faintly.

When the sub-lieutenant moved on to the bridge, he learned that five bombs had landed close by, but none had scored a direct hit. *Pangbourne* had not been seriously damaged.

At this point the sub-lieutenant wiped his face – and noticed that his hand was covered with blood. He looked down and saw that his left trouser leg was even bloodier. Somebody then pointed out that the back of his jacket was missing. Slipping off the remains, he found that a slice of flesh had been carved away. Lowering his trousers, he found his leg full of shrapnel – and then he heard the sound of Stukas coming again. For a moment he enjoyed the thought that he was caught with his pants literally down, before he grew confused. He was in a cabin ... someone was patching up his wounds ... he could not see properly ... there were a lot of people talking at once ...

Beside the mole, meanwhile, *Crested Eagle* was casting off. Hundreds of troops on her upper deck, many of whom had transferred from *Grenade*, *Fenella* and the damaged trawlers, began cheering loudly. They were finally going home. Below decks lay the wounded, in varying degrees of disability. A sailor on board remembers: 'The throb of the engines and the thump of the paddles gave us renewed hope, and a fresh breeze was most welcome as we swung clear and left for the trip back to Dover.'

Because of the falling tide, *Crested Eagle* could not sail directly towards Dover. She had first to head east, parallel to the shore. She sailed for some time past an unbroken stretch of sand crammed with soldiers – but as she came to Malo-les-Bains, she was spotted by another wave of Stukas. The sight of yet more dive bombers was demoralising, but hardly surprising; the conditions were allowing the Luftwaffe its most indulgent day, and a paddle steamer, with its huge wooden wheels, created a wake twice as wide as any other ship. As the planes dived, *Crested Eagle*'s guns jammed, and the bombs fell. Even the brief moments between attacks were filled by machine-gun bursts from the Stukas' rear gunners as they pulled up and away.

Nearby was HMS *Pangbourne*. The wounded sub-lieutenant was now unconscious, but another sailor watched in horror as bomb after bomb fell on *Crested Eagle*, shattering her and setting her alight. He saw oil leaking from the vessel into the sea, and watched men in battledress with full packs jumping into the inches-thick fluid. Some drowned in it; others died when it caught fire, burning them alive.

A sailor on board *Crested Eagle* realised that she had been struck again when he 'felt the ship shudder as if some giant hand had picked us up'. As fire took hold, he watched men running with the skin blasted from their bodies. A lieutenant passed, whom he identified by the emblem on his helmet – but not by his face. That was unrecognisable.

Lieutenant Commander Bernard Booth, *Crested Eagle*'s captain, managed to run her aground near Bray Dunes. Just before he did so, another sailor jumped into the sea, carefully taking off his shoes first, and swimming the short distance to the beach. Only once on land did he realise that the skin was hanging from his hands in melted shreds. Soldiers watched amazed as the ship, her hull burning red-hot for hours afterwards, joined them on the shore.

She is still there, a shocking skeletal presence, emerging from the sea at low tide. At the time of writing, one of her guns is exposed, waiting to be liberated by a 'collector' or by the French government. She is nowadays visited by mussel pickers and those paying their respects to the roughly three hundred men who died on her. One of these was Vic Viner's brother Albert.

Ship losses were very heavy on Wednesday 29 May. Three destroyers and twelve other large ships were lost. And yet over 47,000 soldiers were rescued. By the start of Thursday 30 May, 72,783 men had been rescued in total – considerably more than the Admiralty had anticipated. But that night, a misunderstanding occurred with potentially disastrous consequences for Operation Dynamo.

At about 7 p.m., Ramsay's Dynamo Room in Dover Castle received a telephone call from a naval officer present at Lord Gort's headquarters in La Panne. The officer was, like Charles Goodeve, one of the Admiralty's 'Wheezers and Dodgers', and he made the call without authority. He said that Dunkirk harbour was completely blocked by damaged ships, and that the evacuation must now be carried out entirely from the beaches.

This was not true – and it is unclear why he made the call. Perhaps he had been unduly panicked by the attack on the mole. A little earlier, in the midst of that attack, the Dynamo Room had received a garbled wireless message from a destroyer reporting that it was 'impossible to embark more troops' from the mole. This – at the time the message was sent – *had* been true.

Taking these messages together, Ramsay decided that the mole must now be out of action – but before he could act, he wanted confirmation. Just before 9 p.m., he wired Tennant asking him whether the harbour really was blocked. Tennant replied that it was *not* – but his message never reached Ramsay, who then sent a message to Admiral Abrial at Bastion 32: 'I cannot get in touch with Captain Tennant. Can you inform me whether it is still possible for transports to enter harbour and berth alongside?'

Again, Ramsay received no answer. Rather than take any chances, he ordered all ships to the beaches. Throughout the night – while the weather was excellent and the Luftwaffe almost absent – only four drifters and one yacht came along-side the mole. The chance to evacuate fifteen thousand men, all of whom were ready to depart, was wasted.

The next morning, the evacuation proceeded as before, and ships returned to the mole. But it is clear from these mistaken messages (and others like them) that one of Operation Dynamo's chief problems was communication. This is hardly surprising given the hurriedly improvised nature of the operation. Tennant had made his headquarters in a dug-out near the end of the mole. With him was a signals team, consisting of an officer, an NCO and twenty-four signalmen. Unfortunately, they had brought very little equipment with them: just some hand flags and an Aldis lamp, useful only for signalling to ships immediately offshore.

At first, Tennant's wireless messages had to be transmitted either from the French station at Bastion 32 or from destroyers on the mole. Messages could only be received, meanwhile, at Bastion 32. On 30 May, Tennant took possession of a Marconi TV5 wireless transmitter/receiver set. It could – in theory – transmit by Morse or by voice. But for the first few hours of its life, it failed to transmit, and a few hours later it broke down completely due to sand in the generator.

Tennant's next stab at rectifying the situation involved the establishment of a Royal Corps of Signals wireless station in a lorry next to Bastion 32. This was far more effective; it meant no longer having to rely on a handily sited ship or on French goodwill. It also meant that misunderstandings such as that of 29 May were far less likely to occur.

It is worth noting that while Tennant was struggling to communicate, Lord Gort's headquarters in a villa at La Panne had an excellent cable telephone link with the Dynamo Room at Dover Castle.* Unfortunately, Tennant's only method of communication with La Panne (or with any of the beaches) was by motorcycle dispatch rider, so this was of no use to him. And Tennant's difficulty in contacting his beach parties was mirrored by the beach parties' difficulty in contacting ships offshore. Communication could only be made using

---

* The link had been put in place, months earlier, thanks to the efforts of Ramsay's flag lieutenant. The Admiralty had tried to resist it on financial grounds.

semaphore flags, or the headlamps of cars used as signal lamps.

On 30 May, Tennant received two field telephones with which he set up a link to Commander Clouston on the mole. The two officers may have only been a short distance apart, but for Tennant, the mole was the single most important element of Operation Dynamo. Clouston was also given a loudspeaker for issuing instructions, which showed its value during a lull in the evacuation when Commander Guy Maund, Tennant's assistant, used it to urge on the troops: 'Remember your pals, boys! The quicker you get on board the more of them will be saved!'

The result was instant. The soldiers broke into a run, and in just two hours, eight destroyers embarked 8,528 men, while four passenger ships embarked 5,649 more.

The overall communication picture reveals Operation Dynamo as the improvised – and often ramshackle – endeavour that it truly was. But this is hardly a criticism; it was an eventuality that no one had expected. As the people of Britain were learning to make do and mend, those responsible for their future were doing the same on a more pressing scale.

And because Dynamo was an improvisation, conflicting interests tended to arise. The Admiralty, concerned with the loss of so many destroyers in a single day on 29 May, ordered the withdrawal of its eight most modern destroyers from the evacuation. Just as Fighter Command of the Royal Air Force feared the loss of its Spitfires and Hurricanes, so the Admiralty feared the loss of its most effective ships.

For Ramsay, however, this was a disaster. He now had only fifteen destroyers at his disposal, and these ships were the backbone of Operation Dynamo. By the end of the evacuation, they would have brought off almost 30 per cent of all troops rescued – more than any other kind of ship. Thankfully, the decision was reversed the following day, returning the modern destroyers to full evacuation duties.

Destroyers, first developed at the end of the nineteenth century, were fast, heavily armed ships, well suited to Operation Dynamo – although their speed and size caused difficulty to smaller vessels in the crowded Channel. *Lady Brassey*, a Dover harbour tug, was very nearly struck by a destroyer steaming towards England at over 30 knots. A sailor on board watched troops on the destroyer's fore deck, drenched and helpless, repeatedly deluged by waves as she surged forward oblivious to all around her.

Typically, six or seven hundred men would be crammed onto a destroyer, but there are plenty of accounts of crossings made with more than a thousand soldiers on board. Some destroyer captains deliberately jettisoned their torpedoes and depth charges so that they could take on more men. Leading Seaman Ernest Eldred remembers soldiers crammed into every inch of space on HMS *Harvester*. They were on the upper deck and the mess decks, in the engine room and down the stoke hole. 'The only place we couldn't have them,' he says, 'was round the guns.' The destroyer had to defend itself, after all, and it might also have to fire at enemy batteries on shore.

So weighed down were the destroyers that low tide presented a problem, particularly when a ship's depth-finding equipment failed – as happened on HMS *Sabre*.* The captain's solution was to place a sailor on either side of the

---

* Philip Brown was on board *Sabre* when a shell fired from the shore struck – but failed to explode. 'It was a very lucky escape from certain death,' he writes.

deck to 'swing the lead': that is to drop a line weighted with lead into the water to gauge its depth. The sailors would then sing out the depth in fathoms – 'Mark 5!' – just as sailors on the Mississippi had done in the last century.*

But if many soldiers came home on naval ships (minesweepers as well as destroyers), a similarly vast number – over a quarter of all those rescued – were brought back on civilian personnel ships. These included passenger ferries, car ferries, large pleasure boats (such as *Crested Eagle*), Dutch schuits (flat-bottomed boats designed for Dutch waterways), and countless other varieties of passenger and cargo ship. Twenty were cross-Channel steamers and cargo boats belonging to Southern Railway, five of which were lost. They could take an extraordinary number of soldiers: the Isle of Man ferry *Tynwald*, sailing from the mole at the very end of the evacuation, embarked three thousand soldiers at once.

Anthony Irwin sailed home on board another Isle of Man ferry. When the ship was shelled from the shore, an incontinent officer began screaming for everybody to move to the far side. 'The men, already wetting themselves, lost all semblance of control,' writes Irwin. Fortunately, some level-headed members of the Royal Tank Regiment held the men back while an army chaplain smacked the officer over the head with a lead stick. But as soon as order was restored, six Messerschmitt 110s flew over the ship, machine-gunning the occupants. The scene on deck in the aftermath was gruesome. Next to the gangway was a pile of bodies eight feet high. Irwin and others pulled the dead away and tried to help the

---

* Mark Twain, author of *Tom Sawyer* and *Huckleberry Finn*, chose his nom de plume as a tribute to the sailors' cries. 'Twain' is an archaic form of 'two'.

wounded. A tank corporal with sixteen bullets in his chest and stomach refused morphine, saying that he still had a lot to talk about. He died three hours later.

There was plenty of more prosaic chaos on the large ships. The cook on board *Medway Queen* remembers a crush at the galley doors, and a sudden rush of soldiers pushing billy cans and mess tins in his direction, all expecting to be fed. 'These were not peckish men,' he says. 'They were starving animals, most of them too desperately hungry to be polite.'

Yet politeness and gentility were also evident. Captain Humphrey Bredin boarded an Isle of Man ferry berthed on the mole. To get on board, he had to step over a dead man on the gangplank while bombs fell all around. Once inside, he found himself a corner and settled down. A while later, he was surprised to find a man neatly dressed in a white coat standing over him.

'Are you a steward?' asked Bredin.

'Yes, sir,' said the man. 'Can I do anything for you?'

'Well, would it be possible to produce a glass of beer for me?'

'By all means. But you do know the rules, sir? I can't supply you with alcohol until we're three miles out.'

Once the ship was beyond the reach of licensing laws – if not of Stukas – the steward brought Bredin his beer. 'How could we lose the war,' he laughs, 'with people like this around?'

The stewards, it is worth noting, were not all men. On board the Southern Railway ship *Dinard*, now a hospital ship, was fifty-nine-year-old Amy Goodrich. And on the Southern Railway steamer *Paris* was Mrs Lee, a train carriage cleaner from Brighton. After *Paris* was bombed and sunk on 2 June, Mrs Lee was machine-gunned in the water and picked up by a lifeboat, only to be thrown back into the water when another bomb landed alongside. After another hour and a half in the sea, she was pulled aboard a tug and finally brought back to Dover. Evacuated with her was Gladys Seeley, a nursing sister, who had been badly wounded by shrapnel in an adjacent lifeboat.

The hospital ships all had five or six QUAIMNS* sisters working on board. 'They worked like Trojans,' wrote Captain John White, medical officer on the *Isle of Guernsey*, adding that his job was made easier as none of them ever had to be told what to do. It was made a great deal harder, however, by the Luftwaffe's relentless attacks. The hospital ships were painted white with large red crosses – but not only did this fail to deter the Germans, it seemed to attract them. In his diary, White complained that the red crosses were making the hospital ships sitting ducks. 'Why not paint us grey and put some guns on board?' he wrote.

Isle of Guernsey was attacked while berthed at the mole. As the bombs fell around her, she loaded a thousand men, 490 of whom were stretcher cases. In the chaos, White noticed fit men climbing on board, but he decided not to interfere. As *Isle of Guernsey* sailed away, every bed was full, and the floors, passageways, dining saloon and cabins were crammed with stretchers. Alongside the physically wounded were men suffering from shellshock, 'whose brains had snapped after days and nights of strain, privation and terror'. These men were placed in a guarded cabin and given sedative injections.

Some hospital ships could not get near the mole due to the bombing. Josephine Kenny, a sister on board *St Julien*,

---

* Queen Alexandra's Imperial Military Nursing Service.

travelled to Dunkirk on six occasions, but was unable to reach the mole on four of them. 'We all felt helpless and depressed on the empty trips back,' she writes, 'so different to the elation felt when every inch of deck space was filled with terribly wounded soldiers.' Her words, a strange conflation of exultation and misery, seem to reflect the intense extremes of Operation Dynamo.

Isle of Guernsey, meanwhile, was responsible for picking Flying Officer Ken Newton out of the sea. Newton was an RAF pilot who had bailed out after a dogfight. Like the character Collins in the film, he was helped out of the water by sailors. The sailors were killed, however, by German aircraft raking them with machine-gun fire as they leaned over the side to pull Newton aboard. An account of a hospital ship being machine-gunned as it helped a downed airman surely serves to deflect any suspicions that Hitler was allowing the British to escape. There is little evidence in stories such as these of a golden bridge being built in May and June 1940.

There were, however, a few soldiers who managed to do what Tommy and Gibson attempt to do in the film – take a stretcher on board a ship and remain there to be taken home. Corporal Charles Nash of the Royal Army Service Corps was ferrying stretchers onto the mole when suddenly a military policeman shouted, 'Here! We've got room for a few more! Who'd like to come aboard?' Nash clambered onto a fishing boat, and a few hours later was home. Carrying stretchers was a difficult job, however – particularly given the damage sustained by the mole. Members of the Duke of Cornwall's Light Infantry were given the job of loading a hundred stretcher cases onto the corvette HMS *Kingfisher*. Like Tommy and Gibson, they had to carry their stretchers across a narrow plank bridging a large hole in the mole, even as the bombing continued.

On the evening of Thursday 30 May, William Tennant and Frederic Wake-Walker dined at Lord Gort's headquarters at La Panne, in a villa described by Wake-Walker as a pretentious house overlooking the sea.* The men shared Gort's last bottle of champagne and rounded off the meal with tinned fruit salad. Wake-Walker was infuriated by Gort's comment that while the army had successfully fallen back intact, the navy was making no real effort to help it escape. He tried to underline the difficulties involved, but was interrupted by Brigadier Oliver Leese who spoke of the 'ineptitude of the navy'. Wake-Walker could do little but seethe. Several days into the evacuation, there was no sign of a miracle.

---

* The villa has recently been demolished.

Nine

A Miracle

By the end of Thursday 30 May, the total number of men evacuated stood at 126,606 – almost three times as many as the Admiralty had predicted. The latest news from the perimeter, still held by several thousand men of the rearguard, was that it would probably hold for forty-eight hours. Low visibility had brought respite from the Luftwaffe. And the day had seen, for the first time, more troops embarked from the beaches (29,512) than from the mole (24,311).

In some ways, the beaches were the best place to be. Sand had a curious effect on bombs. If a bomb lands on a hard surface, the shrapnel scatters, and injuries are severe and widespread. 'But going into the sand,' says John Wells, an anti-aircraft gunner aboard *Princessa*, 'there was a thud, and you'd get covered in clods of sand but that was about it.' Arthur Lobb, of the Royal Army Service Corps, remembers a bomb exploding in sand as a strange experience, causing a slow movement of the earth beneath you.

This is not to suggest that the beaches were a safe environment. Many men were killed by bombs on the sand, and as Robert Halliday of the Royal Engineers remembers, it was difficult to find shelter there from a strafing aircraft. And it could be equally difficult getting away from the beaches. There were often no inshore boats to be seen. Sergeant Leonard Howard of the Royal Engineers waded into the water in the hope of getting a lift on 30 May, but soon gave up. There was nothing coming. Even when boats did arrive, soldiers often struggled and vied with one another to get in. When Arthur Joscelyne brought his Thames barge close to shore the same day, troops rushed to get aboard. 'We could have capsized at any moment,' he says. But then a naval officer stood up in the bows, took out his revolver and threatened to shoot anybody who embarked before he gave permission. Like children waiting for an adult to take control, the soldiers calmed down and boarded in an orderly fashion. 'They were in such a state that they just lay down anywhere and slept,' says Joscelyne.

Leonard Howard watched a similar situation escalate. A small boat came inshore, and troops piled onto it so haphazardly that it seemed about to capsize. A soldier was doggedly gripping the stern, and the sailor in charge ordered him to let go. The soldier kept hold of the stern. So the sailor shot him in the head. In Howard's view, this was the right thing to do, however awful it was to watch. 'There was such chaos on the beach,' he says, 'that it didn't seem out of keeping.'

This is not an isolated account, and most examples involve men driven to uncharacteristic extremes of behaviour. The troops were living through an extraordinary ordeal where even the incidental details reminded them of their possible fate. On Thursday, the same day that Leonard Howard watched the shooting take place, Colin Ashford of the Highland Light Infantry remembers seeing the bodies of dozens of young men wash up on the shore. 'There they were, all lying in different attitudes. Some still clutching their rifles. Hundreds of them. As far as you could see.' They came, he believes, from a paddle steamer that had been sunk nearby.* In another man's recollections, the most disturbing aspect of the evacuation was the sight of dead soldiers in the water, moving in and out with the tide. The scene is imagined in the film as a character calmly pushes a floating body away.

Equally disturbing were incidents of premeditated malice. An officer had managed to secure a rowing boat, and he stood up to his waist in water, guarding it, as he waited for his men to arrive. But before they appeared, he was ambushed by a group of soldiers who took the boat from him at gunpoint, grinning as they pushed him away. It is important to remember stories such as these. The whole world was on these beaches, the bad as well as the good, and received wisdom should never obscure that fact.

For at least one officer, however, the situation was quite different. Captain George Ledger of the Durham Light Infantry was queuing on the beach on 1 June. 'You'd think there'd never been a war,' he says. He saw no disorder – although he did notice that, when an aeroplane came over, soldiers ran from the queues to the apparent protection of the sand dunes.

It is certainly true that better organisation led to better behaviour and increased confidence. Twenty-three-year-old Vic Viner was a naval beachmaster, sent to Bray Dunes to 'create order out of chaos'. His job, simultaneously executed by others up and down the miles of beaches, was to keep control of a queue of men. He was told to use his revolver if anybody started to misbehave – 'Shoot to kill, son!'

---

* Quite possibly *Crested Eagle*.

Viner encountered some trouble in his queue when an officer jumped out of line and began yelling, 'I'm a captain! I've got to get in the front!'

'Stay where you are!' said Viner.

'Who the hell do you think you're talking to?' shouted the officer. By this time, Viner had his revolver out, and a large sergeant was offering the captain some advice. 'Do as he bloody well tells you, sir, or you will die!'

The officer stared at Viner, and Viner stared back. The whole queue was watching. Eventually, the officer backed down and returned to his original place.

Twice more Viner was forced to draw his gun, but, as he says, 'They were shell shocked and they wanted to go back to England.' Throughout the days he was on the beach, Viner says, nobody in his queue had to wait more than three days to find a ship – although they sometimes had to spend as much as ten hours in water up to their chests. There were times, he remembers, when the sea became rough and boats could not take soldiers on board. The Stukas usually attacked two or three times a day, although they might strike more frequently. Viner concedes that he was more fortunate than those at other points within the perimeter, for Bray Dunes was not being shelled by German guns.

There is one image that particularly haunts Viner:

So many of them committed suicide. They walked into the water. 'Come on, join up!' 'No, I'm going!' 'Where are you going?' 'I'm going back home. England's over there.' I said, 'I know, but if you walk into that water you'll drown …' And they just did it … They were exhausted and demoralised. It's with me now for ever.

This story painted such a striking image that it served as some inspiration for a scene in the film. And it is a story confirmed by others. Leonard Howard describes men running into the water, overwhelmed by the experience of the beaches. 'They were under terrific strain, and one couldn't do anything for them.'

Sometimes these men were seen swimming far out to sea. On board a lifeboat offshore, troops spotted a fellow soldier swimming towards England with most of his heavy gear still on. Seeing the lifeboat, the soldier started shouting for help – and the troops begged the skipper to pick him up. But the skipper refused. Turning back, he said, would have risked the lives of everyone on board. The soldier was left to his fate.

Though the beach queues increased a soldier's chances of being lifted, not everybody wanted to join them. While Robert Halliday was building his raft from the floorboards of abandoned trucks, all manner of other activities were taking place on the beaches. George Wagner, the young Royal Engineer whose passion was dancing, remembers most people just lying about in the dunes, passing time. He himself found a motorcycle, and drove it up and down the beach. Colin Ashford, an enthusiastic artist, drew a sketch of a destroyer lying offshore.* Rather than join a queue – 'I didn't see the point in it' – Norman Prior spent his time helping others by pushing small boats, already loaded with troops, clear of the shallows where they risked being grounded.

About the most productive thing that any soldier could do was to help build one of the truck piers, another fine example of forced improvisation. It is not clear whose idea these originally were, but there is no doubt that the first one was

---

* He unfortunately no longer has it.

constructed on 30 May at Bray Dunes. Abandoned lorries were driven down to the shoreline, where they were filled with sandbags and their tyres were shot out. They were lashed together, bonnet to tail, and planks were laid across their roofs to form a walkway. When the tide came in, the chain of vehicles stretched far out to sea. At least ten of these piers were built, some fitted with rails along the walkway, and as a result the rate of rescue was dramatically increased.*

Some surprisingly touching behaviour was observed on the beaches as older men counselled their nervous younger comrades. 'We knew the ordeal these weaker-willed boys were going through,' writes an NCO, 'so we helped them as much as we could.' One grizzled old sergeant was even spotted cradling a younger man's head in his lap.

Inevitably, a great deal of fear, anxiety, and downright oddness was exhibited. A terrified officer was seen putting a champagne cork between his teeth every time an aeroplane came near. Should a bomb drop, he explained, he would experience less pressure if his mouth was open. And fear often led to prayer. Some did it privately. George Purton of the Royal Army Service Corps was not religious, but he prayed nonetheless: 'Please God help me!' Others took part in organised services on the beaches. Norman Prior was singing a hymn when an aircraft began machine-gunning the congregation. 'I don't know what happened to the padre,' says Prior, 'but we scattered and those that were on the slow side, caught it and were killed and wounded.'

Some gave up trying to get away. Known as dune dwellers, these men made little homes in the sand, digging holes and

---

* George Wagner and Norman Prior both helped to build the piers at different sectors along the beach.

covering them with corrugated iron and salvaged bits and pieces. In numerous ways, people tried to avoid reality. Dune dwelling was one way, madness was another, suicide was a third. Arriving on the beaches, Patrick Barrass of the Essex Regiment found a fourth. Having discovered an abandoned ambulance on the sand, he climbed in, lay down and went to sleep. 'I left the rattle of war outside,' he says. The beaches were a rabbit hole down which the British army was trying to escape, if not to England then somewhere less tangible.

One notable feature of the retreat and evacuation was the formation of a meritocracy where natural leadership and force of personality won out over rank and hierarchy. Everybody had been reduced to a similar physical condition, they were wearing similar battledress, they were eating similar food, and they had the same prospects of survival. Nowhere is this clearer than in the encounter between a private and Major General Harold Alexander, commander of 1st Infantry Division.

'You look like a big brass hat! Maybe you can tell me where we get a boat for England?' said the private.

Alexander thought for a moment, pointed, and said, 'Follow that lot, son!'

'Thanks, mate,' said the private, 'you're the best pal I've had in a hundred miles!' In the land of Dunkirk misrule, the private felt emboldened to speak to Alexander as an equal. And because Alexander possessed both confidence and an air of natural authority, he was able to answer the soldier without feeling threatened.

Many officers, however, were less formidable than Alexander. With the normal order of things set aside, Dunkirk exposed their lack of substance. George Purton refused to obey the instructions of an officer at Dunkirk. 'Normally I'd have been court-martialled,' he says, 'but that didn't happen.' It may not have lasted very long, but for a period, within the perimeter, the usual rules simply did not apply.

Yet for all the strangeness and danger of their existence, were the soldiers of the British Expeditionary Force scared?

George Wagner claims to have had no fear. 'I always had the feeling that I would get home,' he says. Ted Oates was extremely philosophical: 'When I was on the beaches, I remember thinking, "Well, if I'm taken prisoner, it will be a chance to learn German."'

Arthur Lobb experienced a tense anxiety, a feeling that he might not survive. George Purton wondered how the hell he was going to escape. Vic Viner, who was on the beaches longer than anybody else, admits to having been terrified every time a Stuka came over. Twenty years later, he says, it all came out in the form of a nervous breakdown. And Ordinary Seaman Stanley Allen, serving on HMS *Windsor*, who had a chance to observe the soldiers at close hand, began to suspect that Dunkirk marked the end of the British way of life.

Given these feelings and the prevailing conditions, it is a testament to the optimism, fighting spirit, and determination of the soldiers that their discipline held so well. But this would all be for nothing if the boats and ships were not available to transport them to England.

On Friday 31 May – the sixth day of Operation Dynamo – the British public first learned of the evacuation. Newspaper headlines were relentlessly optimistic. 'Tens Of Thousands Safely Home Already – Many More Coming By Day And Night', shouted the *Daily Express*. The *Daily Mail*'s editorial read:

A Miracle

Today our hearts are lightened. Today our pride in
British courage is mingled with rejoicing. We are proud
of the way the men of our race have borne themselves in
the gigantic battle across the Channel. We rejoice that a
considerable part of the British Army has escaped what
seemed like certain destruction.

But were British hearts really lightened? An examination of
Mass Observation sources reveals a more nuanced and interesting picture. The general morale report for 1 June reports
that people were encouraged by news of the evacuation, but
not overwhelmingly so:

People are not quite clear what to make of the military
situation, but think we must count this as a defeat. There
is an undercurrent of feeling, however, that this will rouse
us, and that we will really show the Germans what the
British Nation is like.

Here we can see that spontaneous creation of Dunkirk Spirit
as a manifestation of people's relief. It did not have to be
imposed from above – and this is underlined by a note sent
by Mass Observation to government ministers the following
day, stating that the vast majority of the British people were
wholeheartedly behind the war, and were anxious to be kept
there. 'But it will only be kept there by bold leadership, and
a forceful, imaginative use of propaganda.'

In other words, the British people were manufacturing
their own spirit – and the government's job became to foster,
encourage and shape that spirit. It was against this background that Churchill made his speech and J. B. Priestley
gave his wireless talk over the coming days.

But it should not be thought that the country was feeling or acting uniformly. The 1 June morale report stresses that while news of the evacuation encouraged the public, reports were also causing anxiety. One Mass Observation diarist, a thirty-two-year-old woman in Birmingham, found herself unable to think, or talk, about anything but the evacuation. A friend had received a postcard from her brother, just arrived back from France, saying that he was going to tell her 'how blasted Hitler blasted the B.E.F.'. The diarist writes that she was not usually one to cry, but she had been crying all the time since learning of the army's fate. Nevertheless, she adds: 'Everybody is cheerful, and in no way cast down. They have momentary spasms of doubt, but it doesn't make them unhappy.'

She was extremely fearful of a German invasion. Most people, she felt, had little idea what this would really mean, the slaughter, the upheaval and terror it would cause. She had spent the day carrying on – but knowing that something nasty was going to happen. It was like, she writes, waiting to visit the dentist for an extraction.

Her conflicted words and feelings, lurching between fear, forced courage and banality, offer a vivid sense of the period. This is how you and I would have behaved on the Home Front. A few days later, like the soldiers on the beach, she was escaping into her own foxhole: 'If I worry and fret, it will only help to wear my nerves a bit more, so I have created a kind of blank in my mind about the battle.'

But like so much of the British population, she tried to channel her fears in a more productive way. 'I would like to engage in local defence work, or something,' she writes. This adds weight to the 1 June morale report, when it notes that people seemed 'willing to do a lot themselves to help the war'.

The tidal wave of volunteerism had begun, that spontaneous unity that was shortly to bind the country and change it for ever.

At home in Britain, as the troops were suffering in France and Belgium, we can observe the birth of Dunkirk Spirit as a reaction to fear, and an alternative to escape. In order to survive, however, fear was going to have to be balanced – and boosted – by hope.

Back in France, on Friday 31 May, Lord Gort handed his command over to the impressive Major General Alexander and returned to Britain.* Gort had been keen to stay to the bitter end, but Churchill would not allow the possibility; he could imagine how Goebbels' propaganda machine would have exploited Gort's capture. The chief of the British Expeditionary Force would have been paraded in front of Nazi film cameras, and photographed looking sheepish alongside Hitler. The prospect was intolerable.

Conditions in Dunkirk on 31 May, meanwhile, were not easy. A fresh wind was causing a sizeable surf, but the greater problem was a shortage of boats. Although significant numbers had actually been arriving at Dunkirk since the previous day, accounting for the fact that almost thirty thousand soldiers had been taken off the beaches on Thursday, many more were needed. Early in the morning, soldiers could only stare at the empty naval and civilian ships offshore. To make matters worse, an artillery bombardment on the mole was sending even more passenger ships to the beaches. But things were about to change.

---

* According to Montgomery, the idea to appoint Alexander as Gort's successor had been his idea. Gort had originally planned to appoint the less able Lieutenant General Barker, commander of I Corps.

This Friday, 31 May, was the day that the Dunkirk legend was born. It was the day that the Armada truly arrived. A procession of coasters, launches, lighters, lifeboats, barges, tenders, trawlers, motor boats, cockle boats, pinnaces, fire floats, tugs, yachts, and goodness knows what else left Ramsgate and made its way to Dunkirk. The line of boats stretched for almost five miles. To Frederick Eldred, aboard HMS *Harvester*, it was a fantastic sight. 'It was almost a holiday scene,' he says, 'with every type of boat afloat.' Flight Lieutenant Frank Howell of 609 Squadron flew low overhead.* In a letter to his brother he wrote: 'The shipping between England and Dunkirk was a sight worth seeing. Never again shall I see so many ships of different sizes and shapes over such a stretch of water.'

The ships did not appear by magic. The possibility that they would be needed for some purpose had been contemplated for a fortnight, initially by Admiral Sir Lionel Preston, head of an obscure Admiralty department known as the Small Vessels Pool. On 14 May, Admiral Preston had placed an item on the BBC radio news (and in a yachting magazine) ordering the owners of self-propelled pleasure craft of a certain size to send their particulars to the Admiralty within fourteen days. This was the start of the requisitioning of yachts and motor boats – but it had nothing to do with the Dunkirk evacuation. At the time, Preston was seeking boats for various home defence purposes, including the sweeping of magnetic mines.

---

* Howell also spotted a lone rowing boat, containing a sailor and eight or ten soldiers. It was hoping to reach England seventy miles away – but was heading in completely the wrong direction, so Howell flew low over it several times in the right direction, trying to communicate the bearing it should follow. On landing he reported its position, hoping that the men would be picked up.

As the days passed, however, the prospect of an evacuation, at first barely feasible, became possible and then likely. And as the prospect hardened, so Admiral Ramsay made it known that large numbers of boats would be needed for an evacuation from the Dunkirk beaches. On 27 May, the day after the commencement of Operation Dynamo, the need became urgent. But sorting through the particulars sent in response to the BBC broadcast was time consuming. Instead, it was decided to take vessels directly from boatyards along the Thames and coastal estuaries. Douglas Tough, of Tough Brothers Boatyard in Teddington, was authorised by Admiral Preston to commandeer any boats he thought suitable. Some were already in his boatyard, others he found on his travels up and down the river. Some owners were happy to give up their boats, others put up a futile struggle. One man, convinced that his boat was being stolen, pursued it up the Thames and called the police.

In the end, Tough assembled over a hundred boats at his yard, while other yard owners and boat builders did the same. Admiral Ramsay's staff was busy, meanwhile, finding boats elsewhere, from assault landing craft to ocean liners' lifeboats. The boats were emptied of inessentials and towed to Sheerness, where crews were found – usually members of the Royal Navy who took temporary control of them.* The unfortunate result was that many boat owners who understood their own vessels were prevented from taking them to France, while retired or reserve naval personnel unfamiliar with small boats were sent in their place. The results were predictable: many of the boats succumbed to engine failure,

---

* A few were crewed by civilians who signed a T124 form, entitling them to £3, and making them Royal Navy volunteers for a month.

while others sank in the shallows. On the evening of 28 May, another appeal was broadcast over the BBC, this time for civilians with knowledge of boats to come forward. The Admiralty was tacitly acknowledging its mistake. It did not merely need boats – it also needed people who could operate them effectively. Of all the improvised elements of Operation Dynamo, none was more homespun than the story of the Little Ships.

The log of one of these Little Ships, the Thames tugboat *Sun IV*, gives an indication how the system operated. On 31 May, she left Tilbury docks for Ramsgate, arriving just before noon. Early in the afternoon, while she was fitted with guns, two naval officers and several ratings came on board to sail her. She then departed for Dunkirk, towing nine small boats.

Several hours later, on her way to France, she was caught in the wash of a destroyer. As her entire port side was forced underwater, three of her ratings were thrown into the sea. One was quickly picked up by a nearby boat, while another drifted away shouting that he could not swim. *Sun IV* swung quickly to port, cast off her boats, and slowed down to look for the missing ratings. One was spotted and pulled aboard, but the other had disappeared. After ten minutes of fruitless searching, *Sun IV* collected her boats and rejoined the flotilla. She had recorded her first fatality before the French coast was even in sight. At 10.30 that night, she anchored off the beaches and began sending her boats to the shore. Between them, they picked up eighty-two soldiers who were brought on board. She then sailed back to Ramsgate, where the soldiers disembarked – and the process began again.

On the same day, a fleet of six cockle boats set sail from Leigh-on-Sea, manned by their civilian crews. One of these boats, *Leona*, was narrowly missed by a stick of four bombs as she sailed towards Dunkirk. 'They were so close,' says crew member Alf Leggett, 'that I could see the yellow stencilling on them as they came down.' Leggett and his fellow fishermen had never seen a bomb before, and they were so shaken that they all went together to the side of the boat and urinated overboard.

Another of the cockle boats, *Renown*, suffering engine trouble early the next morning, was receiving a tow from another cockle boat – *Letitia* – who was herself being towed by a coaster. As the procession neared Ramsgate in the dark, *Letitia* touched a contact mine primed with a delayed action fuse. She sailed past it unawares, but it exploded beside *Renown*, several fathoms behind. Wood splinters rained down onto *Letitia*'s deck, and the tow rope went slack. There was nothing left of *Renown* and her crew of four.

A third cockle boat, *Endeavour*, was also being towed that night due to a smashed rudder. She had successfully ferried soldiers from the beaches and the mole. She arrived safely in Ramsgate with a full complement of soldiers on board. She lives on today – and makes an appearance in Chris Nolan's film.

In fact, a number of original Dunkirk Little Ships appear in the film, testament surely to the film's integrity. It is testament also to the ships' owners, to their many admirers, and to the Association of Dunkirk Little Ships that these vessels remain in such fine health. *Endeavour* is a good example; she sank in 1987 but was raised by members of the Nautilus Diving Club. With luck and a fair wind, she has a long future ahead of her.

Appearing alongside *Endeavour* in the film are the motor yachts *Elvin*, *Hilfranor*, *Mary Jane*, *Mimosa*, *Nyula*, *White Heather* and *Papillon*, the auxiliary ketch *Caronia*, the paddle steamer *Princess Elizabeth*, the motor launch *New Britannic*, and Motor Torpedo Boat 102. Their stories are worth recounting.

When retired lieutenant commander Archie Buchanan listened to the BBC news on the evening of Tuesday 28 May, he heard the Admiralty's call for those with experience of marine engines and coastal navigation. In answer, he showed up at a Suffolk boatyard, where he was given command of the motor yacht *Elvin* and a crew comprising a retired fisherman and an author of maritime short stories.

The three men sailed around the coast without maps, the fisherman guiding *Elvin* from memory. They reached Ramsgate on Friday afternoon – and were promptly told to return to Suffolk. No sooner had they done so than Buchanan received a telephone call ordering them back to Ramsgate – but once there, they were prevented from sailing to Dunkirk. According to the authorities, *Elvin* was too slow to make the trip, and her crew too inexperienced to be trusted. By now, Buchanan and his crew were so frustrated with the treatment they were receiving that they set off anyway.

'We had no idea what the operation was or what we were supposed to do,' says Buchanan. 'With our boat darkened we just followed the general flow of traffic across and then steered straight for the fires of Dunkirk.'

Despite a brief engine failure during the journey, *Elvin* came alongside the mole early on Monday morning. By this time, the majority of soldiers remaining in Dunkirk were French, and a poilu* called out, '*Combien de soldats?*' Buchanan understood what the soldier was asking. How

---

* In the First World War, 'poilu', an adjective meaning 'hairy', came to mean 'a French soldier'.

many men could come on board? And while he did not know the French word for twenty-five, he *did* know the word for thirty. '*Trente!*' he shouted. *Elvin* duly filled up with too many soldiers.

Buchanan was hoping to transfer the soldiers to another ship on the way home, but *Elvin* was moving so slowly that all the other ships pulled away from her. 'We had no idea where the swept channel was,' Buchanan remembers, 'but as we drew only three feet six inches and it was not low water we didn't think that there was much danger from mines.' Arriving safely back in Ramsgate with twenty-five French and eight British soldiers on board, it can be said with confidence that *Elvin* had done her duty. In fact, if a story has ever epitomised Dunkirk Spirit, then it is the story of *Elvin* and her motley crew.

Hilfranor (an unwieldy amalgam of her first owner's three daughters' names – Hilda, Frances and Nora) was one of the ships collected at Teddington by Douglas Tough, who ripped out her cabins in order to make more room for soldiers. When she reached Dunkirk, her frame was cracked by a Stuka bomb, and she was abandoned. But desperate French soldiers pushed her back into the water and set sail in her, bailing her out as they went until she began to sink on the Goodwin Sands. She was finally towed back to Ramsgate by a passing minesweeper.

New Britannic, built in 1930, is a 54ft motor launch with an open deck and a powerful engine. Licensed to carry 117 passengers, she sailed for Dunkirk from Ramsgate on the afternoon of Tuesday 28 May, arriving early on Wednesday morning. On arrival, she began lifting troops from the beach at La Panne, ferrying them to destroyers and passenger ships offshore. Her design made her ideal for the work, and it is thought that she ferried more than three thousand soldiers during the course of the evacuation. She is among the true workhorses of Operation Dynamo, vessels whose importance cannot be exaggerated. She returned to Ramsgate carrying eighty-three men on board.

White Heather carried fewer soldiers than *New Britannic*, but her experience was similar. She sailed to Dunkirk on 1 June, and ferried soldiers from the beaches to larger ships offshore, before making three round trips to England carrying troops. Renamed *RIIS1*, she was later owned by the commodore of the Association of Dunkirk Little Ships.

An Isle of Wight ferry before the war, *Princess Elizabeth*'s first job during Operation Dynamo was as a paddle minesweeper, clearing mines from the channel in front of the beaches on four occasions. This was an exceptionally dangerous job that led to the sinking of three other ships. On 29 May, together with six other minesweepers, she lifted soldiers from the beach at La Panne. She returned twice more to Dunkirk, finally bringing 329 French troops to England on 4 June, at the very end of the evacuation. Over the course of her four trips, she rescued 1,673 soldiers.

It is likely that many Operation Dynamo Little Ships will never be recognised, as their records no longer exist – if indeed they ever did. *Papillon*'s contribution is recorded only in fortuitously preserved notes belonging to a Dover naval commander. A requisitioned motor yacht, she sailed to Dunkirk on 2 June with a crew of four civilian volunteers – despite an official finding that her engines were defective. She returned to Dover the following day.

Caronia was a fishing boat, built in 1927, whose first summer haul of pilchards paid for her construction costs. Requisitioned by the navy, she is one of the Little Ships whose story is likely to remain unknown. Better documented is her role in the 1960s when she was used to ferry supplies to the pirate station Radio Caroline.

Mimosa, *Mary Jane* and *Nyula* are three other Dunkirk veterans whose exploits are relatively obscure. It is clear that *Mimosa* made three trips to Dunkirk and back under the command of Lieutenant Commander Dixon, while *Mary Jane* was a particularly comfortable and well-appointed boat for her time. Uffa Fox, a celebrated British yacht designer, described her as 'one of the cosiest yachts I've ever slept aboard'. One wonders whether her state-of-the-art central heating was turned on for the soldiers of the British Expeditionary Force. *Nyula*, meanwhile, was first seen at the Motor Boat Exhibition at Olympia in 1933, where she was described as 'a very shapely 40ft cruiser, quite one of the most interesting and sea-worthy boats at the show'. Following her service at Dunkirk, she was fitted with a First World War German gun.

MTB 102 is a remarkable survivor. Like a character in a novel who recurs at every pivotal moment, she pops up throughout the story of Operation Dynamo. Equipped with an early form of radar, she was instructed to report to Dover on the opening day of the evacuation. The following day, her crew was told by Admiral Ramsay to 'nip over to Dunkirk and report to Captain William Tennant ... to see what they could do to help'.

On 31 May, she was supposed to bring Lord Gort and his staff back to England, but – as was not unusual – messages went awry and she instead found herself embarking soldiers from La Panne before returning to Dover. The next day, she brought Admiral Wake-Walker off HMS *Keith* and delivered him safely back to Dunkirk. When he then boarded her again to sail to Dover, she hoisted a dishcloth on which a St George's cross had been quickly stained to serve as his flag. Once their duties were complete, she brought both Captain Tennant and General Alexander home to Dover for the final time, but she returned to Dunkirk on 5 June with Admiral Wake-Walker in order to make the harbour unusable for the Germans.

These, then, are the vessels present at a great historical event and at its fictional representation. In that representation, they play themselves. But there are many other vessels whose depiction in the film has a basis in reality. For example, we hear Commander Bolton asking a skipper whether he comes from Deal; he asks because the boat is a simple and elegant clinker-built Deal beach boat. During the evacuation, a Deal beach boat named *Dumpling* made seven trips backwards and forwards between the beaches and larger vessels before she was sunk by the wash of a passing destroyer. This was an ignominious end for a boat built at the time of Napoleon, and whose real-life skipper was over seventy years old. Another Deal beach boat present at Dunkirk – *Lady Haig* – lives on happily today.

It is not merely the boats that owe a debt to reality, of course. Viewers might, for example, see parallels between episodes in the lives of Tennant, Wake-Walker, Clouston and Ramsay. And George, the boy who sails across the Channel in the *Moonstone*, is a particularly interesting amalgam of a number of historical individuals.

One of these is eighteen-year-old Harold Porter, a crew member on board *Renown*, the cockle boat blown up by a contact mine with the loss of all hands. Harold was described in the *Daily Mirror* on 7 June 1940:

Alex (played by Harry Styles), Gibson (played by Aneurin
Barnard) and Tommy (played by Fionn Whitehead) sit on
the beaches of Dunkirk in a scene from the film.

The film's three Spitfires in formation.

British destroyers sailing home to England with
an RAF escort.

In the film, a Spitfire is chased by a Messerschmitt 109
as they pass a representation of HMS *Keith*.

Troops in long hopeful queues waiting for little ships to carry them to larger ships offshore.

A scene from the film: troops queuing for the little ships as casualties are taken away.

Director Christopher Nolan with Fionn Whitehead, playing Tommy.

Allied troops hoping for deliverance.

The mole, intended as a breakwater to prevent sand blocking the harbour, was substantially rebuilt for the film. Here, soldiers stand on part of the surviving mole.

Troops walking along the mole. The wooden walkway, with its high rail, is clearly visible as are the crisscross piles beneath.

A photograph taken by Sub-Lieutenant John Crosby [see Chapter Eight] on board Clyde paddle steamer *Oriole*. It is likely that these soldiers, some up to their necks in water, were standing on one of the submerged lorry piers built by the Royal Engineers.

A lorry pier as recreated by production designer Nathan Crowley and his team. 'It was an enormous learning curve,' says Nathan. These piers were originally built, in May and June 1940, by men such as George Wagner and Norman Prior by driving lorries down to the shoreline, filling them with sandbags, shooting their tyres out, and laying planks across their roofs.

Some of the Little Ships, each weighed down with evacuated soldiers.

In the film, the soldiers load up on one of the surviving Little Ships, the *New Britannic*, recreating the rescue seventy-six years later.

The mole as it looks today at low tide. Only a few of the original crisscross piles are still visible.

Captain William Tennant, later Admiral Sir William Tennant. Arriving on 27 May to coordinate the evacuation as Senior Naval Officer Dunkirk, he encountered a chaotic scene. Later that night, he sent a ship alongside the mole as an experiment. It was a successful experiment: the vast majority of soldiers rescued over the next seven and a half days would be lifted from the mole.

George Wagner photographed at home in Lichfield in November 2016. George was a Royal Engineer, a keen dancer and a beach motorcyclist who helped to build one of the lorry piers. 'We wanted to survive as a country,' he says. 'It was about comradeship and everyone together helping.'

The author stands beside one of *Crested Eagle*'s guns on the beach near Bray Dunes.

A boy of eighteen numbered among the heroes of
Dunkirk was a failure at school. Through ill-health he
never won a prize in the classroom or on the sports field.
But one day he told his father, 'I'm sorry I can never win
any honours at school, but one day my name will be
written on the roll of honour there.'

There are also parallels between George and Joe Reed,
a fifteen-year-old deckhand on board *New Britannic*, the
motor launch that appears in the film. Joe supposedly dived
overboard a dozen times to bring wounded men to the deck
as German aircraft were attacking. On 5 June 1940, his
father told the *Daily Express*: 'He was a brave boy. But my
grandfather, my father and myself have gone across the
Channel and it seemed to me that the boy could look after
himself.'

Reg Vine, meanwhile, another fifteen-year-old, was a sea
cadet whose mother had recently died and whose father had
run off. One day in late May 1940, he was told by a sub-lieutenant that he would be 'going to the seaside' on a launch
called *Rummy II*. The next day, he travelled down the Thames
to Ramsgate, where he was issued with a rifle. The launch
then headed out to sea, towed by a tug. Only now was Reg
told that *Rummy II* would be rescuing British soldiers and
that his role would be to row a lifeboat.

As the launch approached the coast, Reg heard more noise
than he could ever remember hearing. He then saw body
parts floating past – and he was sick. He tried to settle his
stomach by imagining that he was in his uncle's slaughter-
house, and that the bits of bodies belonged to animals.

Arriving at Dunkirk, *Rummy II* was sent to La Panne. The
sea cadets on board, including Reg, spent their days rowing

soldiers from the shore to their launch, which would then motor the men to larger ships further offshore. The whole process was a chain with Reg's lifeboat at one end and a Royal Navy destroyer at the other.

As an interesting aside, Reg remembers seeing French soldiers stripping the dead bodies of English soldiers and dressing in their uniforms.

Gerald Ashcroft, meanwhile, was a sea scout and crew member on *Sundowner*, a 62ft naval pinnace. His skipper was Charles Lightoller, the most senior officer to have survived the sinking of the *Titanic* in 1912. The navy wanted to commandeer *Sundowner* – but Lightoller persuaded the relevant authorities that with his experience (he had commanded a destroyer in the First World War) he was the man to take her to Dunkirk. 'I'll warn you it's not going to be a pleasure cruise,' Lightoller told Gerald, 'but if you'd like to come with us, we'd be pleased to have you.' *Sundowner* would eventually rescue 130 soldiers from a stricken destroyer; Ashcroft remembers the men being very low when they came on board, continually saying that they'd let the country down. 'But we tried to let them understand that they *hadn't* let the country down,' he says.

A final historical figure with parallels to George is Albert Barnes, who at fourteen was probably the youngest civilian involved in Operation Dynamo. At the time, he was working as a galley boy on the Thames tug *Sun XII*. As he was given no warning that the tug was leaving for Dunkirk, he had no time to tell his parents that he would be away. When he finally returned home, he took a bath and slept for twenty-four hours. 'Then it was back to work as usual,' he says, 'scrubbing and cleaning and brewing up tea.'

Like all the characters in this film, it seems that George is not based on any one individual. He is an amalgam, a representative of a type of young man who existed in 1940.

One of these young men was seventeen-year-old Jim Thorpe. As I write, Jim is almost certainly the last man alive to have gone over to Dunkirk on one of the Little Ships. Born in November 1922, he now lives in Maryland in the United States. When I spoke to him in late March 2017, he explained that his brother, Arthur, was a boating enthusiast who lived alongside the River Thames. In late May 1940, Arthur got in touch asking Jim for help. 'What do you need?' asked Jim. 'I need a man like you for the weekend,' said his brother.

When the time came to leave, Jim still had no idea where they were going. 'We're going to help someone,' is all that Arthur would say. But the weather was good, and Jim arrived safely on the French coast, surrounded by many other boats. He was impressed by the number of soldiers on the beaches and the fact that they were queuing up to their chests in water.

They took the boat as far inshore as they dared, and shut off the engine. Immediately men started trying to board. 'It was a little bit on the frantic side,' says Jim. 'There were a lot of people trying to get on at the same time. So I would say, "Wait a minute! Wait a minute!"' Once the men were on board, Jim would tell them where to go, pushing them up front and clearing the back of the boat so that the engines could be started.

Jim remembers travelling across the Channel many times. He recalls German aircraft strafing the boat, and the soldiers on board firing back with their rifles. But did he realise the importance of the job he was doing?

'No. You don't think about that sort of thing. You think about – just get those men. They were trying to do something for us. You think, Let's get them out!'

So far in our story, we have encountered various kinds of Little Ships and their personnel, but in the improvised and tumultuous environment of Dunkirk, there were some very strange vessels on the water, crewed by a remarkable range of individuals. As Robert Newborough was sailing away from Dunkirk in his Fleet Air Arm vessel, he spotted a canoe going the other way.

'What the hell are you doing?' shouted Newborough.

'I can take one other!' explained the canoeist.

But perhaps the least reassuring mode of transport in the Channel was observed by the master of the steam yacht SY *Killarney*. He sailed past a French officer and two Belgian soldiers attempting to reach England on a door. And balancing on the door, between the three passengers, were six large bottles of wine.

Another unusual Little Ship, though for different reasons, was *Advance*, a motor launch crewed by three bearded civilians who looked very much like pirates. As somebody commented at the time, 'Only the Jolly Roger was missing.' But far more unusual than their appearance was the fact that within forty-eight hours of *Advance*'s return to England, two of her crew members had been detained by the police under Regulation 18B as members of the British Union of Fascists.

And yet for all the different sorts of people aboard the Little Ships, there were, it appears, no women. The Association of Dunkirk Little Ships certainly has no record of a woman – notwithstanding an article in *The Times* of 6 June 1940 headed 'Women Among Volunteer Crews'. The piece alleges that at least one woman received permission to take a Little

Ship across to Dunkirk. She did this, it claims, by telephoning the Admiralty in such a deep voice that she was mistaken for a man. There is, unfortunately, no corroboration for this story. There was a prodigious amount of unsubstantiated rumour flying about in the days after Operation Dynamo, and *The Times* seems to have been as likely to repeat gossip as anybody else.

Just as rumours can take hold in the aftermath of an event, so can received wisdom. Not so long ago, the received wisdom was that the miracle of Dunkirk was achieved solely by the legendary Little Ships, crewed by stout-hearted Englishmen, men such as Clem Miniver,* who left the pub on a warm summer's evening, jumped in their boats, and returned two days later, tired and bearded, never to speak of the terrible things they had seen. This, of course, was a cliché, an exaggeration with little basis in fact. Yet the revisionist view that the Little Ships hardly rescued any soldiers, that they were an insignificant coda to an evacuation achieved by the Royal Navy, is equally misleading.

The reality is that the Little Ships, a surprising number of which were manned by civilians, played a vitally important role in Operation Dynamo. At a basic level, the entire evacuation was invigorated by the arrival of the flotillas. But beyond this, the Little Ships actually brought more soldiers home to England than has ever been acknowledged. This is because many Little Ships, packed with soldiers, were towed across the Channel by larger ships. When the procession reached England, each smaller ship would moor alongside

---

* Clem Miniver is the husband of Mrs Miniver, the title character in a 1942 film about a suburban British housewife. Clem takes his own motorboat across to Dunkirk.

the larger ship, the soldiers would climb from the smaller ship onto the larger ship and from there onto the dock, and the smaller ship would not be credited with rescuing anybody at all. It might not even be recorded as having taken part in Operation Dynamo.

Yet even if a Little Ship did nothing more than ferry men from the beaches to the larger ships, it was still responsible for rescuing every single man that it ferried. Without its contribution, that man would have remained on the beach to be captured by the enemy. Considered in these terms, the contribution of the Little Ships seems very significant indeed – and this is without tackling the theoretical question of how far Dunkirk Spirit was influenced by their story.

As the flotillas began to arrive on Friday 31 May, however, and the evacuation gained momentum, the perimeter around Dunkirk was shrinking. The immediate result was that six thousand men at La Panne had to march along the beach to Bray Dunes. Colonel Stephen Hollway of the Royal Engineers remembers standing on the beach at La Panne. He was told that there would be no more boats coming in. He then passed out, either from a shell blast or from exhaustion, and when he came to, early on Saturday morning, there was not a living soul left on the beach. The eastern beaches had been abandoned.

As far as the film is concerned, this is a telling moment. In a no-man's-land such as this, Tommy, Gibson, Alex and the Highlanders settle down in the grounded Dutch trawler. Allied troops have disappeared and German troops are shortly to arrive. And while there is little evidence of Dutch ships (other than the ubiquitous schuits) taking part in Operation Dynamo, there *is* a record of a Dutch eel boat – *Johanna* – arriving in Dunkirk at the end of May.

On Friday 31 May, meanwhile, Winston Churchill flew to Paris in his customary Flamingo to meet members of the Allied Supreme War Council. The French and British sat around a table, facing each other, and Churchill was able to offer some rare good news. As of lunchtime, he said, 165,000 troops had been evacuated – far more than anyone had expected.

'How many French?' asked Weygand.

'So far, only fifteen thousand,' said Churchill. Not such good news.

Weygand wondered how he could face French public opinion with such a disparity. More French would have to be evacuated. Churchill agreed. Desperate to keep France in the war, he had already decided that Anglo-French relations must improve. From this point, he explained, British and French troops would embark in equal numbers.

A telegram was then drafted to send to Admiral Abrial in Bastion 32. It noted that once the perimeter had collapsed, British forces would embark before French forces.

At these words, Churchill exploded with righteous emotion. *'Non! Partage – bras dessus, bras dessous!'* he shouted. His meaning was clear as he mimed two people clutching each other as they departed. But he went further. Carried away in the moment, he promised that the British would defend the perimeter to the bitter end to allow the French to escape.

In truth, this was never likely to happen. It was almost inevitable that the French would end up defending their own country as the British returned to theirs. Churchill's promise would, in time, be remembered by the French as a classic example of English perfidy, as serious as the concealment of their intention to evacuate.*

---

* See Chapter Seven.

Relations between British and French soldiers always depended on the individuals and the circumstances. There had undoubtedly been ill feeling on both sides, the French focusing on supposed British betrayal, the British on the apparently poor standard of the French army. And during the evacuation, that ill feeling often revealed itself. As represented in the film, French soldiers were prevented from joining queues and boarding boats. Robert Newborough remembers trying to pick British troops ahead of foreign troops. He believed it to be his duty. 'Sometimes,' he says, 'one got a bit ruthless and said, "British only!"' Yet it seems that after Churchill's order that French and British troops be evacuated together, genuine efforts were being made to follow his instruction. And despite the shrinking of the perimeter, Friday 31 May was Operation Dynamo's most successful day in terms of evacuations. A total of 68,014 men were lifted, 22,942 from the beaches and 45,072 from the mole. The running total was now 194,620 men rescued.

The first loaded ship to depart Dunkirk the next morning was the *Whippingham*, an Isle of Wight paddle ferry with 2,700 troops on board. Such huge numbers suggest a knowledge that time was running short. And *Whippingham* very nearly capsized when shell fire caused troops to rush to the sheltered side of the ship.

A little later, at about 8 a.m., Admiral Wake-Walker was on the bridge of the destroyer HMS *Keith*, off Bray Dunes, when a formation of Stukas appeared in the distance. Three of them came down directly at *Keith* – and so began the first of five consecutive bomb attacks. The first ended in near misses, the closest bomb landing ten yards away. The second sent a bomb down the central funnel, blowing out the under part of the ship. Sitting nearby was *MTB 102* – and seeing

Keith's difficulty, it drew near. Admiral Wake-Walker chose his moment and transferred across. The third and fourth attacks weakened her further, and at 9.15 a final attack sunk her. All that remained of HMS *Keith* was a large oil slick in which soldiers struggled, vomited and drowned.

Later that day, the decision was taken to abandon all daylight evacuation from the mole and the beaches. German batteries now commanded sections of the Channel and all necessary embarkations could be carried out under the relative safety of darkness.

Saturday was a mixed day for the Allies. Shipping losses reached their highest level, but the number of troops rescued was almost as high as the previous day. The number of soldiers evacuated was 64,429, of whom 47,081 were picked up from the mole. The accumulated total had now reached 259,049.

The end was in sight – but it is worth standing aside for a moment to try to imagine life within the perimeter during Operation Dynamo. Perhaps the greatest initial shock to a newcomer would be the noise. Dunkirk was very loud. Guns of all types were being fired, shells were flying overhead and bursting, Stukas (so long as they were fitted with sirens) were screaming. This would not all have been going on at once, of course, but the ambient noise was loud enough that 'Dunkirk throat', a relentless sore hoarseness, was a near-universal complaint.

A sound common on the beaches during quieter spells was a soft sighing, similar to the wind passing over telegraph wires. This was actually the sound of wounded men moaning. Singing could often be heard; popular songs at Dunkirk include ironic favourites like 'Oh I Do Like to Be Beside the Seaside', 'We're Going to Hang Out the Washing on the

Siegfried Line' and 'Three Hundred Men Went to Walk, Walk along the Sand Dunes' (to the tune of 'One Man Went to Mow'). A patriotic favourite was 'There'll Always be an England', while 'Home on the Range' was also popular. The French, meanwhile, could often be heard singing 'La Marseillaise'.

Common expressions among soldiers included 'It's a Blighty move', meaning 'I'm going back to England', and 'Make for the black smoke', meaning 'Head for Dunkirk'. Whatever the men were discussing among themselves, bad language helped them to make their point. And one of the most startling noises heard at Dunkirk was the silence that came in the aftermath of an attack. 'The quiet, when the firing ceased,' writes an anonymous QUAIMNS nurse, 'was more noticeable than the continuous noise had been.'

On Sunday 2 June, as the British effort reached its culmination, Major General Alexander was told to hold on for as long as possible so that the maximum number of troops could be evacuated. Captain Tennant believed that five thousand British troops remained, in addition to the four thousand men on the perimeter, who were currently withdrawing. Ramsay suspected that an additional two thousand men could be found hiding in the town (where some might have remained since Anthony Rhodes departed his cellar a week earlier). Nevertheless, it was hoped that they could all be evacuated within the next twelve hours.* With this aim, Ramsay sent out a Nelsonesque call to destroyers and minesweepers: 'The final evacuation is staged for tonight, and the nation looks to the Navy to see this through. I want every ship to report as soon

---

* Churchill's promise to defend the perimeter as the French evacuated was clearly not a factor in Alexander and Tennant's thinking.

as possible whether she is fit to meet the call which has been made on our courage and endurance.'

At 5 p.m. a huge armada of ships set out from Dover to mop up the British Expeditionary Force – and to take as many French troops as possible. The first vessels reached Dunkirk at 6.45 p.m. and began boarding large numbers. From the mole, the Clyde steamer *King George V* brought 1,460 home, while the destroyer *Venomous* lifted 1,500. The last of the British rearguard, 2,000 men, was brought to England on the Channel Islands steamer *St Helier*. It left Dunkirk at 11.30 p.m. Captain William Tennant promptly sent the signal 'B.E.F. evacuated', and embarked for Dover in *MTB 102*.

But that did not mean that the evacuation was at an end. It continued in an effort to rescue as many French troops as possible. The very last ship to depart the mole, at 3.05 a.m. on 4 June, was the Isle of Man steam packet *Tynwald* with her astonishing haul of 3,000 men on board. Twenty thousand French soldiers were taken off that night, and the very last ship left Dunkirk at 3.40 a.m. with the Germans only three miles away. About 12,000 French troops remained to be taken prisoner.

At 2.23 p.m. on Tuesday 4 June, Operation Dynamo was terminated.

Ten

Where's the Bloody RAF?

As we have seen, many elements came together to create the miracle of deliverance. Some had more effect than others, but all played their part. The counter-attack at Arras; the several halt orders; Gort's decision to evacuate; the defence of the corridor's strongpoints and the perimeter around Dunkirk; the calm sea, cloud cover and smoke over the harbour; the degaussing of ships; Tennant's discovery that the mole could be used to load troops; Churchill's refusal to consider making peace; the efforts of the Royal Navy and the Merchant Navy; the valuable work of the Little Ships – all of these factors together create our story. But another crucial factor has not yet been explored: the performance of the Royal Air Force.

Strafed and bombed by the Luftwaffe, soldiers on the beaches and the mole were often heard to ask, 'Where's the bloody RAF?' They carried on asking once they had returned to England. But the RAF was in France and its aircraft were parked up on French airfields long before this question first arose. RAF light bomber and fighter squadrons were sent out as part of the Advanced Air Striking Force, a joint French and British organisation that had been created in anticipation of war. 'We went out as soon as we could in September,' says

Billy Drake of 1 Squadron. 'We flew across in our aircraft. All the ground transport went by sea.' His first job as a pilot was to ensure that the troop ships were protected as they crossed to France.

Life was quiet at first. Drake was stationed on an airfield that his squadron shared with a nunnery. His mess was in Le Havre – where things were racier. 'We took over a brothel,' he says, 'and two of the girls stayed on as waitresses to look after us.' And as the BEF dug trenches and settled down to its strange holiday, the RAF, too, had little to do – mainly haphazard reconnaissance. 'We had no early warning,' says Drake. Most operational sorties were carried out in response to the noise of enemy aircraft. 'Our activity consisted of endless patrols,' says Roland Beamont of 87 Squadron, 'and there was no radar to help. It was just a question of eyeballs.'

There was confusion in London, meanwhile, about German intentions. Was the Luftwaffe going to come for the capital? And if it did, would anybody survive? This was no foregone conclusion. In 1932, Stanley Baldwin had told the House of Commons, 'I think it is well also for the man in the street to realise that there is no power on earth that can protect him from being bombed. Whatever people may tell him, the bomber will always get through.' In fact, believed Baldwin, it was going to wipe out European civilisation. Harold Macmillan, writing in 1956, explained that the pre-war generation thought of air warfare 'rather as people think of nuclear war today'.

So as Britain steeled itself for a catastrophic bombing campaign, many wondered why the Royal Air Force was not pre-empting Hitler by bombing Germany first. 'We in Britain had organised a Bomber Command,' wrote the aerial commentator J. M. Spaight. 'The whole *raison d'être* of that

Command was to bomb Germany ... We were not bombing her. What, then, was the use of Bomber Command? Its position was almost a ridiculous one.'

Other voices urged caution; there was no need to initiate an unnecessary fight. But why, Winston Churchill asked in January, did the Germans not attack? Perhaps they were apprehensive of starting a war they could not be sure of winning, or perhaps they were 'saving up for some orgy of frightfulness which will soon come'.

On the morning of 10 May, the orgy arrived. The Luftwaffe appeared over France. The night before, Joe Pengelly, an NCO at the RAF Forward Air Ammunition Park in Reims, was having a relaxing evening at an Ensa concert.* He got back late and fell asleep in his clothes. Woken at dawn by the sound of explosions, he went to the door and looked out. 'It was a German aircraft,' he says. 'I went to the Lewis guns and started blasting away.' Roland Beamont's airfield came under low-level attack that morning, while for Billy Drake, 10 May brought a dramatic change of pace – but no information. 'All that our HQ could say was take off and patrol such and such an area. I was bloody frightened,' he says, before correcting himself: 'No, I was apprehensive.' For Beamont, that day marked the beginning of a ten-day battle. 'Eighty-seven Squadron were in the thick of it,' he says, 'until we were pulled out on 20 May because we hadn't enough aeroplanes or pilots to carry on.'

The Royal Air Force was still flying some almost obsolete planes – such as the Hawker Hector, an army cooperation biplane in the process of being phased out. (Any that were

---

* Entertainments National Service Association, an organisation providing live entertainment to the armed forces.

left after Dunkirk, however battered, were sold to neutral Ireland.) The enchanting-sounding Fairey Battle was a light bomber introduced in 1937, but already outclassed by 1940. Like the Spitfire and Hurricane, it had a Rolls-Royce Merlin engine, but it also carried a bomb load and a three-man crew. In combat against the Luftwaffe, it was slow and vulnerable. Vivien Snell, a Fairey Battle pilot of 103 Squadron who bombed the bridges across the River Meuse in a vain effort to prevent the German advance, was no fan of his aircraft: 'It was unmanoeuvrable and had one .303 machine gun firing rearwards. It was kamikaze. Our losses were huge.' The Fairey Battle was withdrawn completely by the end of 1940.

Through a combination of surprise and superior machines, the Luftwaffe overwhelmed the RAF in these opening days, in the air and on the ground, where they targeted aircraft on airfields. The pressure on pilots became enormous. Beaumont says his squadron of Hurricanes was on continuous patrol, such that 'people were just not able to write up reports – there was too much action'. His squadron's losses were heavy and its records were lost in the move from one base to another. 'It was difficult to know what was happening,' he says.

In the meantime, a sense that German pilots did not play by the rules was growing among their British counterparts. Beaumont witnessed deliberate German attacks on civilians. 'If you jam the roads with refugees and overturned vehicles and slaughtered horses,' he says, 'the allied reserves are going to take longer to reach the front.' Belgian refugees fleeing the invasion remember these aerial attacks. Louis van Leemput, then aged thirteen and escaping with his family, remembers being fired at on more than one occasion, once even *after* Belgium had surrendered. 'The war was over!' he says, still astonished nearly eighty years later. 'There was a deep ditch nearby and we just had to jump in and the bullets went, "Tuck! Tuck! Tuck!" over the cobblestones. We could have been killed, even in that moment.'

Allied pilots were beginning to hear other disturbing reports. Arriving in Lille, Harold Bird-Wilson of 17 Squadron made a bleak discovery: the Germans were shooting at pilots bailing out. 'It was obvious that the esprit de corps and the rules of war were going to be very different in comparison with the fighting that took place in World War I,' he says. He remembers that the pilots were shaken and angered by this and he took it as a warning to protect any parachutists who descended.

By 15 May, the RAF had already lost 250 planes. Sir Hugh Dowding, the commander-in-chief of Fighter Command, lost patience and notified Winston Churchill that no more Hurricanes would be going to French airfields. If losses continued at this rate, Dowding feared that Fighter Command would be left unable to defend Britain. It was a decision Churchill struggled to accept. Desperate to keep the French fighting, he overruled Dowding, insisting on four further squadrons being sent out. A shambolic reorganisation resulted, as these new squadrons were created out of eight existing squadrons, with the result that pilots with different training and little mutual understanding were thrown into action together. Sir Cyril Newall, chief of air staff, subsequently ruled that no further squadrons would be sent to France; instead they would move to airfields in the south of England, from where they could make sorties over France.

Neither Churchill nor the French leaders were pleased with this decision. In Whitehall, Roland Melville, Newall's private secretary, was approached by a French liaison officer with a message from General Gamelin: without a further four squadrons being sent immediately, the battle would be lost. Melville told him there would be no more squadrons for France. The officer was clearly desperate so Melville telephoned Newall's assistant, asking him to reconsider. But the answer, again, was no. 'I reported it to this man who burst into tears,' says Melville, 'and he spent the rest of the night walking up and down the corridors outside my office weeping.'

By resisting requests from the Prime Minister for more fighters to be sent to France, Sir Hugh Dowding shows himself to have been a brave and determined man. Nicknamed 'Stuffy' by his men, Dowding cut a very different figure to his flamboyant German counterpart, Hermann Goering. A socially awkward* widower, Stuffy cared deeply for his men, and they respected him back. He often referred to his airmen, including his son Derek, as his 'chicks'. Goering could be energetic, inspiring even, but he was significantly less paternal. In persuading Hitler to allow the Luftwaffe to finish off the BEF† against the advice of his senior commanders, he placed personal ambition above the welfare of his men. Both Wolfram Freiherr von Richthofen, commander of Fliegerkorps VIII, and Albert Kesselring, commander of Luftflotte 2, objected. Kesselring complained that many of his *gruppe* were now heavily reduced in strength, and his bombers were

---

* His personal assistant, Hugh Ironside, remembers the 'gruesome' sherry parties Dowding used to throw with his sister. 'Stuffy would have one sherry,' he says, 'and he used to play his ancient tunes on his ancient gramophone and after a time I used to find it most difficult to get anyone to come.'

† See Chapter Six.

still operating from Germany, which allowed for only one sortie a day. But Goering would brook no dissent, however sensible. He desired the prestige.

These contrasting men, Dowding and Goering, led the war over Dunkirk, but what of the aircraft at their disposal? Another single-seat British biplane was the Gloster Gladiator. Described by one man as 'no aircraft to go to war in', this is precisely what a number of pilots did. James Sanders of 615 Squadron had been flying Hurricanes, but after falling out with a squadron leader, he was placed on Gladiators as punishment. The honorary commanding officer of his squadron was Winston Churchill, who visited the airfield with his wife, Clementine. When Mrs Churchill asked if she could sit in his Gladiator, a flattered Sanders agreed. She eased herself into the seat and began poking the controls, as curious non-flyers frequently do. Churchill, meanwhile, stood in front of the aircraft, looking down the barrels of the machine guns. Sanders did not realise until later that the guns were cocked and ready to fire. Had Mrs Churchill shown just a touch more enthusiasm, she would have removed her husband's head.

On 23 May, Sanders, now a Gladiator veteran and flight commander, took command of a detachment at Manston airfield in Kent. In the early days of the evacuation, 'G'-Flight made eight patrols over the Channel, protecting ships, large and small, from attack. Sanders survived this dangerous period, and after the flight was disbanded on 30 May, he was placed back on Hurricanes. Gladiators remained in service, however, defending the Royal Navy Dockyard near Plymouth during the Battle of Britain.

In the years leading up to the war, Dowding oversaw the introduction of the two great heroes of British fighter aviation – the Supermarine Spitfire and the Hawker Hurricane. The Spitfire entered service in 1938. A monoplane, single-seat fighter with a Rolls-Royce Merlin engine, it was loved by pilots for its handling and speed, and by the British public for its distinctive engine note, its elliptical curves and the confidence it inspired. Al Deere, a pilot officer with 54 Squadron who started out on Gladiators, remembers his Spitfire training as basic: 'You learned the cockpit drill, you read the pilot's handbook, and it felt right. It looked fragile but it was an amazingly tough aircraft.'

Tough it may have been, but it was also responsive. George Unwin, a sergeant pilot of 19 Squadron, found the Spitfire so sensitive on the controls that he never needed to heave it or force it. 'You just breathed on it,' he says. 'If you wanted to turn, you just moved your hands slowly and she went.' For James Goodson, an American who flew with 43 Squadron later in the year, piloting the Spitfire 'was like pulling on a tight pair of jeans'. Against regulations, Goodson would smoke his cigar in the cockpit, and when he dropped his lighter, he would move the stick a fraction of an inch, roll the Spitfire and catch the lighter as it fell from the floor.

For Chris Nolan, the section of the film dealing with the war in the air is 'all about the Spitfire':

It's such a magnificent plane, one of the greatest vehicles ever designed. I went up in a Spitfire myself and the feeling of speed and power is unique. You feel very close to the elements, like you're in a kite with an amazingly powerful motor. You feel the air rushing past the wings, and when you touch the stick, when you turn it, when you roll it, the responsiveness, its relationship with the atmosphere, is really quite incredible. But the confinement in the small cockpit, being strapped into that. There's the feeling of power and control but there's also isolation.

One problem it posed was how to bail out. On 25 May, James Leathart of 54 Squadron (known as 'Prof' on account of his academic ability) was over Gravelines and Calais, when fellow pilot Johnny Allen's Spitfire was hit by anti-aircraft fire. 'Oh hell, my engine's packed up,' Leathart heard Allen say over the R/T. Moments later, with Allen's plane now on fire, Leathart heard him again: 'Yippee! There's a destroyer downstairs. I'm bailing out. But how?' Allen managed to execute a roll and drop out upside down. Three days later, according to Leathart, Allen showed up in the 54 Squadron mess wearing bits and pieces of naval uniform.

While the Spitfire is the iconic British fighter of the Second World War, the Hawker Hurricane was just as important in the earlier part of the war. More angular and less structurally innovative than the Spitfire (it had a wooden-framed and fabric-covered fuselage as opposed to the Spitfire's all-metal body), it was nevertheless an extremely agile and impressive aircraft.

Geoffrey Page of 56 Squadron says, 'The Hurricane was a bulldog and the Spitfire a greyhound. One was a tough working animal, the other a sleek, fast animal.' He considered the Hurricane easier to fly but lacking the Spitfire's speed and climb. 'They were both lovable in different ways,' he says. In the end, it is safest to say that those who flew Spitfires tended to prefer Spitfires, and those who flew Hurricanes tended to prefer Hurricanes.

Another single-engine aircraft also made an impression during the Dunkirk evacuation: the Boulton Paul Defiant. Its partially rotating gun turret behind the pilot harked back to the Bristol Fighter, one of the most successful aircraft of the First World War – except that the Bristol Fighter also had a forward-facing machine gun. The Defiant had no forward-facing armaments; it was designed to position itself alongside a bomber and shoot it out of the sky. It was never intended to engage in hectic dogfights against Messerschmitts. We will soon discover how it fared.

The most effective German fighter aircraft during the Battle of France and the Dunkirk evacuation was the Messerschmitt Bf 109. A single-seat fighter, it was less tight in the turn than the Spitfire and the Hurricane, but it had one distinct advantage – its fuel injection system. This meant that it could dive faster than either of the British fighters.

The Bf 109's job was to protect the slow, unwieldy bombers such as the Heinkel He 111, with its distinctive glass nose, and the Dornier Do 17, nicknamed 'the flying pencil' for its sleek lines. Both of these were originally introduced as commercial aircraft. But the Heinkel, unlike the Dornier, had been designed to be converted easily into a military plane, at a time when, under the terms of the Treaty of Versailles, Germany was not allowed an air force. The most feared German bomber during this period, as well as the most vulnerable, was, as we have seen, the Junkers Ju 87 (Stuka) bomber.* With its Jericho trumpets sometimes operating and its ability to aim its bombs by aiming the aircraft itself, the Stuka terrorised civilians and soldiers on the ground. Yet it delighted opposition fighter pilots, who viewed it as easy prey.

As the evacuation began on 26 May, it fell to Fighter Command's 11 Group to combat the German attack on the port, shipping and the Dunkirk perimeter. Air Vice-Marshal

---

* See Chapter Four.

Keith Park had just sixteen squadrons a day for Dunkirk. But the first meeting between a Spitfire and an Me 109 had already taken place on 23 May. In a patrol early that morning, Francis White, leader of 74 Squadron, shot down an observation aircraft, a Henschel Hs 126. But the Henschel put a bullet in White's radiator, forcing him to land at Calais Marck aerodrome, which was still in Allied hands.

The Germans were poised to capture Calais, so the RAF launched a rescue mission: a Miles Master (a two-seater, flown by 'Prof' Leathart), protected by two Spitfires, was sent to collect White. They all crossed the Channel, and the Master landed at Marck aerodrome to fetch White, while the Spitfires stayed airborne. One, flown by New Zealander Al Deere, maintained a patrol of the airfield, while the other, flown by Johnny Allen, went higher to check for German aircraft. Almost immediately, Allen radioed Deere that he had spotted Messerschmitts. He quickly shot one down and damaged two more, sending them into the clouds streaming smoke. Deere tried to warn the pilots on the ground that Messerschmitts were about but, as the Master had no radio, could only waggle his wings.

As he was doing this, an Me 109 flew directly in front of him, heading towards the Master, causing Leathart and White to run for shelter. Higher up, Allen was now surrounded by 109s, and radioed Deere for help. Deere shot down the 109 directly in front of him before climbing to meet Allen, firing at one Messerschmitt and chasing another away. Once the Master was in the air, all three aircraft headed for home.

Thinking back to the action, Deere has no memory of being afraid. 'It was the thrill of the thing really. There was no sense of danger at that stage.' So excited was he that he carried on chasing the final 109 even when he had used up all his ammunition. 'That shows you how really green I was,' he says. But the combat gave him confidence, convincing him that there was no reason to fear the 109. He also learned to watch his fuel – a crucial theme in Chris Nolan's film.

There were skirmishes throughout the day on 26 May, but many British patrols were cancelled due to poor weather. And there were losses due to friendly fire.* John Nicholas remembers: 'My great friend, Flying Officer Johnny Welford was shot down by a British destroyer and killed, on 26 May off the Goodwin Sands. He bailed out – his parachute streamed but it didn't open and he was killed. By the time they realised what they had done and dragged him out, it was too late.'

On the same day over Dunkirk, Peter Parrott of 145 Squadron spotted a Heinkel 111 and broke formation to go after it. He started firing and 'it very rudely shot back'. Parrott realised that the Heinkel's gunner must have hit his radiator because his cockpit filled with steam. He turned for home and was halfway across the Channel when his squadron caught up with him: 'There was a lot of chatter on the radio about what was wrong with me. As I got over the coast at Deal, my engine stopped.' The plane dropped to three or four thousand feet and Parrott tried to find somewhere to land. He saw uneven areas, and people out for their Sunday evening walk, before picking a field and shoving the stick forward. He hit a few sheep, turning them to mutton. People started to gather around the Hurricane, and a policeman showed up. Parrott asked him to keep the crowd away from the loaded guns, and asked where he could find a telephone. A farmer came by on a horse and trap. 'Who's gonna pay for them sheep?' he said to Parrott. 'Try the Air Ministry,' said

---

* An expression in use since 1918.

Parrott. The farmer rode off but Parrott still needed a tele-phone and realised the nearest was the farmer's. When he reached the farmhouse, the farmer and his wife were having tea and there was a large, juicy ham on the table. Parrott put in a call to Manston airfield and asked to be collected. Then the farmer pointed down the hallway and said, 'You can sit there!' Parrott sat on his own. He wasn't offered any ham.

Living lives of such unpredictability, pilots did what they could to boost morale. A flight commander of 610 Squadron remembers an officer who, having worked at Harrods before the war, called in his contacts. A Harrods van arrived every morning with food and drink for the day; the pilots had fillet steak for lunch, lobster thermidor for dinner, and immense danger between meals. And despite their lack of preparation and experience, pilots seemed eager to see action. When names were drawn from a hat for the honour of making 19 Squadron's first patrol over Dunkirk, Brian Lane recorded George Unwin's reaction on being the man left behind: 'He stood looking at me with a hurt expression on his face, for all the world like a dog who has been told he can't come for a walk.' From that day until his death in 2006, Unwin was known as 'Grumpy'.

The following day, 27 May, the evacuation was fully under way. But only 7,669 British troops left Dunkirk. And in the meantime, despite the pessimism of Goering's commanders, the campaign began promisingly for the Luftwaffe with the almost complete destruction of the inner harbour.* And though the pilots of Fighter Command were enthusiastic, few had yet seen an enemy plane.

---

* This, of course, was why the mole was pressed into service for embarkations, on the night of 27–28 May, by Captain William Tennant.

George 'Grumpy' Unwin had a surprisingly common experience when he first encountered the enemy: he froze. 'I just sat there in a turn,' he says, 'not petrified, but frozen for about ten to fifteen seconds.' When enemy gunfire struck his fuselage, the moment was broken – and it never happened to him again. 'I always regarded the first time you got mixed up as being the most dangerous. One isn't used to being shot at in any walk of life.' A sergeant pilot of 222 Squadron found himself admiring Me 109s on his first engagement. 'They looked so pretty!' he says. But by the time *his* moment was broken, the pretty machines had got on his tail and his engine was pouring smoke.

Pilots were learning to ignore official rules and guidelines. They stopped flying in the old First World War Vic formation, for example – with a leader and two wingmen – and instead began copying the German formations learned while flying in the Spanish Civil War and the Polish campaign. In terms of experience – and therefore tactics – the Germans were well ahead of the British.

And it paid to ignore another guideline – concerning height. Pilots were initially told to stay at 20,000 feet, and never to fly lower than 15,000 feet, as the anti-aircraft gunners were supposedly able to take care of enemy planes at lower levels. But this had disadvantages. For one thing, it meant that Stukas were all out of range, as they started their dives at 15,000 feet; for another, it meant that Royal Air Force aircraft were too high to be seen by British soldiers on the ground. These factors led to British aircraft flying lower – even if it meant being shot at regularly by British naval guns.

On 27 May, the Germans' large formations threatened to outnumber the RAF. 'The norm was for up to twelve Hurricanes to be attacking 40 to 50 German aeroplanes,' says Roland Beamont, 'but sometimes the odds were greater than that.' The numerous bombers were able to drop hundreds of tons of bombs on the town and the beaches – though many hit the sand where their energy was dissipated and much of their destructive power wasted.

Yet the RAF had considerable success on this day. Thirty German aircraft were lost, and the Boulton Paul Defiants excelled. Early in the morning, they brought down two Me 109s, and on their next patrol, at least another three, possibly five – without loss. German pilots did not yet appreciate the particular danger these aircraft presented with their turret gunners.

The next day, Tuesday 28 May, the bombers of Fliegerkorps I, II and VII were set to work over Dunkirk, protected by the fighters of Jagdfliegerführer 3. On the same day, a message came from the chief of the British air staff warning that the RAF must make 'their greatest effort'. Fighter Command was instructed to protect the Dunkirk beaches 'from first light until darkness by continuous fighter patrols' and, critically, all patrols would be 'at a strength of at least two squadrons'. The Luftwaffe was about to face its first serious air battle.

Faced with *gruppe*-sized opponents, the British had little choice but to send up larger units – but this meant that fewer patrols could be made, and longer gaps were left between each. These gaps could be exploited by the Germans. Fighter Command was also facing its first serious challenge.

54 Squadron made a dawn patrol on the morning of 28 May. Spotting a Dornier, Al Deere led the chase. 'I was firing a burst at him,' he says, 'and suddenly I could see return fire from the rear gunner.' He felt his Spitfire judder and guessed that a bullet had pierced his glycol tank. With his cooling system hit, he couldn't continue, and had to come down. He

crash-landed on the beach. He did, in other words, what the character Farrier does in the film. As Deere made impact with the ground, he was injured, gashing his eyebrow. He had landed wheels up on the water's edge and the tide was coming in. He wandered up the beach towards a café and looked back to see the tide already rolling in around his Spitfire. A woman in the café helped him with his bleeding eyebrow, sticking it together with plasters.

Deere returned to the beach and took in the chaos he had previously seen from several thousand feet: 'It was pretty hectic. The bombing, the strafing. We were taking cover.' And then he noticed something that disturbed him greatly. British gunners were firing at British planes. He tried to intervene but to no avail.

After a while, he made his way to the mole and tried to get on a ship, but an army major stood in his path and told him to get in line. Deere argued he had to get home as quickly as possible to rejoin his squadron. 'For all the good you chaps seem to be doing over here,' said the major, 'you might just as well stay on the ground.' The major kept Deere off one ship, but the New Zealander managed to board the next – where the atmosphere was no less tense. The soldiers were angry.

'Where the hell have you been?' they said.

Deere had been flying for ten days straight. He had nothing to apologise for. 'We were there but you, perhaps, didn't see us!'

The soldiers were unpleasant – but Deere managed to stay calm. And he was asked to help with aircraft identification. He came on deck and saw the ships' guns were firing at British aircraft.

The morning rain gave way to heavy cloud. Because of this, the Luftwaffe was forced to stay inland, targeting the town and port. John Ellis of 610 Squadron remembers carrying out two patrols that day, but visibility was poor and he spotted no enemy. Without the Luftwaffe to worry them, his squadron 'flew low over the beaches from time to time to give the Army a bit of encouragement and show them we were about'. South African Hilton Haarhoff was the rear gunner in a Lockheed Hudson, a four-man reconnaissance aircraft. His pilot, fellow Springbok Ronald Selley, also tried to instil confidence in the troops, by flying low over the ships. 'Whenever we did this the troops on the ships would give us a wave and grin as we sped past,' says Haarhoff, adding that Selley was an exhibitionist who liked to fly closer to the water than any other pilot. His navigator did not like it at all, but skimming so low across the Channel paid off when they spotted an upturned table floating in the Channel with three men on top of it, and managed to guide a trawler towards it.

Having been held up by the weather on 28 May, the Luftwaffe was again hampered by low cloud the following morning. Goering was infuriated but, for all his temporal power, he could not roll back the clouds. An improvement in the weather at midday, however, allowed the Germans to launch consecutive major bombing raids, two of which met with no resistance. This was the day when *Crested Eagle*, as well as many other ships, was sunk, and the mole was mistakenly abandoned for several hours. So successful was the Luftwaffe on the afternoon of 29 May that its chief of staff, Hans Jeschonnek, changed his opinion. He now believed that the Luftwaffe *could* destroy the BEF in its Dunkirk pocket.

For Eric Barwell of 264 Squadron, a Defiant pilot, the war began in earnest on this day. 'Four Stuka dive bombers were flying along,' he says, 'more or less line abreast, and three of us Defiants formatted under the gaps. And they just exploded.

They had fuel tanks between the pilot and his navigator – they were easy meat.' It was an extraordinary day for his squadron. It claimed an astonishing thirty-seven enemy aircraft destroyed. A Hurricane pilot who met the Defiant pilots later that day remembers them as 'cock-a-hoop'. He pointed out that the Germans had probably mistaken them for Hurricanes, and were unlikely to make the same mistake again. The pilot was right – this sortie marked the height of the Defiants' success. Once the Germans understood that the Defiant's turret posed its only danger, it became the easiest of kills for German fighters. It would soon be withdrawn from daylight action to become a night fighter.

The exact figures of how many planes were brought down on 29 May conflict heavily. Over-claiming was inevitable and happened on both sides. But an unacknowledged kill can rankle, even years later. John Nicholas of 65 Squadron came across Messerschmitt 110s in their trademark defensive circle. He fired at one and pulled away to the right, only to see in his rear-view mirror that three had broken out of formation to follow him. 'I decided the only thing I could do,' he says, 'was whip round and go down for the centre one. Which I did.' He fired at it and at the last minute pulled up, but when he looked back, he couldn't see any planes at all. He returned to Hornchurch and described the scene to his intelligence officer: 'But he didn't give me a combat report.' In 1992, Nicholas found out that another pilot had been credited with this head-on attack. 'It irritated me at the time!' says Nicholas. 'After a while, I thought, Oh what does it matter, it was fifty years ago!'

For Denys Gillam of 616 Squadron, the main problems of flying over Dunkirk were the limited amount of time he could remain there (a little over half an hour) and the difficulty in chancing on the right altitude to intercept the enemy. An afternoon such as this, when the weather conditions suited the Germans, offers a stark glimpse of what might have happened had good weather lasted for an unbroken week.

On Thursday 30 May, sea mist, fog and smoke from burning Dunkirk meant the Stukas were unable to function once again. By the end of the day, almost 54,000 British troops had made it off the beaches or the mole – the most successful day so far. But this did not mean that British squadrons and pilots were finding the operation easy work. 'To maintain a standing patrol,' says Gillam, 'meant that one was flying two or three times a day – about five hours a day starting in the early morning and going on until dusk.' And in order to encourage the efforts of men such as Gillam, Lord Gort sent a message of gratitude to the RAF. He said their presence was 'of first importance in preventing embarkation being interrupted'.

All the same, some could not stand the strain. 'We had the odd case of pilots proving unsuitable,' Gillam remembers. 'We had one that went to pieces on the ground just as he was getting into his aeroplane, so the doctor went and hit this chap on the chin – hard. Knocked him out. He didn't fly again.'

Friday 31 May was, as we have already seen, the most successful day of the evacuation. Eric Barwell, the successful Defiant pilot, was back over Dunkirk. On his first patrol, he saw a fellow Defiant break up into four pieces after its tail was sliced off by another Defiant. He saw no parachute emerge. He went out again later in the day and found himself surrounded by enemy aircraft. He shot one down, but when he attacked another three Heinkel bombers, his coolant system was hit and the cockpit filled with fumes. Jettisoning his hood, he aimed for home – but it soon became clear that he would have either to bail out or to ditch the Defiant on the water.

There were ships below who could pick him and his gunner up – but Barwell was worried that if they bailed out, they risked drifting away from the ships, possibly into a minefield. He chose to ditch the plane into the sea.

Looking down, Barwell saw fishing boats. He could ditch close by – but, even with his survival at stake, it crossed his mind that the fishing boats would be too smelly. He then spotted two destroyers about half a mile apart and figured that if he hit the water between them, one would probably bother to pick him up.

As he descended he was surprised by how difficult it was to gauge his height over a calm sea – and the next thing he knew he was in the water, trying to swim towards the surface.

Once on top, Barwell spotted his gunner, swam over to him, and discovered he was unconscious. He started to swim to the destroyer, a sort of sidestroke pulling the gunner by his parachute. One of the destroyers, he was delighted to see, was making its way towards him.

When he was near, one of the sailors from the destroyer dived into the water and swept the gunner away from Barwell and brought him on board. Once Barwell reached a climbing net near the stern, he was too weak to pull himself up. But somebody helped, and he was safe.

Barwell soon discovered another miracle – the Defiant pilot whose aircraft had broken up into four pieces was standing on deck. Alive and well. He must have parachuted out so low that Barwell had failed to see him. And, at that moment, Barwell's gunner regained consciousness.

For a while the gunner had no idea where he was. As he looked up, the first thing he saw was the pilot – whom he thought had died – standing in front of him framed by a deep red glow. He was utterly convinced that he was in hell.

He was thankful to discover, soon afterwards, that he was alive – as was the pilot, who was standing in a doorway that reflected the sunset.

In terms of the film, this is an interesting account; the character Collins ditches into the sea in his Spitfire, tries to break through his canopy with his flare gun, and is freed when the canopy is smashed from the outside. Barwell, in his Defiant, seems to have been thrown clear – which distinguishes his scenario from Collins's. So, is it really possible that a Spitfire could stay afloat long enough for a pilot to free himself or be freed?

Jack Potter, a sergeant pilot, was on patrol with 19 Squadron on 1 June. When the squadron flew into twelve Me 110s, he set his sights on one – but his ammunition ran out. There was no reason to stay around, so he started for home, before realising that his Spitfire was damaged. About fifteen miles from the English coast, Potter's engine seized. He figured his chances of being picked up if he bailed out were poor, but ditching in a metal Spitfire was also highly risky. On balance, though, he felt that this was his only chance, and he aimed towards a small boat.

Straightening out to land, Potter undid his Sutton harness, and inflated his life jacket. 'On first touching the water,' he says, 'the machine skimmed off again, and after one more such landing it dug its nose into the sea.' He stood up in the cockpit and found that the aircraft was still afloat.

The Spitfire stayed afloat for about ten seconds. Potter tried to keep hold of his parachute because he had been told it functioned like a lifebuoy, but it got caught on the sliding hood and as the Spitfire sank he was pulled down. He managed to break free and started to swim up, and was struck by the tailplane as the Spitfire went down.

The little boat he'd spotted was French, the *Jolie Mascotte*, and its crew spoke no English. They were trying to get to Dunkirk but were lost. Potter helped them to find the right course.* In return, they gave him food, drink and dry clothes.

The fact is, therefore, that a ditched Spitfire stayed afloat long enough for a pilot to free himself, become trapped, free himself again and survive.

Graham Davies, of 222 Squadron, went out on dawn patrol on 31 May, but began to lose height after being hit by anti-aircraft fire. He remembered the advice of a Hurricane pilot that it was possible to land wheels down on Dunkirk beach due to the hard sand. Thinking that he might be able to fix his Spitfire and take off again, Davies landed to the west of Dunkirk, in order to avoid the thousands of troops to the east. But as he came down, he was fired on by the French guns at Fort-Mardyck. He landed safely nevertheless and, after meeting the artillery men who had shelled him, he eventually managed to set fire to his aircraft, and received a lift into Dunkirk.

At the end of the mole, Davies could see a minesweeper and a paddle steamer. German planes were strafing from time to time, and a bomber was dropping its load in the harbour. Dead bodies were lying everywhere. In the midst of this, an angry British soldier was storming back up the mole, furious

---

* Potter does not mention his feelings on the subject – but it must have been galling, after such an ordeal, to discover that the boat was heading for Dunkirk, and not for the safety of England.

that the Navy would not let him come aboard a ship with a German prisoner he was frogmarching around.

On the morning of 1 June, the weather cleared. The return of the Stukas en masse coincided with the return of the modern British destroyers. A number of unopposed Luftwaffe attacks were launched in the morning, resulting, as we have seen, in the sinking of HMS *Keith* as well as a number of other destroyers and naval ships. British soldiers seethed at their apparent lack of protection. Harold Bird-Wilson tells of Ken Manger, a fellow 17 Squadron pilot who bailed out of his Hurricane over the beach. Attempting to board a destroyer, he was bluntly informed by an army officer that ships were not for the Royal Air Force. But Manger, it turned out, was an excellent amateur boxer. He knocked the officer into the sea, and stepped gingerly on board. The following day, Manger was back in the air over Dunkirk.

Arthur Taylor of 13 Squadron received so many threats from soldiers that he hid his uniform. 'I wore gumboots to cover the lower part of my Air Force uniform,' he says, 'and a black oilskin jacket to cover my Air Force jacket.' Sufficiently disguised, Taylor was evacuated home. Flying Officer Peter Cazenove, meanwhile, who had been forced to land his Spitfire on the beach, was turned away from three different destroyers. 'The Navy said that all accommodation was reserved for the Army, and the Air Force could go fuck themselves,' Cazenove's friend Tony Bartley wrote in a letter to his father. Cazenove was captured and ended up in a POW camp.

There are many reasons why soldiers did not see members of the Royal Air Force. For one thing, the RAF ended up employing large formations which meant gaps were necessary between patrols. For another, the Germans had observers behind Dunkirk who were able to call up attacks. This allowed the Luftwaffe to arrive shortly after the RAF disappeared. Third, the RAF was patrolling inland to cut the Germans off *before* they could reach the beaches. This makes sense. Once the Luftwaffe was over the beach, it was too late to prevent an attack. Fourth, the RAF was often flying at 20,000 feet or higher. At this height planes simply could not be seen from the ground. And fifth, since British guns were firing at almost every friendly aircraft that flew overhead, nearby soldiers would have mistaken these British aircraft for German machines.

Hilton Haarhoff's squadron patrolled Dunkirk on the afternoon of 1 June. He noted that the beaches 'were now nearly deserted, but the sand showed a mass of shell holes and shelter trenches which were hastily dug by our troops'. He was also able to see the line of lorries that had been driven out into the sea to form a jetty for the boats. On their way home, Haarhoff's Hudson crew witnessed a dogfight between Spitfires and Stukas. The Stukas were attacking ships returning to Dover. Haarhoff saw one Stuka dive, release its bombs and rise again. 'I looked for his target,' he says, 'an inoffensive tug towing a barge loaded with troops.' A huge wall of water rose up in front of the tug, blotting it from view. 'I did not expect to see the tug again,' he remembers, 'but in less time than it takes to tell, the tug was still steaming forward and the shower of water decreasing as it fell; the gallant little tug was quite unharmed and I gave it a cheer.'

The morning of 2 June started quietly for Fighter Command, with their patrols meeting little resistance. Tony Bartley remembers his squadron dropping to 9,000 feet

– against orders – where it encountered thirty Heinkel 111s, destroying about eighteen of them. Even further below, Bartley could see Stukas diving. But the Stukas had not succeeded in thwarting the BEF's escape. And they had made a liar of their commander-in-chief. It turned out that Hermann Goering's Luftwaffe could not destroy the British Expeditionary Force – whatever he had told Adolf Hitler.

On 2 June, 611 Squadron experienced their first day over Dunkirk. Squadron Leader John McComb remembers they had planned a drinks party for their wives in the mess that day. When the order came through to go to Dunkirk, they decided not to cancel the party, as 'we could not have Hitler interfering with our drinking habits'. The squadron was about to take off on patrol when one of the pilots, Donald Little, leapt briefly onto the wing of McComb's aircraft and asked him to feed his dog that night. McComb and his wife shared a cottage with Little and his wife, and another pilot, Ralph Crompton and his wife. 'That morning,' remembers McComb, 'we ran into a cloud of Messerschmitts and got into all sorts of trouble and lost these two young pilots.' The squadron arrived back in ones and twos. 'Meantime the party had started, broken with a cheer as someone else turned up. Came the time when Lil Crompton realised with June Little that no more were coming back.' The two young women asked for no help or support. 'Without a tear or a word they quietly slipped out of the ante-room and went back to the cottage.'

Over the entire period of the Battle of France and the evacuation, 931 British aircraft (of which 477 were fighters) failed to return from operations, were destroyed on the ground, or were irreparably damaged. Over the same period, 1,526 airmen were killed, wounded or taken prisoner.

For the period of the evacuation, the numbers are less precise. 11 Group gives a figure of 258 German aircraft destroyed. The 1953 Official British History offers a figure of 177 British aircraft destroyed or damaged, of which 106 were fighters. Whatever the precise figures, however, it seems clear that the Luftwaffe lost more aircraft during the evacuation than Fighter Command. And while mistakes were made by both sides, they were both severely hamstrung. The British by the fact that many of their aircraft were unavailable to them, the Luftwaffe by the fact that the task thrust upon them by their chief was unrealistic. And both sides were constrained by the battle's distance from their airfields; they only had limited time in the air.

Ultimately, however, whether or not its task was realistic, the Luftwaffe had failed to destroy the British Expeditionary Force. It had failed in its stated aim for the very first time. And not only that, it failed to make a large dent in the Royal Air Force.

The RAF, on the other hand, had demonstrated that the much-feared Luftwaffe could be nullified. It had gained experience for the great air battle ahead. It had shot down large numbers of the enemy, and, with a great deal of help from the weather, it had protected the British Expeditionary Force. Most importantly – it had not lost.

So we can add, with some confidence, the final great element that contributed to the miracle of deliverance: the performance of the Royal Air Force.

Eleven

A New Dunkirk

Operation Dynamo is not well known in the United States. It is not particularly well known anywhere outside the United Kingdom. But that is a great shame – because it has huge international significance. If the BEF had been captured or destroyed at Dunkirk, Britain would almost certainly have been forced to surrender. She would then have become, as Churchill warned his Cabinet, a slave state, allowing Hitler to concentrate all his efforts on the Soviet Union. And without Britain as a partner, it is difficult to see how the United States could have opened a second front.

But let's set any conjecture aside – because none is necessary. Had Britain surrendered we would all be living in a very different world today. My family would not be alive because all the Jews would have disappeared from Britain many years ago. And without Britain to preserve freedom and the rule of law, the totalitarian norms of Nazi Germany would have bled throughout Europe. Barbarism, intolerance and coercion would be the natural order of things.

The closing ceremony of the London 2012 Olympics featured a vignette of Winston Churchill, played by Timothy Spall, emerging from a model of Big Ben. Here we all are, the organisers seemed to be suggesting, enjoying a free Olympics, in a free United Kingdom, in a free world – and it's all thanks to this man. Or thanks to this period, more accurately, these few weeks when Churchill held his ground and the British army got away.

That is the message at the heart of this book. The tale of the retreat and evacuation is not a parochial British story, that bit of history that happened before America and Russia joined in. It is the story of the global preservation of freedom, of the prevention of a new dark age. It deserves to be remembered.

And all this can be said before we have even discussed the return of the BEF to Britain. Once the ships were under way, the world still had a chance.

On ships on the way home, many men fell asleep. Some tried to find quiet corners where they would not be disturbed. 'We'd arrive back in England, discharge everybody and get back to the beaches again,' says Lieutenant Commander John McBeath of HMS *Venomous*, 'and then a soldier would suddenly appear. He'd made the trip back to Dunkirk without knowing it.'

Leon Wilson, a French artilleryman, crossed to England on a destroyer whose captain welcomed the large French contingent on board with the words, 'Come on, Frogs! Sit down and have something to eat!'

'It was a good joke!' says the magnanimous Wilson, who sat and ate properly for the first time in days. 'I don't think the Savoy could have given us such a meal.'

The vast majority of returning British troops understood that they had suffered a terrible defeat. Many felt that they had shamed their country. This attitude is demonstrated by the character Alex towards the end of the film. But a surprise was in store for those who felt this way. 'In England, the reception was amazing,' says Ian English, a Durham Light Infantry officer, who witnessed a public euphoria that made the returning soldiers feel like heroes. Humphrey Bredin boarded a train at Dover, fell asleep, and woke up at a place called Headcorn, where, he says, 'the women almost gave us a party. They invaded the train with tea, coffee and buns.' Anthony Rhodes was minding his own business when a complete stranger pressed money into his hand. 'Well done, you lot! Jolly good job!' shouted members of the Women's Voluntary Service as Captain Gilbert White's train passed by. Oranges and cigarettes were shoved through the carriage window at Private William Ridley. At one point he looked up to see 'Welcome to the Dunkirk Heroes' painted on the side of a building. When Sergeant Ted Oates had a chance, he wrote to his family: 'We had a marvellous reception here & it seems as if we are heroes or something, I don't know very much about all this.'*

For Bredin, the public's reaction was embarrassing. 'We felt, damn it, that we'd run away!' Ridley, too, talks of feeling ashamed. And plenty of soldiers were angry at what they saw as betrayal, by the politicians, by their officers or by the army itself.

On 2 June, Anthony Eden, the Secretary of State for War, was loudly booed as he addressed troops at Aldershot. At around the same time, Basil Dean, head of Ensa, sat in a Bridport pub listening as 'seething' soldiers outdid each

---

* In the same letter, Sergeant Oates apologises for 'not getting anything for Martin's birthday but all the people were refugees & shops were shut also there were no post offices working'.

other with accounts of their experiences. One man complained loudly that the junior officers in his unit had grabbed the vehicles and fled to the French coast, leaving the NCOs and men to look after themselves. Others angrily backed him up. In mid-June, eighteen-year-old Colin Perry was told by a soldier of how his officers had deserted their men when their ship was sunk by Stukas. And seventy-seven years later, Maurice Machin of the Royal Army Service Corps remains furious about what happened: 'They say Dunkirk was a victory. It wasn't – it was a disorganised mess. If it hadn't been for the British people coming to our aid, I would have died along with many more.'* George Purton is more subdued in his criticism, but his point is similar. 'We were sent,' he says, 'into something we could not cope with.'

Yet the public reaction to the evacuation, whether miracle or disorganised mess, was neither contrived nor imposed. It was a spontaneous demonstration of relief. Friends and relatives were safe, and the war was going to continue. Nurse Eileen Livett began looking after returning soldiers at her hospital in north London. She considered them heroes 'because we all realised, here at home, how tight the situation was ... It was really touch and go.' This was the mood that Winston Churchill tapped into so effectively when, speaking to the House of Commons, he admitted that wars might not be won by evacuations, but that 'a miracle of deliverance' had been achieved.

---

* After the evacuation, Machin was sent straight to a training camp where the officers in charge – none of whom had been in France – accused the men, many of whom were near-starving and without uniforms, of being untidy and dirty. Machin was – and still is – furious.

For some people, Dunkirk became a personal inspiration. It made Nella Last feel part of something 'undying and never old … I felt glad I was of the same race as the rescuers and the rescued.' For long-time pacifist Dennis Argent, it was the spur to changing his beliefs. He could now imagine the circumstances where killing an enemy 'can be obviously and directly the means of saving the lives of civilian fellow-workers, and maybe even friends and family'.

In a speech given several months after Operation Dynamo, the historian Lord Elton described Dunkirk as the turning of a tide. People were now learning 'that the things which really mattered were not the complicated and exclusive things. It was not the stocks and shares or exclusive nightclubs which mattered now, but having a roof and a meal and the sound of children's laughter around one.'

Elton's impression of Dunkirk as a national wake-up call may be slightly simplistic (and extremely sentimental) but there is no doubt that the British social and political climate began to change at once. Before Dunkirk, the government could not afford to provide free milk to mothers and children. On 7 June, it introduced a scheme offering precisely that. Money was suddenly no object.

Days later, Harold Nicolson, Parliamentary Secretary at the Ministry of Information, delivered a paper to the Cabinet describing how the old order was changing. 'Every effort must be made,' he wrote, 'to provide real equality of opportunity for the younger generation.' In reply, Lord Halifax, a relic of another age, acknowledged that human values now seemed more important than financial purity.

If Britain were to survive, after all, she would need the help of her ordinary people as never before; she would need them to fight, to work long hours in factories, to volunteer their services in aid of the war effort, and to tolerate all manner of regulation and restrictions.

In return, there would have to be compensations. Her people would be offered better wages and increased protection. But their newfound importance would also gain them a greater stake in society. This was acknowledged, on 1 July, in a leader in *The Times*:

> If we speak of democracy, we do not mean a democracy which maintains the right to vote but forgets the right to work and the right to live. If we speak of freedom, we do not mean a rugged individualism which excludes social organization and economic planning. If we speak of equality, we do not mean a political equality nullified by social and economic privilege. If we speak of economic reconstruction, we think less of maximum production (though this too will be required) than of equitable redistribution ... The new order cannot be based on the preservation of privilege, whether the privilege be that of a country, of a class, or of an individual.

A fight to resist Nazi iniquity, it seemed, made little sense if Britain failed to acknowledge her own inequalities. Dunkirk turned abstract ideas like freedom and equality into realisable goals, which the wartime government would shortly start to embed into British life. The sudden shock of Dunkirk was the spark for the creation of modern Britain.

None of this would have come as much consolation, however, to those taken prisoner in France, or brought back wounded. At her hospital in Barnet, Eileen Livett tended to men suffering terribly. One young man in his late teens, of whom she was very fond, had third-degree burns. He had been in such good physical condition before being wounded that the burns started to heal very quickly. But when Livett removed the bandages around the man's head, his charred ear came away with the dressing. The following day, Livett was off duty, and when she returned to the hospital she was told that the young man had died. The dressing around his eyes had been removed – and he had discovered that he was blind. 'Although he was healing so beautifully,' says Livett, 'the shock was just enough to really finish him.'

The fact is that Operation Dynamo did not bring home the entire BEF. More than 140,000 British troops remained in France. Some had failed to reach Dunkirk, while members of 51st (Highland) Division – sent to help man the Maginot line – remained south of the Somme, cut off from the remainder of the BEF by the German advance. The division continued fighting after Operation Dynamo, but was surrounded by the Germans and captured on 12 June at St Valery-en-Caux.

On the very same day that 51st Division was being marched into captivity, two fresh divisions – 52nd (Lowland) Division and 1st Canadian Division – were arriving in France as part of a second British Expeditionary Force, sent to help the French resist the Germans. This 2nd BEF, however, was never likely to succeed. Its own commander, Lieutenant General Brooke, wanted to evacuate his troops after only two days, but Churchill was so keen for France to stay in the war, and so concerned about the effect of another evacuation on French morale, that he ordered the divisions to stay where they were. Then, on 14 June, German troops entered Paris. It became clear that the French were truly beaten, and the order was finally given for the 2nd BEF to evacuate from Bordeaux, Cherbourg, St Malo, Brest and St Nazaire.

Astonishingly, just weeks after the first, a second chaotic retreat to the coast took place, again involving the abandonment of supplies, and ending in a further call for ships and boats. It also led to the greatest single maritime disaster in British history, as the Cunard liner *Lancastria*, bringing over 6,000 people back to England, was sunk by German aircraft as she left St Nazaire. Up to 4,000 men, women and children died, most of them drowned. Churchill refused to allow news of the *Lancastria*'s sinking to be released; the press had published enough bad news that day, he believed. Operation Ariel (the code name for the evacuation of the 2nd BEF) brought huge numbers of Allied troops to Britain.

On 22 June, France signed an armistice with Germany. The signing took place in the same railway carriage, in the same clearing near Compiègne, as the armistice of 1918. Hitler wanted his revenge, he wanted to humiliate the French, even if that meant ripping an old railway carriage from the wall of a museum and transporting it into a field.

Reporting from Berlin on 14 June, American journalist William Shirer noted that diners crowded around a loudspeaker in his hotel bar as news of the Germans' entry into Paris was announced. They smiled and seemed happy. But there was no undue excitement, and they all returned to their tables to carry on eating. The next morning the Nazi Party newspaper, *Volkische Beobachter*, reported: 'Paris was a city of frivolity and corruption, of democracy and capitalism, where Jews had entry to the court, and niggers to the salons. That Paris will never rise again.'

Shirer arrived in Paris three days later to find the streets deserted and the shops closed. At night, the streets he remembered as being full of laughter and music were dark and empty. But there *were* sightseers. Every German soldier seemed to carry a camera, and they acted like naïve tourists. 'I saw them by the thousands today, photographing Notre-Dame, the Arc de Triomphe, the Invalides.'

The majority of French troops who had arrived in Britain as a result of Dynamo and Ariel, meanwhile, chose to return to France. One of those who stayed was Leon Wilson. Evacuated to Dover at the beginning of June, Wilson had been held at White City Stadium until he changed his name and joined the British Army. Stationed in Wiltshire, he was sent to a children's school where he sat by the door almost every day learning English. 'I didn't take long until I started talking,' he says, 'and after a while I could speak quite well.'

On a break from school, Wilson attended a dance at the Astoria on Tottenham Court Road. There were more women than men present, and he noticed 'one gorgeous young lady, very little, about five foot, but fantastic'. He asked her to dance, and at the end of the evening, walked her towards Hyde Park, where he tried to kiss her. This was how he met his wife.

In the meantime, he had begun training at various locations around England, and was sent to Egypt in 1943 as a lance bombardier. Months later, he was transferred to the Intelligence Corps, with whom he went to Italy. In August 1944, he arrived in his native city of Paris just two days after its liberation. He went straight to his old family home at 8 Rue des Bois, 19th Arrondissement. But Wilson's family was Jewish, and much had changed in the city since he had been there last:

I rang the bell. I walked into the concierge, and when she saw me, she fainted. She thought I was dead! And I was in a British uniform! After a couple of minutes, I said I

wanted to go up to see my parents, as I said I didn't
know what had happened to my family. And of course,
while I was talking, somebody probably heard me, and
they went up to the First Floor, and they alerted the
people who lived there now. I went up there and I saw a
plastic swastika on the right hand side. I knocked – the
lady was crying and three or four kids were crying.
People were shouting in the street, 'Why don't you arrest
them?'

The new occupants had been placed in the apartment by the
Nazis, but Wilson was not interested in them. He only wanted
to find his own family. For several days he searched, but
learned nothing. He went to the family's old factory on Rue
Belleville, to find it closed. In the end, he returned to the
apartment and gave the concierge his address in London.

After a long wait, news arrived that his father and one
brother had shown up in Paris. They had survived the camps
together. But his mother, his grandmother and his other three
brothers (the youngest of whom was only two years old) had
died in Buchenwald.

Two weeks after he heard the news, Wilson's father came
to London – without his brother. 'I'm glad he didn't come,'
says Wilson, 'because my father showed me a photo and he
was just a skeleton and nothing else.' His father told him that
the camp guards had separated the men and women, but he
said little more. 'I've never *ever* asked my brother what kind
of a life he experienced when he was deported,' says Wilson,
'because why restart it all over again?'

Since the end of the war, Leon Wilson has lived in England.
But in 1950, he returned to Dunkirk. He wanted to visit a
village outside the town where he and his comrades had

stopped on the retreat and stolen bicycles from a shop. His bicycle had helped to save his life, but he had long felt guilty for taking it.

After searching for a while, Wilson found the shop. It was still there. He stood outside for a while. 'But to be honest, I was a coward,' he says. 'I couldn't go in to say that I was sorry for pinching some of your bicycles. But I was very upset for seeing the place that really saved our lives.'

Leon Wilson's life has taken any number of turns since his evacuation from Dunkirk, but it remains the defining event of his life. The same is true for many of those evacuated and taken prisoner. But the importance of Dunkirk spreads beyond those who were there, or even those who can remember it. It is a cultural event, an icon, whose significance has changed over the last seventy-seven years as society has changed. And we are now approaching the point where Dunkirk turns from living memory into history. Soon there will be nobody left who can tell us what it was really like. The politicians, historians and journalists will be able to invoke the story completely freely, whether to confirm a prejudice, further a career, or present it truthfully for its own sake. And it is now that Chris Nolan has chosen to make a survival film, set during the evacuation. I wanted to speak to those involved in making it – to learn what they felt about Dunkirk the historical event, how they approached it as a subject, and how they went about turning it into a film.

Emma Thomas is Chris Nolan's producer as well as his wife. She has often brought ideas for movies to him in the past. 'Ninety-nine per cent of the time,' she says, 'he might be intrigued by it but he doesn't see a way into it for him as a director.' But this time was different. Emma had been reading about Dunkirk, and she said there hadn't been a recent film on the subject. 'He saw the void,' she says, 'which made me very happy.'

Dunkirk is a story that Chris grew up with, and once Emma had reminded him of the story, he began to read around the subject. He closed himself away, just as he had done with Batman, another iconic and beloved institution. 'Privately, in my own time, I find my feet in terms of the story that I think needs telling,' he says. He needs to distance himself from pressures and influences.

But the process of writing the Dunkirk script was an unusual one. 'I did a lot of historical research, I read many first-hand accounts, which I don't usually do, whether I'm dealing with real life or not.' This was because he wanted to understand the mechanics of the event. And then he started on *how* to tell the story. 'Once I felt that I had the mechanics of the event in my bones, then I could put the structure together.'

But he didn't pitch the idea to a studio immediately. He sat down and wrote the script first. And then he took a long walk. In Dunkirk.

Chris asked production designer Nathan Crowley to meet him there in August 2015. It seemed the obvious place to start, and nobody had any idea why they were there. Or, indeed, who they were. As Nathan says, 'If you put Chris in a baseball cap, no one knows who the hell he is.' But this walk would define the look and feel of the film. Nathan (who has worked with Chris on the *Dark Knight* films and *Interstellar*) has a wide-ranging job. 'Anything you see in front of camera, anything physical, the production design team is responsible for it. From location picking, to the way the ships look, or whether the hospital ships have outlooks to the beach, the planes, the mole, the destroyers, half-scale destroyers – we're responsible for everything. Except for costumes and special effects, we create the world that the film is based in.'

Nathan and Chris walked from the harbour to Bray Dunes, although they didn't make it to La Panne. 'We were a bit tired by then,' he says. But the walk was essential to their understanding of the film. They tried to study the mole to establish what it was made of. And they soon realised they *had* to film in Dunkirk. 'You can't fake this, it's unique,' Nathan says, 'the tide, the beach, the buildings in the town, the mole itself.'

But it wasn't just the atmosphere of the place that they were after. It was also the integrity. 'We just felt like we *should* shoot there, it was important.' And then they started wondering whether they could get real Mark I Spitfires, and any Little Ships that had really taken part. 'We felt there should be a sort of return. Get some of the original items, rebuild the mole in its original position. It was partly a search for accuracy – but it also seemed the right thing to do. For the movie and for the event.'

The further they walked the more they learned. 'Seeing that tide go in and out, the scale of it – you realise it's a really difficult beach to get off,' he says. And once they started building, the difficulties piled up. 'It was difficult to rebuild the mole, and we found it difficult to berth a ship at the rebuilt mole. And when we built our truck pier, that was really difficult too! You really start to understand the task, get a sense of what they had to deal with.'

Nathan is quick to stress that he and his team weren't under shell fire, there weren't any Stukas above them, and the enemy wasn't attacking the perimeter as they worked. 'We were just trying to moor boats on the mole. But we learned it's not simple. The mole wasn't built for that.'

This, in a sense, is what occurred to Captain William Tennant late on the night of 27 May 1940, and to many ships' crews in the days that followed. 'Recreating these real events gave everyone a taste of what the men went through at the time – and added to the sense of responsibility.'

The next stage for Chris and Nathan took them back home. 'I set up a mini-art department in his garage,' says Nathan. 'Just me and him. Chris wants to figure out how to make the film before anyone else comes on board.'

Eventually Chris and Emma put the idea to Warner Bros. 'We went to them with the script all ready,' says Emma, 'and we could say "This is how it's going to be" and they were very excited about that.' But Dunkirk is not only an event that's little known in America. It's a story of failure, of a military catastrophe. These were two elements likely to challenge any American film company. 'But I think that the universality of the story, how relatable the dilemmas are, means that everyone can understand that wherever they come from.

'It felt like the right time to do this,' Emma says, 'because we're in a fortunate position.' The fact is that Chris and Emma have made some hugely successful films, which places them in a strong position with the studio. 'They tend to give Chris the benefit of the doubt – at the moment!' says Emma. 'It was similar with *Inception*, a totally unconventional film that it would have been hard for anyone else to get made, but Chris was coming off an enormous success. We were in the same position with this, and they got what it was about the story that excited us.'

So now, with a studio behind them, Chris and Emma assembled their team. They went to Nilo Otero, first assistant director, a man they've worked with before, on *Inception* and *Interstellar* among other films. Nilo describes his role: 'I'm like number one on a ship. Chris, as captain, thinks about strategy and overall goals. I make the ship run. That's the best analogy. I used to have a second assistant director who quoted *In Which We Serve* a lot, and would say to me, "More cocoa, Number One?"'

Nilo describes his first task on a film. 'I get the script and I break it down into its components. For scene one, its description, what's needed for it and where it's going to take place.' He then works out a series of 'strips' (they used to be actual cardboard strips; now the process is computerised), each representing a scene or piece of action, and decides how many strips will be shot on each filming day.

With this breakdown, Nilo and Chris create a provisional schedule – how to get the story on film in the time available. 'We start horse trading,' he says. 'This day is too light, this one is too heavy, and in the process of going through the components as, essentially, individual manufacturing elements, we pound out a schedule.' And they factor in geography. 'Where are we going to do this? Where exactly on the beach at Dunkirk? What's going to be shot in the UK, what's to be shot on stage in the US, what's going to be on the sea?' This was a daunting project for Nilo, who has a passion for history and particularly for the Second World War: 'I've been on the English Channel and it's a difficult stretch of water. The first miracle of Dunkirk for me is the weather. What made it possible at all was the fact that it was this ridiculous clock-face calm sea – like the Channel *never* is. It was reasonable for Hitler to believe this evacuation could never succeed, because who would expect you could float across the Channel in a row boat?'

The team now grew to include, amongst others, set decorator Gary Fettis, costume designer Jeffrey Kurland, special effects coordinator Scott Fisher and props master Drew Petrotta. Each has a specific responsibility, but they work closely together and their roles interconnect. Gary Fettis explains that his team 'provides all the details – the props and the dressing that define the characters and support the storyline'. There is typically minute attention to detail on a Nolan film; on *Interstellar*, for example, the young girl was living in a bedroom that had a wall of books, and Gary, Emma and Chris chose every single book on the shelves. But for *Dunkirk*, the process was a little more organic. 'The emphasis was on the sweeping panoramic canvas of Dunkirk itself – the beach, the industrial areas, the mole.' Gary's primary rule is that nothing should distract. Rather, every detail should serve the story, the director's vision, the actors' imaginations. Gary says that Chris didn't want to push the destruction and carnage of war to a level that would overwhelm. 'His mandate was to keep it simple and lean. So the challenge for me was how to make a statement in those vast spaces where any military hardware could be easily dwarfed.'

Jeffrey Kurland and Drew Petrotta, costume and props respectively, work closely together, as what they both do is personal to the film's characters – how they dress and what they own, handle or use. Drew describes his job: 'If you have a table in a room and characters are eating dinner, we wouldn't do the table, but we might do the dishes and the food.' In a historical setting such as Dunkirk, he must stay as close to what he discovers in his research as possible. 'And in a military movie like this,' he says, 'it's pretty much laid out what the guys had. We just had to think about quantities and that depended on how many people, and how much money, we were going to have.'

While Jeffrey had to organise the making of hundreds of costumes, even to the extent of building looms to weave accurate period fabric for the uniforms, so far as Drew's department was concerned 'there was not a lot of manufacturing to be done, other than some rubber guns and life jackets.' Drew found real life jackets from the period, in different styles, and showed them to Chris who picked his favourite. 'Then we recreated them as new.'

For Jeffrey's department, using original costumes was out of the question. 'With the wear the uniforms had to take, in and out of the water, blasted with sand, they would have fallen apart. It would have been totally impractical.' Drew, however, could use original items. 'We had some great binoculars that we used for a colonel on the mole – actual World War Two binoculars. We had some actual navigation tools too. And some of the rifles were real, from the period.' His department also recreated the leaflets used in the opening moments of the film. 'We showed some copies of the original leaflets to Nathan and Chris. Then they designed their own version – close to the real one, but with some things, like colours, augmented to help them tell a story on film.' He laughs. 'And then we made five thousand of them.'

Jeffrey and Drew also work closely with Scott Fisher on special effects. Scott is responsible for all the physical effects except those created in post-production through computer graphics. As technology advances, so Scott's department evolves – but not in its dealings with Chris.

'Chris wants to get as much stuff in camera as he can and then use CGI to fix the few things that you don't get,' says Scott. 'For him, everything is traditional.' Which means that

Scott takes a different approach on a Nolan movie. 'I'll read a script of his very differently than I will for another director. With other directors, you can kind of assume that things will get done with CGI, but you can never make that assumption with Chris.' It means that Scott has to combine traditional methods with new. 'The basic stuff is tried and true. Then I use whatever technology I can to achieve what we're trying to get.' Recreating bomb explosions, for example, is very traditional and something that Scott has a lot of experience with.

Scott thinks CGI can change how a film feels to an audience. 'It can be so heavy when it's used in whole sequences,' he says. 'Everyone knows those movies – a computer-generated world has a very distinctive look. CGI's a fantastic tool to go back and remove the wires from the stunt guy when he's getting pulled out of an explosion, or if we're missing a boat that should be there. But we have all these real assets in the shot – full-size ships, the mole, all the extras – that if we just add stuff in the back of the frame, it's much less noticeable. It's just cleaning up.'

One of the big advantages with shooting for real is the genuine impact the event can have on an actor's performance. 'Something happens to the reactions,' Scott says. 'With *Interstellar*, Chris wanted the robot right there on set delivering lines and interacting with the actor, otherwise that actor would be staring at a green screen, faking an eye line and pretending to interact.' This is even more true, he thinks, when filming the impact of a bullet, or an explosion. The effects may be stage managed and completely safe, but the reactions are visceral. 'I've been on shows where things were meant to be done with CGI, and we'll stage something simple like a little air mortar, just for a reaction, and you'll see a light go on in a director. They're like "Whoa! That reaction was real!" So you start doing more and more of it.'

Scott also believes that CGI has a sensory and emotional effect on an audience – it can allow them to step back from the film. 'People's eyes are trained to it now. It can take you out of the moment because you know it's not reality based. It changes it in your mind, I think.' But for Chris and Nathan, the audience has to have an authentic experience, a first-person perspective. It has to be a soldier under fire on the beach, or a Spitfire pilot flying against the Luftwaffe – so anything that allows it to step back is unwelcome. Chris wants the film to have a documentary feel. As Nathan says, 'We want to make it about being with them.'

The script features three storylines through four elements – land, sea, air and, crucially, time. In many ways, time is the most fundamental. There is a ticking clock running through the whole story which poses relentless questions. Will the men make it away? Will the ships survive? Will the planes run out of fuel? Chris and Nathan worked together on finding defining images for these four elements. Nathan started by making a model of the mole. 'We realised that it's a road to nowhere,' he says. He first thought the defining image would be men sitting around on the seafront, but with more research and as their ideas developed, that changed. 'There's nothing new to that image, the public knows it already. It's not interesting enough. So we were happy to open the film with it and then leave it behind. That was an early decision.'

The film starts with Tommy making his way through the perimeter towards the beach. 'We defined the town of Dunkirk with the chase through the old, mysterious streets, the low buildings. Then you break onto the seafront, you understand the size of it – and you've done it.' The key image for the land element was 'the white mole with troops, three men wide, endless helmets as far as you can see, going to nothing, just out into the sea – that's the desperation of the event. No boats. Just men on the mole. It says "This is the end of the road." You've been chased to the water and there's one bridge. But it won't get you to England.'

For the sea, the defining image was of a soldier sitting on the hull of an upturned boat, stranded in the English Channel. The boat is derelict, its broken propeller rocked by the wake of the sea. It's been bombed, too far from the beach to get back, too far from home to swim. For Nathan, this caught 'the circular motion of the film, the never-ending Groundhog Day for those soldiers who got off the beach but their ship was sunk, and they had to keep coming back. And here's this broken soldier sitting on a wreck in the middle of the sea. He's exhausted, he's giving up, nothing can save him. The man sitting between a big sky and a big sea.'

This image inspired another decision: 'It helped us choose IMAX, because it's such a good format to cover the sky.' The Little Ships also define the sea element. The film features one in particular, *Moonstone*, a boat found on Loch Ness. 'We're with this small ship for an entire day of the film's timeline,' says Nathan. 'It's a well-known image but it's absolutely key – that's the really human part of the story, the *Moonstone*.'

For Emma, this is what makes the story so relatable. 'Any film that is going to appeal to a modern audience has to be a story about humanity,' she says. 'You can watch any number of war films and feel distanced from them because you can think "I'm not in the army. I haven't done military service and never will", but what differentiates the Dunkirk story is it's also the story of civilians. It's the story of everyday heroism. That's why it's appealing as a film – soldiers waiting to be rescued and the people on the Little Ships coming across to save them.' For Chris, civilians willingly going into a war zone is what makes Dunkirk 'one of the great stories of all time'.

The Spitfire, meanwhile, unites two elements – air and time. Cameras were placed inside the cockpit to capture both a view of the pilot at work and the pilot's view of the outside world. 'It was about being with the pilot,' says Nathan. 'Rather than always seeing these planes from the outside, we wanted the audience to really experience this piece of machinery. The task was to get cameras on a real plane, which we did, and on the wings, and actually shoot banking over Dunkirk. When you bank over, you see the scale of the event from the plane's point of view, rather than a "God shot". It was always about being with them.'

Chris and Nathan flew in a Spitfire themselves, and this informed the film for them. 'The fuel will only allow you to fly for a short time over Dunkirk, and there are so many other considerations – apart from being attacked by the Luftwaffe – there are so many other things you have to control to make sure you can get there and get back.' Nathan thinks the challenges for a Spitfire pilot were similar to those of the men on the mole or the Little Ships: 'It's time running out, chances running out. People don't realise how many planes were lost trying to protect that beach.'

As he did his research, Nathan was also struck by the industrial nature of the area. 'It's not a quaint seaside town, it's a big industrial port. No one's portrayed how industrial it is before. We wanted that in our story, the unromantic modernity of it.' He says the original mole, built only two years before the event, was an extremely modern structure.

'This was not about people in deckchairs, it was about this huge industrial area – and a lot of it on fire.' They chose an area where the oil spills were burning for the Spitfire's landing. 'I was very pleased to get that brutalism into our film,' he says.

Recreating the black smoke that hung over Dunkirk, and guided the RAF from the English coast, was Scott Fisher's task. He did it by burning diesel, but the city of Dunkirk imposed restrictions. 'Our permit to create that smoke,' he says, 'was based on which direction the wind was blowing because it was so thick. It wasn't toxic, it was just so dense there were concerns for motorists on nearby roads.' But the wind is an unreliable cast member. 'There was a local factory and the whole building started filling up with smoke. They couldn't work. And another time the smoke went into the town. So there were a few incidents where it was a problem.' Scott and his team just had to keep working round it, 'positioning the diesel in different areas until we got the desired effect'. The diesel was passed through a high-pressure pump and lit in a containment reservoir. 'There were some days when the wind was blowing in a really bad direction and we just couldn't do it.'

Nathan remembers that one day, foam suddenly appeared on the beach. 'It was like *Doctor Zhivago* or something, these guys walking through this foam.' Utilising such unforeseen moments was all part of making the film. 'To us, this was how we wanted to tell the Dunkirk stories. The event itself was all about improvisation, organised chaos. There were so many different things happening, so many individual events, there are as many versions of Dunkirk as there were men on the beach. And there were the small ships, the mole, the destroyers, the minesweepers, the planes, Dutch trawlers, thousands of men – it was such an event! The film is all about being thrown into this event visually, not sitting outside it. Chris has these concepts in his mind, then I come in and just help him visualise the whole thing – that's my job in the first six months.'

There is one last crucial element of the film that is both ever-present and permanently absent – the enemy. Chris understood that there was no personal contact between the soldiers on the beach and the enemy, and he wanted to reflect this in the film. 'That is the way war is experienced,' says Nilo Otero. 'When you talk to old soldiers – they didn't see the enemy. For one thing, when somebody's shooting at you, you don't stick your head up and look! You get in a hole and you stay there. It's a frightening experience. I think that revelation of mortality is really what the picture's about. That, and the simple effort to avoid dying.'

For Chris, making the threat faceless frees the event from its geopolitical ramifications – it becomes a timeless story of human survival. He didn't want to take a classic war film approach because in so many ways, the story of Dunkirk is not the story of a conventional battle. 'It was death appearing from the sky,' he says. 'U-boats under the Channel that you can't see. The enemy flying over and rising up through the waves to pick people off, to sink ships.' The soldiers cannot understand their own predicament, and the audience experiences the same horror. This is why the action never leaves the beach. 'If you're continually showing the Germans as Germans and generals in rooms talking about strategy, you are lifting the veil.' The audience would then be more informed than the soldiers. 'Standing on a beach, trying to interpret what's going on, "How do I get out of here? Should I stand in these lines? Should I go into the water?" That's the experiential reality I want the audience to share. You see herd behaviour, primal, animal behaviour – people standing in lines in the water because they see other people doing it, not because they know there is a boat coming. I think that is fascinating and frightening.'

Emma agrees. 'The enemy is scarier when you're not seeing them. You don't *need* to see them. It's such a simple notion, what these people were going through – tanks and soldiers over there, planes above, submarines and mines below – that's all you need to know really. When you think about *Jaws*, you don't need to see the shark to understand the threat of it.'

Rebuilding the mole was one of the first tasks for the production department. Despite research and studying photographs, Nathan felt he hadn't understood the mole until he got to Dunkirk and saw what is now left of it. 'The concrete part is still there,' he says, 'and we rebuilt about a thousand feet onto the end of it.' Emma remembers how difficult the process was. 'The work on the mole was massive and time-consuming. It involved all sorts of work, dredging around the mole, rebuilding. We were incredibly lucky in that the city of Dunkirk were very helpful. They're very film friendly, it made all the difference.'

Even the process of rebuilding the mole was influenced by how Chris wanted the audience to feel. 'What had been there in the first place was a mixture of wood and free-cast concrete – those big Xs that you see on all the photos,' says Nathan. 'We had so much trouble finding out what it was originally made of. If you took a boat out to the end of the pier, you see that it's concrete, but people also talked about wood. We decided to build the part we added on out of wood for two reasons: we needed to get it up in a decent amount of time but it was also a cinematic decision. We could have faked concrete using wood but decided not to. Chris and I both thought we didn't want the audience wondering what we'd done, "What is that made of?" So we decided to play it as wood.'

In the end, they didn't want to draw the audience's attention away, to remind them they are in a cinema. So the trademark crosses were made out of enormous twelve-by-twelve timbers, harvested from a local forest. Each beam was milled and pre-cut and had to be put up with steel plate. 'It was the biggest challenge of the entire film,' Nathan says, 'because we were dealing with the tide. There is a three- to four-hour window to put your base plates in and then to crane the structure in place. We built it in sections on the side of the dock, and using a crane barge placed each section. But with only four hours to actually bolt it down, to get it secure from the sea before that tide came in – that was hard.'

During filming, a storm damaged the rebuilt mole and ripped off the wooden walkway on top. 'The sea is hard out there,' Nathan says, 'which we found out. It was a huge worry. Our Warner Brothers engineer said, "This is an incredible structure, stronger than most permanent piers I've stood on." But because it was an open structure, the waves crashed in underneath and punched the boards off.' Extra boards had been set aside in case of emergency. 'It was all fixable,' Nathan says, 'but it was about getting out there in safe weather and putting them back so we could carry on filming.'

Chris and his crew did not have the miraculous good weather of the evacuation – but they were pleased artistically if not historically. 'Rough weather looks much better on film,' says Nathan. 'Having sun on film is no good even though it was more historically true.' And the bad weather made it a very difficult beach to work on. 'We tried hard and we had lots of problems – the mole, the truck pier. And it's not easy to land a priceless Spitfire on that beach.'

The Spitfire landing on the beach is a crucial moment in the film. Dan Friedkin, a Spitfire owner who flies his own aircraft, was prepared to attempt it and the area was walked many times in order to find the right place to land. The RAF pilots in 1940 discovered that Dunkirk beach made a surprisingly decent landing strip. 'That tide washes the beach pretty flat, and it's hard-packed sand, so it's pretty good,' says Nathan. 'The chosen area was cordoned off and the pilot did many "touch and go" practice runs, all of which we filmed.'

Nathan vividly remembers the moment of landing: 'To see a Spitfire Mark 1 land on Dunkirk beach – incredible.' But after landing, the aircraft stuck in the soft sand. The tide was coming in, and everyone had to run and help push it out. Suddenly, the Spitfire's safety became everybody's concern.

Two major issues were crowding in at once – the relentless twenty-foot tide, and sunset. And this was significant because the pilots had to get back to their airfields before dark. Nathan was at a distance when this happened. 'I just saw this commotion, people running to the Spitfire. You can push a Spitfire around, you can lift it out with enough people. So a lot of people went down and got it out. It took off and got home before sunset. But I'll never forget seeing a real Spitfire land on Dunkirk beach.'

As far as the Spitfire's German counterpart, the Messerschmitt Bf 109, was concerned, Nathan made an artistic decision. 'I really needed to use the yellow nose of the Messerschmitt,' he says, 'even though it's historically inaccurate. They didn't have them until August 1940, and Dunkirk

happened in May and June.'* But it was a visual consideration. 'We have to be able to identify them quickly, because if
we're with the pilot and these things are moving so fast, we
have to understand who's who. The obvious thing to do was
stick a big yellow nose on the enemy. And also, it looked
much better.' They decided not to specify the Spitfire squadron. Nathan found genuine squadron numbers that hadn't
been used. 'The numbers on the Spitfire were real. When the
war was done, they had spare squadron numbers at the
Ministry that hadn't been used yet. So we had real numbers.'

After rebuilding the mole the next great challenge for
Nathan was recreating the truck pier. 'There's no account of
how to actually build one,' he says. 'We tied the trucks
together, real, solid truck bases – there were logistical
concerns even about that. We had to take the oil out because
the city didn't want any chemicals in the water. But when we
towed them into the sea and the tide came in, we realised,
"Oh shit, they're floating!" The first tide that came in, two of
them floated off!' Nathan and his team had to think fast. 'We
got our knives out and stabbed all the tyres before the whole
lot went. So it was an enormous learning curve.' This was
pretty much the same learning curve undergone by the Royal
Engineers on 30 May 1940. They too had to deflate the tyres
– although, back then, the city was in no fit state to issue
restrictions on oil pollution. 'You appreciate it's not easy
building a truck pier,' says Nathan, 'there are so many unforeseen details and it's got to be long enough to reach the tide,
which is enormous.'

---

* The film's historical advisor (also the author of this book) remembers
phoning associate producer Andy Thompson to ask why the
Messerschmitts had yellow noses. Now he knows.

Nathan was very keen to get hold of HMS *Cavalier*, a 1943 destroyer, now in dock at Chatham Dockyard. Although not at Dunkirk, she was similar to ships that were, but she couldn't be brought out of dry dock. The team did get other original ships but they had to disguise any later developments. They also made half-scale destroyers. 'We have ships that get sunk in the film,' says Nathan, 'and we wanted to make sure they had accurate markings. I felt that I needed to make every number you see on a ship, to recreate a ship that was actually there.'

He was also very keen to use original Little Ships if possible – and any paddle steamers that could be found. 'Our first day walking the beach,' he remembers, 'we saw the remains of *Crested Eagle* out there. Then you go to the end of the mole and at very, very low tide, you see the remains of *Fenella*. It was very important to get a Thames paddle steamer because it's such an oddity to see one moor up. It didn't have its engines but they towed the *Princess Elizabeth* out for us.'

Gary Fettis remembers how much work had to be done on the boats to make them historically accurate. 'There was always so much to do,' he says. 'Even for the smaller craft. And then there were the hospital ships, all the Red Cross supplies. We did a lot of re-rigging with rope ladders.' The amount of work needed led to some interesting collaborations. 'The big fenders on the ships, they use giant rubber balls nowadays, but back then they were made out of rope, woven in thick hemp. We had to make about ten of them.' They found a Dunkirk man who had re-rigged a ship for a local museum. 'He knew how to weave these bumpers. And he employed prison labour to make them. First-time offenders, kids, they weren't hard-core criminals. I hope the producers know,' Gary adds, 'because we saved a lot of money that way.'

Gary also needed a team on the beach, known as 'set dressers'. 'I have to be ahead getting the next set ready,' he says, 'so I can't stand around where they're shooting or I won't get tomorrow's work done. So we wanted set dressers, but not having the budget, we found this local hockey team. It was in between their seasons, and they were great – nice, intelligent guys, we gave them direction and they were unbelievable.' Later on in the shoot, when Gary and his assistant, Brett Smith, were driving through Dunkirk they saw a poster featuring the hockey team. 'They were like local movie stars! We had no idea. But they took direction so well, and they said it was an experience they'll never forget.'

One of the biggest sets for Gary to dress was the interior of a destroyer. This set was built on stage in Los Angeles, in a huge water tank. His assistants sourced components for the interior from the largest ship-wrecking yard in the United States. 'It's in Texas,' says Gary. 'They brought back all these parts, doors and valves, bunks. And it's only a page and a half of script, but it's a key scene.' Then he had to dress the interior of a trawler with fishing gear. 'But with the exteriors, on a war movie, there were a lot of sand bags, and artillery, ammunition crates, trucks and parts.'

Gary had also to recreate the human carnage. 'We used a lot of dummies for long shots. Chris would lay actors and extras closer to camera.' Gary confounded Chris at one point; he had dressed the beach for the first reveal, near Malo-les-Bains, as Tommy first arrives. 'We had dressed forty trucks and ammunition crates from the point of view of the camera in the dunes. To stretch it out, we used a forced perspective. We had a walkie-talkie so we could tell the person on the beach, "Move this, move that" until we got it just right. When Chris pulled up in his car, he walked straight to me, like a man on a mission. He looked at the beach and what we had dressed and he said, "When I was driving down the beach just now, I saw this stuff spread out and it meant nothing. I couldn't understand what I was seeing. It looked sporadic. But now I understand – you made it work for the camera."' Gary says this is how you compose a frame. 'You take a position, and you start stacking things and spreading them out. You can cheat with things fifty feet apart, but from the camera's angle they look like they are closer. It makes your eye feel there's more there. We did that several times in different areas to get the bang for the buck.'

Scott was responsible for organising the sinking of ships, explosions and shootings. He used more high-yield explosives on this movie than normal. 'All those World War Two explosions have such a distinctive look, you need a lot of explosive to replicate that. We used those more in the distance and as we got nearer to the actors, we used air mortars so we could be right on them and still be safe.' Air mortars are tanks of air connected to high-pressure air guns that blow the surface of sand or water. 'It's very repeatable,' says Scott, and being able to reset an effect is a crucial part of his work. 'It's safe so you can have a stunt man or actor in close proximity, we can test it and work in a little closer, and there's no worry of anything dangerous hitting anyone.'

The men being blown through the air work with Tom Struthers, in charge of stunts. 'Tom has a crane with a wire rig. He can ratchet the stunt man away incredibly fast, as if it's the power of the explosion. But it's his rig doing all the work and he's in charge of them.' Back in the States, on set, there were 'dump tanks' filled with water to film both the sinking of interior holds and the exterior portion of a ship that could roll over by about ninety degrees and sink to twenty-five feet.

Scott had to create the effect of bullets striking the sides of boats. This was a challenge, as Chris wanted bullets to blast through the trawler's sides and water to enter through the holes while sunlight came through above the water's surface. It was a complex effect. Scott's team drilled holes in the side of the boat and filled them with disguised squibs that could be blown out on cue. Behind the wall, they built a clear tank that they filled with water, and behind that they carefully positioned lights.

Squibs are also used to create the effect of a man being shot. 'They are really tiny,' says Scott, 'just for the movie industry. You always want to have as much continuous action as you can, so we link the squibs to remote control devices. At the start of the movie, there are guys running down the street, they get shot, they go down, they continue on, climb over a wall, then bullets hit the wall.' The squib is shielded from the actor's skin and packed with fake blood or red dust, and it has enough power to blow through the material of their shirt. 'You can trigger it remotely, fifty, sixty feet away if you want, so you can be behind camera when the thing goes off – or two or three – however many you want on a person.'

Dealing with the actors and extras were Nilo and his team of assistant directors. 'You're painting with people,' he says. 'Chris is loath to use CGI, so there's a lot of art involved on set, a lot of fooling the eye.' On the biggest crowd days, there were 1,380 extras. 'And they are all human beings,' Nilo says, 'they wander off.' He remembers saying, in a production meeting with other department heads, 'You may think we're

doing Dunkirk but to me this is two hundred pairs of pants!'
'What I meant was, with our budget we had two hundred
pairs of correct British Expeditionary Force pants. In order
to be close up, in other words to see people, we could use two
hundred guys at any given time. We have to pay a man to
attend a costume fitting for this uniform, and they only had
enough money to do two fittings each. So this is a movie
about vast numbers of people and we have two hundred
pairs of pants, two fittings each – you're going to have the
same four hundred guys in front of the camera all the time
– you're going to see the same faces too often! I just kept
repeating this, in one context or another, "This is two
hundred pairs of pants, guys. That's the movie we're
making."'

Nathan Crowley and his production team created 'fake
men', a row of soldiers painted onto canvas that could be
rolled out and pinned in position with stakes in the ground,
to fill the frame. 'If you have a living, moving person at either
end,' says Nilo, 'in the middle and in front or behind it – that
changes everything visually. Because it's all about fooling the
eye. It's all about how people perceive things.' Nilo remembers how the beach 'ate' men. 'It was daunting. The scale just
swallowed them. And when you look at the pictures of the
real event, the sheer density of people, especially on the boats,
we just couldn't do that safely. Even if we'd had the people,
we couldn't do it safely.' This made him think about the realities of war. 'You can't do what people do in war. You can't
fly aeroplanes the way they flew them, you can't operate
ships the way they operated them. You can't have men fling-
ing themselves to the ground the way they did, because it's
dangerous. It turns out war is a very dangerous thing! And
the only reason people do these incredibly dangerous and

risky things, is because the alternative is being killed.' Certain things, in other words, can never be entirely recreated.

The size of the beach created practical, as well as artistic, difficulties. 'The scale is hard to register on film,' says Chris. 'Walking to scout the various locations, you can walk seven or eight miles just to get to the next location along.' This had to be made clear to the team of assistant directors responsible for ensuring that the cast and supporting artists were where they needed to be in good time. 'I had to explain to the assistant directors that the fact you could see the mole from every point along the beach didn't really make the beach one location. To go from where we were shooting one scene to the base of the mole, for example, was what we call a "company move". Everybody had to be put in vehicles, driven up onto the roads and into the town to come back out. So the simple geography of a beach setting is paradoxical, because it feels like everything is close and should be in one place, but it's not.' This made Chris focus on the 1940 Dunkirk experience: 'Entire little communities, temporary villages of people on the beach appearing and forming during the evacuation. Then people just disappearing, individuals disappearing.'

Chris has described the characters in this film as 'present tense', since they do not have pasts and back stories, and this meant that fine character differentiation was something for Jeffrey Kurland to work up in his costume design. 'It is my job to give a director as much detail and reality as possible,' he says, 'then he can do with it as he feels best.'

Jeffrey started by researching the uniforms for historical accuracy. Then he thought about the characters as individuals – who these boys were, their ages, their experience. 'I tried to humanise them,' he says. But, of course, by the time they had made it to the beach, a lot of the soldiers had been retreating for a fortnight. Their uniforms were dishevelled, kit had been discarded, weapons lost. This gave Jeffrey room for character. 'There's an ease to the character of Tommy, reflected in the way he wears his uniform. And that's different to the way that Alex wears his – he's more of a "tough", for want of a better word.' And then there's a character who wears an ill-fitting uniform. This is not accidental. It is part of the story-telling – and the essence of Jeffrey's job.

Casting the film, meanwhile, was an unusual process because it required unknowns for the younger characters. 'Our casting directors, John Papsidera and Toby Whale, put actors' auditions on tape, and we looked at that material,' says Emma. 'Then Chris met in person with some of the actors he liked.' Emma found putting together the ensemble for this film to be one of her most interesting casting experiences. She has a degree in history, the subject has always fascinated her, and she felt as though 'we were bringing history to life with this film, with its rich tapestry of characters and faces.' But meeting these young actors brought home to her one of the realities of Dunkirk. 'It was shocking to me how young everybody was. When we met Fionn Whitehead, he's wise beyond his years and incredibly mature, but he's very young, he's only four years older than my oldest child, and it really made it clear to me how young some of these people were, caught up in these terrifying events.'

As well as the newcomers, there are some very experienced actors in the cast – Kenneth Branagh and Mark Rylance, to name two. There's a sense that these men play the reliable old warriors, while the newcomers play the untested young kids of the BEF. Emma acknowledges the parallel. However, although one actor in the film may be making his movie debut, he is currently one of the most famous young men on the planet: Harry Styles. Was it a risk to cast someone so well known, and yet such an unknown quantity? 'It didn't feel risky at all,' says Emma, 'because he auditioned the same way everyone else did. Over the course of days of coming back to audition, giving it his best, Harry was absolutely right for the part, and it didn't feel any more a risk casting him than it did casting anyone else.' Emma appreciates that his fame might get in the way for some: 'there's always the risk that people can't get past the persona, but the truth is he's a great actor. I think when you watch him in the movie he utterly sucks you in. He's not Harry Styles any more, in the same way that Fionn isn't Fionn Whitehead any more – he's Tommy.'

For Nilo Otero, the chance to work on a film set during Operation Dynamo was the chance to indulge his interest in this period of history. Or as Chris put it in his thank-you note: 'At last you got a chance to put some of your arcane knowledge to good use.' Nilo says, 'I've been a distant student of war my whole life somehow.' When he first did a breakdown of Chris's script, it was brought across the US and hand-delivered by Andy Thompson. The script was codenamed 'Bodega Bay', as Chris is very protective of his scripts.

'I'm from San Francisco,' says Nilo, 'so I just ran with that. And it became the Germans invading northern California. If I'd been captured with my schedule and interrogated, that's what it would have looked like.'

Nilo scheduled twenty-five days of filming on the beach. They finished in twenty-three. 'I've done a lot of military movies,' he says, 'and you often have serving officers acting as advisors, and for the first couple of days they laugh at you. But after four or five days, they sidle over to me and say, "This is a lot like what we do."' Nilo is aware of the crucial difference between war and war films, but he points out the similarities. 'You have a working unit of people who go out and perform a very specific job, in varying circumstances and environments. This unit must be flexible enough to adapt but be specific to what you're doing that particular day.' The shooting days on the beach were eleven hours long, with everyone exposed to the weather. They had to wear goggles to protect their eyes from the sand. 'There aren't many jobs now where you are absolutely at the mercy of the elements,' he says, 'and with two tides a day, that beach appears and disappears. I was astonished because the photos show vast numbers of men on the beach – well, let me tell you, that beach disappears! And all those guys had to keep moving back and forth.'

Nilo is probably, in the last seventy-five years, the man who has come closest to understanding how to organise an evacuation from Dunkirk; he has dealt with large numbers of people, the tides, the weather, limited resources, the challenge of bringing ships into the mole and onto the beaches, the truck piers – the list goes on. He was in no danger of dying, but he was under pressure to work within a time frame, effectively and safely. And while he would be far too modest to mention the names Tennant, Ramsay or Wake-Walker, his job was not entirely disimilar to theirs. In effect, he's trying to coordinate thousands of people. 'I am a field guy,' he says, 'and I depend on good staff work. Which is what the production manager and line producers do. I schedule the things in micro time, as it were. It's that minute-to-minute working your way through the day, that's what I do. And in the process of that, I run a film set.'

Nilo is interesting when he discusses the meritocracy that formed at Dunkirk as units were broken up and men had to manage their own survival. It is reflected, he believes, in the microcosm of a film set, which also has its own natural order. His authority on set is granted to him for the same reasons soldiers follow leaders. 'You obey your officer because he's the guy who's going to save you. You don't obey him because you're afraid of him. At Dunkirk, the environment was one of total chaos and everything was unknown – who knows if enough ships are going to come? It's absolute uncertainty and therefore acting with an interest in the future is very difficult to do. I've worked with directors who come to me the first week and say, "Should we fire somebody just to show that we're serious here?" People do that! And it's foolish! You don't flog your way to a good ship. You lead by example.'

Nilo believes that in real combat, when everybody has a gun, the army becomes fiercely democratic. 'Anyone who thinks he can put people's lives at risk because of the insignia on his hat – that guy's going to get shot in the back of the head.' When he thinks about how the evacuation was conducted, he is in awe of the BEF and the Royal Navy. 'I'm so impressed it didn't turn into horrible chaos. It's an example of discipline, but not the discipline of the army in peacetime. It's the discipline of circumstance.

'Chris commands a film like no director I've ever worked with,' Nilo says. 'He's the best, he really is. He knows his material inside and out, he has a very clear idea of what he wants.' Even though their relationship is that of captain and number one, Nilo offers suggestions to Chris if he thinks they're useful. 'A lot of assistant directors are really just assistant producers, they worry about a schedule and a budget. I pride myself on actually being an assistant *director*. I've been at this a while and I know the job of directing is a lonely one because only the director is worrying about the story. Chris and I trust each other, and he understands that you can't micro-manage making a film. Eventually you're going to be standing there with some actors and a cameraman and it's going to be a collective process.' He acknowledges that ultimately, it's Chris's vision that everyone is there to serve. 'But if you want things to be exactly the way you want them,' he says, 'go paint. Chris has as certain and focused a cinematic vision as anybody I've ever worked with and at the same time, he can experience what is going on in the moment and adapt that to what he originally desired, in a way that's just a joy. It's wonderful to be able to contribute occasionally. And he is open to it. Or he'll just say, "No, never mind that."'

Gary Fettis says, 'Chris just loves movie-making. He's in love with movies. And this movie wasn't easy and there were times when he thought he had a particular series of boats and then all of a sudden found out, "Well, I can't have those two, because the harbour isn't dressed", or whatever it was. And he looks like this kid that's just sad for a moment. Five minutes later, he's re-directing, saying "How do we solve this, how do we ..." He's moving forward. And you have to jump, you have to be on your game to keep up with him.'

Even though this is a multi-million-dollar film, as Emma notes, 'There is never enough money. We actually made this film for a lot less than people will realise when they see it.' When Chris and Emma pitched the script to the studio, they simultaneously asked for the amount of money they needed – and it was significantly less than their previous films. 'We thought the studio would go for that. But it meant we definitely had to be imaginative. It's a vast story and scope, and we had to do an awful lot for the money we had and we had to be clever about how we scheduled things and shot things. We had to be incredibly efficient.' Emma believes having such an accomplished and resourceful team made a huge difference, but also that financial limitations can be creative. 'Setting yourself a challenge like that, in some ways, it frees you to come up with interesting ideas that you wouldn't have if you could just write a cheque.'

The very first films Emma and Chris made together with a pittance of their own money may seem very different from these movies made for many millions of dollars, 'but ultimately it's all the same. On those very small films, we had no money and never enough money. But honestly, you never do, because you're always trying to push the limits of what you're able to do within the parameters that you have. And so the experience of making all of those films is remarkably similar.'

One of the things that struck Nilo Otero as he worked on the film was how semi-religious Dunkirk was as an experience for the British people. 'It was the first time anything went right in this fucking war,' he says. 'It literally was a miracle. An actual miracle. And I think the British people took it as a sign that this can go right.' He thinks that an American audience will spot this ('How can they miss it?' he says) but believes it's compelling drama either way. 'War brings out the best and worst in men. If you're going to make a movie, you have to make two hours worth watching – nobody wants to watch two hours of people eating dinner, unless it's a really great meal. You need to make those two hours an incandescent two hours of human experience. And war certainly fits that bill.'

He thinks the fact that Chris has not chosen to give a history lesson and has told the Dunkirk story as a survival movie, adds to its impact. 'When you're in the middle of what turns out to be history, you don't know it's history. It's not history for you. It's another day for you, it might be a more dangerous day than usual, but it's a day. And then you hear Winston Churchill talking about you and your life. Turns out that you were present at the beginning of something.'

Chris hopes that by distilling history into a personal experience for the audience, the film will become something of a Rorschach test. He does not want political interpretations to be forced on the audience. That is not something that interests him. As Dunkirk moves beyond living memory, and veterans become fewer, he wants to make a universal film that places us in the shoes of the protagonists. That way, he says, 'people will find the Dunkirk that they want to find.'

Illustration Credits

Alex, Gibson and Tommy on the beach in a scene from the film. (© *Warner Bros. Entertainment Inc.*)

The film's three Spitfires in formation. (© *Warner Bros. Entertainment Inc.*)

British destroyers sailing home to England with an RAF escort. (© *Popperfoto/Getty Images*)

In the film, a Spitfire is chased by a Messerschmitt 109 as they pass a representation of HMS *Keith*. (© *Warner Bros. Entertainment Inc.*)

Troops in long hopeful queues waiting for little ships to carry them to larger ships offshore. (© *Hulton Deutsch/Corbis Historical via Getty Images*)

A scene from the film: troops queuing for the little ships as casualties are taken away. (© *Warner Bros. Entertainment Inc.*)

Director Christopher Nolan with Fionn Whitehead, playing Tommy. (© *Warner Bros. Entertainment Inc.*)

Allied troops hoping for deliverance. (© *Ullstein Bild/Getty Images*)

The mole, intended as a breakwater to prevent sand blocking the harbour, was substantially rebuilt for the film. (© *Warner Bros. Entertainment Inc.*)

Troops walking along the mole. (© *Popperfoto/Getty Images*)

A photograph taken by Sub-Lieutenant John Crosby on board Clyde paddle steamer *Oriole*. (© *Time Life Pictures/The LIFE Picture Collection via Getty Images*)

A lorry pier as recreated by production designer Nathan Crowley and his team. (© *Warner Bros. Entertainment Inc.*)

Some of the Little Ships, each weighed down with evacuated soldiers. (© *Hulton Archive/Stringer via Getty Images*)

In the film, the soldiers load up on one of the actual surviving Little Ships. (© *Warner Bros. Entertainment Inc.*)

The mole as it looks today at low tide. Only a few of the original crisscross piles are still visible. (© *Joshua Levine*)

Captain William Tennant, later Admiral Sir William Tennant. (© *Popperfoto/Getty Images*)

George Wagner photographed at home in Lichfield in November 2016. (© *Joshua Levine*)

The author stands beside one of *Crested Eagle*'s guns on the beach near Bray Dunes. (© *Paul Reed*)

Acknowledgements

I have a very large number of people to thank. First of all, I have received a huge amount of encouragement and support from Chris Nolan, Emma Thomas and Andy Thompson. I have admired their skill and energy, and enjoyed sharing their vision.

I have greatly enjoyed working with the team at William Collins – Joseph Zigmond, Iain Hunt, Tom Killingbeck and Steve Gove. Every morning, I have looked forward to our chats – notwithstanding the time constraints. Meanwhile, my agents at United Agents, Jim Gill and Yasmin McDonald, have guided me through this unusual project very ably.

Many people have offered their time and advice. Paul Reed, whose knowledge of both the story and the landscape is unrivalled, was as generous as ever. Nobody knows more about the Junkers 87 than Peter C. Smith, and I enjoyed corresponding with him. I spent a fascinating day with Clive Kidd, the curator of HMS Collingwood's Heritage Collection, who showed me all manner of radio and communications equipment. Giles Milton was very kind in sharing his information on degaussing; Dan Wybo was similarly generous in relation to King Leopold. Dipping my nervous toe into the film world, meanwhile, has brought me into contact with delightful people such as Desiree Finnegan, Con Gornell and Jason Bevan.

Max Arthur reassured me when this task seemed impossible in the time available, while Peter Hart tried unsuccessfully to turn me into a more clubbable historian. Andy Saunders has been a helpful sounding board, and Julian Wilson allowed me to share the benefit of his labours. My thanks go to Terry Charman, Steven Broomfield and Peter Devitt. The National Archives have provided some of the most important and interesting documents in this book. The National Maritime Museum has been extremely helpful, as has been the Dunkirk 1940 Museum. And the Imperial War Museum Sound and Documents archives which have been, as usual, mines of superb information.

From the IWM, I would particularly like to mention Richard McDonagh, Richard Hughes, Jane Rosen, Madeleine James and the museum's agent, Barbara Levy. I was very kindly allowed to use significant quotes from the Sound Archive's collection of interviews. These related to William Harding (6323), Edward Watson (7194), Thomas Myers (10166), John Williams (11939) and Leon Wilson (20137).

I would also like to acknowledge the help I have had from the Association of Dunkirk Little Ships. The archivist, John Tough, answered my questions, while I enjoyed the company of past commodore Ian Gilbert, as we travelled to visit a number of Dunkirk veterans.

This book was written in a number of different places. The London Library (in particular, the fifth floor by the window, but please keep this to yourself) is an excellent place to work, as well as a treasure trove of books from this period. I have spent many hours in the British Library, and many other, rather less expected hours, in the atmospheric library of *Queen Mary 2* as she sailed the Indian Ocean. Desperate writing was done in other places, from Quatermain's Camp in the Eastern Cape to the Brooks's spare bedroom to the maternity unit at University College Hospital – all places where I should have been paying more attention to matters in hand.

Over the last year I have been fortunate to meet a good many veterans. Two of those I visited with Ian (Eric Roderick of the Royal Army Service Corps and Harold 'Vic' Viner of the Royal Navy) have since passed away. So too has Philip Brown (who served on HMS *Sabre*, and was introduced to me by his daughter Joanna Wortham) and Charlie Searle (of the Royal Army Medical Corps who was introduced to me by Nic Taylor).

As I write, I learn that Colin Ashford of the Highland Light Infantry is recovering well from a fall and that Les Gray of the Royal Engineers is recovering from pneumonia. I am delighted, meanwhile, to report that Arthur Lobb of the Royal Army Service Corps, Arthur Taylor of the Royal Air Force, Robert Halliday and George Wagner of the Royal Engineers, Ted Oates and George Purton of the Royal Army Service Corps, and Norman Prior of the Lancashire Fusiliers are all fit and well. So is Jim Thorpe, almost certainly the last surviving man to take a Little Ship over to Dunkirk, who now lives in a Maryland nursing home. I thank Dave Wilkins of the University of Maryland for bringing Jim to my attention. We owe all of these men a great deal. Long may they thrive.

I have also recently visited two Battle of Britain pilots – Tim Elkington and Tom Neil – both of whom vividly described the realities of air fighting. I thank both of them, as well as Margaret Clotworthy and Tim's wife, Patricia, for their wonderful hospitality. I also thank Louis van Leemput, a retired officer of the Belgian Air Force who, as a boy in May 1940, had been one of countless Belgian refugees fleeing from the Germans, and who touchingly shared his memories. And there were others who shared family memories. Susan Cooper, for example, shared the recollections of her father, Jim Baynes, while Lorraine Gill spoke movingly of her father, Cyril Roberts.

At a personal level, there are many to whom I am grateful. I would like to thank Keith Steane, my history teacher at Lyndhurst House School, who retired this year. He was a superb teacher who passed his enthusiasm on all those years ago. I would also like to thank the school's current headmaster, Andrew Reid, for showing me such generosity earlier this year.

I would also like to mention Santo Massine, an expert on many facets of Dunkirk, who has inspired me with his patience and good humour. And my thanks go to others – Osian Barnes, Turtle Bunbury, Will, Anna, Beau and Gracie Brooks, Lucy Briers, Alexandra Churchill, Richard Clothier, Marshall Cope, Victoria Coren Mitchell, Ruth Cowan, Bob and Susannah Cryer, Simon Dinsdale, Ian Drysdale, Bill Emlyn Jones, Bridget Fallon, Megan Fisher, Simon, Robert, Gillian and Lionel Frumkin, Tanya Gold, Edward Grant, Meekal Hashmi, John Hayes Fisher, Nigel Hobbs, Mishal Husain, Simon Irvine, Katie Johns, Edward, Mollie, Olivia, Rosalind and Lillian Keene, Suzy Klein, Paul Lang, Lionel Levine, Judy Levine, Kim Levine, Marshall and Sue Levine (and James, Katie and Georgie), Mhairi Macnee, Charles Malpass, Emily Man, Dru Masters, Jon Medcalf, Paul Miller, David Mitchell, Harry Mount, Duncan Neale, Fred Perry,

Jess Redford, Dora Reisser, Andy Robertshaw, Malcolm Rushton, the Rowes (Chris, Sara, Charlie and Matti), Dorothy Sahm, Tanya Shaw, Michael Sparkes, Chris Spencer, Prem Trott, Orlando and Miranda Wells, David Weston, Mike, Annabel, Henry and Arthur Wood, and all those whom I've shamefully forgotten to mention.

Above all, I would like to thank Claire Price who has combined a great deal of (unpaid) work on this book with a sparkling acting career – and managed, at the same time, to carry our first child. This is multi-tasking of the highest order.

A full essay on sources can be found on Joshua Levine's website –

joshualevine.co.uk

Select Bibliography

Addison, Paul, *The Road to 1945: British Politics and the Second World War* (London: Pimlico, 1994)

Addison, Paul and Crang, Jeremy A. (eds), *Listening to Britain: Home Intelligence Reports on Britain's Finest Hour – May to September 1940* (London: Vintage, 2010)

Barclay, C. N., *The History of the Royal Northumberland Fusiliers in the Second World War* (London: William Clowes and Sons, 2002)

Beaton, Cecil, *The Years Between: Diaries 1939–44* (London: Weidenfeld and Nicolson, 1965)

Blake, John, *Northern Ireland in the Second World War* (Belfast: Her Majesty's Stationery Office, 1956)

Blaxland, Gregory, *Destination Dunkirk: The Story of Gort's Army* (London: Kimber, 1973)

Blitzkrieg in Their Own Words: First-hand Accounts from German Soldiers 1939–1940 (South Yorkshire: Pen & Sword, 2005)

Blythe, Ronald, *The Age of Illusion* (London: Hamish Hamilton, 1983)

Bond, Brian and Taylor, Michael (eds), *The Battle for France and Flanders 1940: Sixty Years On* (Barnsley: Leo Cooper, 2001)

Bourne, Stephen, *Mother Country: Britain's Black Community on the Home Front 1939–45* (Stroud: History Press, 2010)

Brann, Christian, *The Little Ships of Dunkirk* (Cirencester: Collectors' Books, 1989)

Brayley, Martin J., *The British Army 1939–45 (1)* (London: Osprey, 2009)

Brayley, Martin J., *The British Home Front 1939–45* (London: Osprey, 2005)

Bullen, Roy, *History of the 2/7th Battalion, The Queen's Royal Regiment 1939–1946* (Guildford, 1958)

Calder, Angus, *The People's War: Britain 1939–1945* (London: Pimlico, 1994)

Calder, Angus and Sheridan, Dorothy, *Speak for Yourself: A Mass-Observation Anthology, 1937–1949* (London: Cape, 1984)

Chappell, Mike, *British Battle Insignia* (London: Osprey, 1987)

Churchill, Winston, *The Second World War, Volume 2: Their Finest Hour* (London: Cassell & Co, 1949)

Collier, Richard, *The Sands of Dunkirk* (London: Collins, 1961)

Colville, John, *The Fringes of Power: Downing Street Diaries 1939–1955* (London: Hodder and Stoughton, 1985)

Darrieus, Henri and Quéguiner, Jean, *Historique de la Marine Française 1922–1942* (Saint-Malo: Editions l'Ancre de Marine, 1996)

Darwin, Bernard, *War on the Line: The Story of the Southern Railway in War-Time* (London: The Southern Railway Company, 1946)

Davis, Brian, *British Army Uniforms and Insignia of World War Two* (London: Arms and Armour, 1992)

Select Bibliography

Dean, Basil, *The Theatre at War* (London: George G. Harrap & Co, 1956)

Dickon, Chris, *Americans at War in Foreign Forces* (Jefferson, N. C.: McFarland & Co., 2014)

Dildy, Douglas C., *Dunkirk 1940: Operation Dynamo* (London: Osprey, 2010)

Ellan, B. J. (Lane, Brian), *Spitfire! The Experiences of a Fighter Pilot* (London: John Murray, 1942)

Ellis, L. F., *The War in France and Flanders 1939–1940* (London: Her Majesty's Stationery Office, 1953)

Emsley, Clive, *Soldier, Sailor, Beggarman, Thief: Crime and the British Armed Services since 1914* (Oxford: Oxford University Press, 2013)

Engelmann, Bernt, *In Hitler's Germany: Everyday Life in the Third Reich* (London: Methuen, 1988)

Fowler, David, *The First Teenagers: The Lifestyles of Young Wage Earners in Interwar Britain* (London: The Woburn Press, 1995)

Franks, Norman, *Air Battle for Dunkirk: 26 May–3 June 1940* (London: Grub Street, 2006)

Fraser, David, *Knight's Cross: A Life of Field Marshal Erwin Rommel* (London: Harper Collins, 1993)

Frieser, Karl-Heinz with Greenwood, Joan, *The Blitzkrieg Legend: The 1940 Campaign in the West* (Annapolis, Maryland: Naval Institute Press, 2005)

Gardner, W. J. R. (ed.), *The Evacuation from Dunkirk: 'Operation Dynamo' 26 May–4 June 1940* (London: Frank Cass, 2000)

Gaulle, Charles de, *War Memoirs, Volume One: The Call to Honour* (London: Collins, 1955)

Gilbert, Martin, *Finest Hour: Winston S. Churchill 1939–1941* (London: Heinemann, 1983)

Godfrey, Simon, *British Army Communications in the Second World War: Lifting the Fog of Battle* (London: Bloomsbury, 2013)

Graves, Charles, *The Home Guard of Britain* (London: Hutchinson, 1943)

Griehl, Manfred, *Junkers Ju 87: Stuka* (Airlife, 2001)

Grundy, Trevor, *Memoirs of a Fascist Childhood* (London: Arrow, 1999)

Guderian, Heinz, *Panzer Leader* (London: Penguin, 2009)

Hadley, Peter, *Third Class to Dunkirk: A Worm's-Eye View of the B.E.F., 1940* (London: Hollis and Carter, 1944)

Halder, Franz, *The Halder Diaries: The Private War Journals of Colonel General Franz Halder* (Boulder Colorado: Westview Press, 1976)

Harrison, Ada May (ed.), *Letters from the War Areas by Army Sisters on Active Service* (London: Hodder and Stoughton, 1944)

Harrison, Tom, *Britain Revisited* (London: Victor Gollancz, 1961)

Harrison, Tom and Madge, Charles, *Britain by Mass Observation* (London: The Cresset Library, 1986)

Hayward, James, *Myths and Legends of the Second World War* (Stroud: Sutton, 2003)

Henrey, Madeleine, *The Siege of London* (London: J. M. Dent and Sons, 1946)

Herzog, Rudolph, *Humor in Hitler's Germany* (New York: Melville House, 2011)

Hill, Christopher, *Cabinet Decisions on Foreign Policy: The British Experience October 1938–June 1941* (Cambridge: Cambridge University Press, 1991)

Hinton, James, *Nine Wartime Lives: Mass Observation and the Making of the Modern Self* (Oxford: Oxford University Press, 2010)

Hodson, James Lansdale, *Through the Dark Night: Being Some Account of a War Correspondent's Journeys, Meetings and What Was Said to Him, in France, Britain and Flanders during 1939–1940* (London: Victor Gollancz, 1941)

Hollingshead, August, *Elmtown's Youth and Elmtown Revisited* (New York: John Wiley & Sons, 1975)

Horne, Alistair, *To Lose a Battle: France 1940* (London: Macmillan, 1969)

Irwin, Anthony, *Infantry Officer: A Personal Record* (London: B. T. Batsford, 1943)

Jewell, Brian, *British Battledress 1937–61* (London: Osprey, 2005)

Johnson, Donald McIntosh, *Bars and Barricades* (London: Christopher Johnson, 1952)

Kennedy, John Fitzgerald, *Why England Slept* (New York: W. Funk, 1940)

Keyes, Roger, *Outrageous Fortune: The Tragedy of Leopold III of the Belgians 1901–1941* (London: Secker & Warburg, 1984)

Langley, J. M., *Fight Another Day* (London: Collins, 1974)

Lestrange, W. F., *Wasted Lives* (London: George Routledge & Sons, 1936)

Levine, Joshua, *Forgotten Voices of Dunkirk* (London: Ebury, 2011)

Lord, Walter, *The Miracle of Dunkirk* (London: Allen Lane, 1983)

Lowry, Bernard, *British Home Defences 1940–45* (London: Osprey, 2004)

Mackay, Robert, *Half the Battle: Civilian Morale in Britain during the Second World War* (Manchester: Manchester University Press, 2007)

McKay, Sinclair, *Dunkirk: From Disaster to Deliverance – Testimonies of the Last Survivors* (London: Aurum Press, 2015)

Martin, T. A., *The Essex Regiment 1929–1950* (Brentwood: The Essex Regiment Association, 1952)

Marwick, Arthur, *Britain in the Century of Total War: War, Peace and Social Change 1900–1967* (London: The Bodley Head, 1968)

Maschmann, Melita, *Account Rendered: A Dossier on My Former Self* (London: Abelard-Schuman, 1964)

Montgomery, Bernard, *The Memoirs of Field-Marshal The Viscount Montgomery of Alamein, K.G.* (London: Collins, 1958)

Mosley, Leonard, *Backs to the Wall: London Under Fire 1939–45* (London: Weidenfeld and Nicolson, 1971)

Mosley, Leonard, *Battle of Britain* (London: Pan, 1969)

Newlands, Emma, *War, the Body and British Army Recruits, 1939–45* (Manchester, Manchester University Press, 2014)

Newman, Philip, *Over the Wire: A POW's Escape Story from the Second World War* (South Yorkshire: Pen & Sword, 1983)

Orwell, George, *The Road to Wigan Pier* (London: Victor Gollancz, 1937)

Perry, Colin, *Boy in the Blitz: The 1940 Diary of Colin Perry* (Stroud: Sutton, 2000)

Plummer, Russell, *The Ships that Saved an Army: Comprehensive Record of the One Thousand Three Hundred Little Ships of Dunkirk* (Wellingborough: Patrick Stephens Ltd, 1990)

Pownall, Sir Henry and Bond, Brian (ed.), *Chief of Staff: The Diaries of Lieutenant-General Sir Henry Pownall Volume One* (London: Leo Cooper, 1972)

Pratt Paul, William (ed.), *History of the Argyll and Sutherland Highlanders, 6th Battalion* (London: Thomas Nelson and Sons, 1949)

Price, Dr Alfred, *Britain's Air Defences 1939–45* (London: Osprey, 2004)

Priestley, John Boynton, *Postscripts* (London: Heinemann, 1940)

Prior, Robin, *When Britain Saved the West: The Story of 1940* (London: Yale University Press, 2015)

Rhodes, Anthony, *Sword of Bone* (London: Faber and Faber, 1942)

Roberts, Andrew, *Eminent Churchillians* (London: Phoenix, 1994)

Roland, Paul, *Life in the Third Reich: Daily Life in Nazi Germany 1933–1945* (London: Arcturus, 2016)

Saunders, Andy, *Battle of Britain, July to October 1940: RAF Operations Manual* (Somerset: Haynes, 2015)

Savage, Jon, *Teenage: The Creation of Youth Culture* (London: Chatto and Windus, 2007)

Sebag-Montefiore, Hugh, *Dunkirk: Fight to the Last Man* (London: Penguin, 2015)

Sharp, Nigel, *Dunkirk Little Ships* (Stroud: Amberley, 2015)

Shirer, William, *Berlin Diary: The Journal of a Foreign Correspondent, 1934–1941* (London: Hamish Hamilton, 1942)

Smalley, Edward, *The British Expeditionary Force, 1939–40* (Basingstoke: Palgrave Macmillam, 2015)

Stewart, Geoffrey, *Dunkirk and the Fall of France* (South Yorkshire: Pen & Sword, 1988)

Stewart, Patrick Findlater, *The History of the XII Royal Lancers* (Oxford University Press, 1950)

Sumner, Ian and Vauvillier, François, *The French Army 1939–45 (1)* (London: Osprey, 2008)

Thomas, Donald, *An Underworld at War: Spivs, Deserters, Racketeers and Civilians in the Second World War* (London: John Murray, 2004)

Thompson, Julian, *Dunkirk: Retreat to Victory* (London: Sidgwick & Jackson, 2008)

Titmuss, Richard, *Problems of Social Policy* (London: Her Majesty's Stationery Office, 1950)

Tubach, Frederic, *German Voices: Memories of Life during Hitler's Third Reich* (Berkeley: University of California Press, 2011)

Walmsley, Leo, *Fishermen at War* (London: Collins, 1941)

Warlimont, Walter, *Inside Hitler's Headquarters 1939–45* (London: Weidenfeld and Nicolson, 1964)

Waugh, Evelyn, *Put Out More Flags* (London: Chapman and Hall, 1942)

Wilson, Patrick, *Dunkirk – 1940: From Disaster to Deliverance* (South Yorkshire: Leo Cooper, 2002)